BUSINESS LEADERS EDITION

MISSION MATTERS

World's Leading Entrepreneurs Reveal their
TOP TIPS TO SUCCESS

ADAM TORRES AND
TIM KINTZ

CENTURY CITY

Beverly Hills, CA

MISSION MATTERS

PODCAST

WITH

Adam Torres

© 2023 Adam Torres. All rights reserved.

Copyright © 2023 by Mr. Century City, LLC. All rights reserved. No part of this book may be used or reproduced in any manner whatsoever without written permission except in the case of brief quotation embodied in critical articles and reviews.

For information, visit **www.MissionMatters.com**

Managing Editor:
Adam Torres / @AskAdamTorres

Graphic Design:
Kendra Cagle

Beverly Hills, CA 90212
www.MissionMatters.com

The Mr. Century City Logo is a trademark of Mr. Century City, LLC.

Mission Matters, Beverly Hills, CA

This publication is intended to provide general information regarding the subject matter covered. However, laws and practices often vary from state to state and are subject to change. Because each factual situation is different, specific advice should be customized to the particular circumstances. For this reason, the reader is advised to consult with his or her own adviser regarding that individual's specific scenario.

This book was created as a collaborative effort. Each author's opinion is solely their own. The authors have taken reasonable precautions in the preparation of this book and think the facts shown in the book are accurate as of the date it was written. However, neither the authors nor the publisher assumes any responsibility for any liability resulting from the use or application of the information contained in this book, and the information is not intended to serve as legal or professional advice related to individual situations.

DEDICATION

To my wife Kristi, my daughter Maddyn, and my son, Cooper: I am so proud, and I love each of you with all my heart. Thank you for supporting me on this journey.

To all the hardworking managers who are willing to work through the grind, pay the personal price to create a culture of growth, and help their people achieve more than they ever imagined.

To the leaders who sacrificed their time, energy, and often sanity to challenge me to improve and get out of my comfort zone. I wasn't easy to manage and probably gave you gray hair, but the lessons I learned from you are priceless.

TABLE OF CONTENTS

Acknowledgments i
Foreword By Adam Torres iii
Introduction By Tim Kintz v

CHAPTER 1: 1
Meet Business Challenges and Build an Inspiring Business
By Brad Weber

CHAPTER 2: 9
From Flipping Tires to Flipping Houses
By Brooke Sousa

CHAPTER 3: 15
Find the Best Print Service Provider to Launch a Successful Franchise
By Bryan Vielhauer

CHAPTER 4: 23
Traveling the Road From Corporate to Entrepreneur
By Carlton Millinder

CHAPTER 5: 31
Putting Kids First: Leveraging Pediatric Telemedicine for a Healthier Future
By Chelsea Johnson

CHAPTER 6: 41
Tangible Assets You Can Hold
By Collin Plume

CHAPTER 7: 49
The Reluctant Entrepreneur
By Curt Maier

CHAPTER 8: 57
Life Lessons and Legacy
By Cynthia Gallardo

CHAPTER 9: 63
The Observationist: Success in Business and Life—It's all about People Through the Lens of a Business Leader and Professional Magician
By David Reich

CHAPTER 10: 73
Understanding the Grief Caused by Career Transitions
By Diana Stephens

CHAPTER 11: 81
The Mindset of "Get to" Rather Than "Have to"
By Greg Johnson

CHAPTER 12: 89
Modernize or Die: 8 Principles for Doing Business the Way Your Customers Want
By Jason Kennedy

CHAPTER 13: 99
Activating the Power of Authentic Leadership
By Jennifer A. Ingram

CHAPTER 14: 107
From Strategy to Execution: How a Full-Service Marketing Agency Can Boost Your Business
By Jennifer Johns Sutton

CHAPTER 15: 119
Small Businesses, Community Cornerstones
By Jessica Z. Brandenburg

CHAPTER 16: 129
Become a Full-Time Feminist and Change the World
By Jessica Nava

CHAPTER 17: 139
Redefining Success
By Joseph Fannin

CHAPTER 18: 147
Want to Win? LEAD and Build a Great TEAM!
By Keith Angell

CHAPTER 19: 155
Life and Business Lessons from a CEO & Dad of Seven
By Kevin M. Campbell

CHAPTER 20: 163
The Power of Behavioral Science to Improve Leadership
By Kurt Nelson

CHAPTER 21: 171
Your Gifts Will Make Room for You
By Lanise Block

CHAPTER 22: 179
Rooted Perspective
By Lee Ann Schwope

CHAPTER 23: 187
Driving Excellence and Transcending Mindsets in CEO Leadership and the C-Suite
By Leigh Priebe Kearney

CHAPTER 24: 197
Life Lessons Learned from the Man in the Mirror
By Mansour Khatib

CHAPTER 25: 205
Revolutionary 4-D Brand Alignment: Putting the "Human" Back in Human Resources
By Mark A. Mears

CHAPTER 26: 221
Creating the Most Valuable Retirement Asset: Oneself
By Mark Andrew Thiede

CHAPTER 27: 231
Don't Take No for an Answer
By Mark R. Warren

CHAPTER 28: 239
A Health Awakening Awoke the Entrepreneur in Me
By Matthew J. McCarl, Sr.

CHAPTER 29: 247
Make it Matter
By Meghan Mackay

CHAPTER 30: 255
The Power of Delayed Gratification
By Mher M. Vartanian

CHAPTER 31: 263
Mental Health is the Driving Force Behind the Success of Your Business or Product
By Myntillae Nash

CHAPTER 32: 271
Think Like a Venture Capitalist
By Oksana Malysheva

CHAPTER 33: 281
The Secret to Leadership Success
By Petria McKelvey

CHAPTER 34: 289
My Road to Humanity
By Philip Ayles

CHAPTER 35: 297
Building a Stronger and More Sustainable Bottom Line
By Sally Handlon

CHAPTER 36: 307
Engineer From the Outside-In
By Scott E. LeBeau

CHAPTER 37: 315
The Marketer's Guide to Digital Transformation
By Shamir Duverseau

CHAPTER 38: 323
Motivate the Unmotivated
By Tim Kintz

Conclusion 331
Appendix 333
Listen to Our Podcasts 341
Other Available Titles 343

ACKNOWLEDGMENTS

I would especially like to thank the following people who made a huge difference in my life:

- Bernice Kintz—amazing and patient MOM

- Bill Todd—My high school baseball coach who knew what made me tick

- John Kazanas—My college baseball coach and mentor (Advanced Scout, Chicago White Sox)

- Dan Schumacher—My first sales manager who took me under his wing

- Huey Burnham—Great friend, fellow dreamer and entrepreneur

- Doug Dingman—Business mentor and friend (Co-Founder, ProConsulting Inc.)

- Kathleen Rittmaster—Former boss who made a difference (General Manager, Joe Verde Sales & Management Company)

FOREWORD

By **ADAM TORRES**

As I look back at the collaborations Mission Matters has had the pleasure to be part of, it amazes me. When we started, we didn't have a website or a brand. We also didn't have any background in publishing or podcast production. All we had was a deck for our company, describing an idea for entrepreneurs to come together into an anthology book series, and a dream of something bigger. I thought this book series would simply be a way to drive new business. Boy, was I wrong.

At that time, I was still a financial advisor, managing money, and our original brand was called Money Matters Top Tips. Once our co-founder, Chirag Sagar, decided to come onboard, we broadened our scope and vision. The idea became simple. We would create a platform for business leaders, entrepreneurs and executives, so we could collaborate, create and contribute our best thoughts, our best ideas, our best stories—all for the benefit of others. This platform, now known as Mission Matters, encompasses podcasts, thought leadership, website content and extensive social media. We now offer strategic and collaborative avenues to create more content, by adding virtual and live events into the mix.

Looking back, with 300-plus authors published, 5,000-plus podcast interviews recorded and 100,000-plus pieces of content distributed, I'm shocked and amazed to look at the support that the business community has given us. And let's not forget the stories that our authors have entrusted us to craft, promote and distribute.

We are now releasing the 10th edition of our Mission Matters Business Leaders book, where we have brought together, once again, the best of the best in different industries and backgrounds. In these pages you will read stories of success, failure and the ups and downs that come from chasing dreams and career success. In compiling these stories, it's my hope that you will be inspired and motivated to pursue your own passions in life.

For those with a dream that may defy logic or seem unreasonable, keep reaching for the unattainable, enjoy the bumps in the road and continue pushing for greatness, just like these amazing entrepreneurs, business leaders and executives.

If you have a dream, go for it.

To your success,

Adam Torres

P.S. We'd love to hear your story and Mission. Learn more at **www.MissionMatters.com**.

INTRODUCTION

By **TIM KINTZ**

Welcome to the Mission Matters Business Leaders Edition! In the pages that follow, you will find an array of valuable insights from a diverse group of authors. They share their most empowering and humbling personal experiences in business and in life, to provide you with some essential building blocks that will help you succeed and lead.

One of the major themes in this book is leadership. There are people from my life who I look back on and think, if it wasn't for that person, if they were not a leader in my life, who knows what would have happened to me. I can name a few: Coach Kazanas, Bill Todd, Kathleen Rittmaster and Dan Schumacher. They all showed up at different points in my life. But every one of them learned what made me tick and cared more about me getting better than I cared about me getting better. Being a leader is a great opportunity. And it's also a great responsibility.

What does it mean to be a successful leader? Success is a choice. Survival is instinct. When you wake up in the morning, you don't wake up thinking, "I am successful and I'm going to kill it today." You have to choose to think that. When you wake up, you think, "I need water. I need food. I need to use the restroom." That's survival. Success is a choice you make at the beginning, middle and end of your day, and throughout your day. Whether you're a leader, a salesperson, or somewhere in between, it's a choice. There are a lot of interesting choices in this book.

In my chapter, I talk about how to motivate the unmotivated. Everyone today is complaining that they can't find good people to hire. They complain about millennials and how younger generations don't want to work. I believe our current environment is an opportunity to do something different that will gain market share, while your competitors are focused on what's not working. I share specific strategies on not only how to motivate the unmotivated, but also how to be the leader you need to be to make a difference in both your business success and the lives of the people you lead.

I am passionate about leadership, because I know there are salespeople out there giving it all they have, working bell to bell, putting in twelve-hour days, missing their kids' birthdays, working on holidays, working weekends, and they don't necessarily have leaders who are there for them. I'm very empathetic to salespeople, because there are so many managers who got to that position like people get ahead on the TV show "Survivor": out wit, outplay, out last, don't get voted off, and eventually, you are going to be the manager.

In managers' defense, it's typically the least trained position in any company. And, there was probably very little training when they were an employee or salesperson. There was just enough, but nothing great. When they get promoted into management, there's very little people skills or leadership training. They get thrown to the wolves and have to figure it out on their own. Your people deserve a fearless leader. Someone who is not going to just tell them what to do, but work with them as they do it, no matter what level they achieve. Top producers still need effective management. You have to understand how to motivate people at different levels. Laker's coach, Phil Jackson, was that unique golden unicorn who had the ability to develop young players, as well as lead and motivate players at all levels, from rookies to superstars like Shaq, Kobe, and Michael Jordan. Unfortunately, we can't all be Phil Jackson as leaders. But the reality is, Phil Jackson had to learn it, too. Phil Jackson wasn't Phil Jackson when he started.

In today's world, there's no such thing as job security. There's only employment security. What are you going to do to make yourself employable? And as a leader, what are you going to do? If you believe you can't find good salespeople, maybe you just can't find someone who is turnkey and brilliant at what they do from the minute you hire them. But you can hire good people and develop them. That's the leader's job.

I've spent many years training both salespeople and managers. And what inspires me most about what I do is when I get that phone call or email from a person telling me how it's changed their life. They had a better Christmas because of it, or they accomplished something they never thought they could do. Zig Ziglar said it best: "You can have everything in life you want if you will just help enough other people get what they want." If you have that mindset, it makes what you do easy.

My wife went to work for Zig when I was still early in my training career. I asked Zig one day, if you had to give me one tip, what would that be? He said, "Every time you get up to do a seminar, or work with people, I want you to prepare as if that's the first class you've ever held. For most of the people sitting there, it's the first time they've heard you. Whether they're investing an hour or eight hours in you, don't waste their time. Time is the new commodity. They will never get that one hour or eight hours of their life back. So, make it worth it." That was one of the best pieces of advice I've ever received.

Thank you for making the choice to read this book. I hope you enjoy all the stories and information in these pages and that they inspire you on your entrepreneurial journey. I wish you success in your work and in your life.

Tim Kintz

CHAPTER 1

MEET BUSINESS CHALLENGES AND BUILD AN INSPIRING BUSINESS

By **BRAD WEBER**

Developing software is a technical pursuit and one that I love, so much so that I have made it my career for more than 25 years. But doing what you love only takes you so far. If you aim to become an entrepreneur and grow a company, you must meet complex business challenges with inspirational leadership.

In this chapter, I share some portions of my entrepreneurial journey and highlight a few memorable challenges and the lessons learned in addressing each one.

After earning my MBA, I took a job as an application developer for Andersen Consulting, a global software development and change management firm. I left the comfortable confines of the company a few years later to pursue a career as a solo entrepreneur building software for small businesses. In doing so, I found the administrative aspects of running the company to be simple, given that I was the only person on the payroll.

Desiring to take on more challenges, I started my company, InspiringApps, in 2007, to design and build custom software for large enterprises. While the software development was more complex, so were the business growth challenges—far more than I ever anticipated or imagined.

Growing a Company is Fraught with Risk

An entrepreneurship professor in my MBA program said, "All of the risk in business is in fixed cost." That made sense at the time, and it stuck with me when founding InspiringApps. If you invest in equipment, a building or employees in my case, the risk is in generating enough revenue to cover those costs.

Having employees with regular payroll obligations, regardless of available billable work, was risky. At first, I only hired contractors to reduce my liability. As a new business formed the same year Apple introduced the iPhone, it didn't take long to see enough steady work that I was comfortable converting a few contractors into full-time employees. But we grew to a team of 30 very quickly, although most were still contractors.

That is when I learned that not **all** business risk is in fixed cost. There were plenty more. First, although the new iPhone app era was a boon for our business, it also created plentiful opportunities for independent contractors who could develop apps for that platform. They would join our team when we had an interesting project, but quickly jumped ship when things got hard or when presented with a more interesting opportunity on another project. That left us holding the bag. We didn't have continuity throughout our projects, we missed deadlines and the quality of our work suffered.

While most of our costs were variable with our contract team, we thought we'd be able to sell projects more easily to customers on a fixed-cost basis instead of time and materials—and we were right. Customers appreciated that. However, we then had projects with fixed revenue and unlimited cost potential from the hourly team of contractors delivering the work. It was a disaster. The company lost money during that time.

The lesson for today's MBA students and entrepreneurs is that there is tremendous risk when the structure of your revenue and costs are not aligned. You can be profitable on projects when both are variable. You can be profitable when both are fixed. But having a mix of the two can create a financial mess.

Cultivating a Winning Culture Requires an Employee-based Team

As an independent software developer, I earned a reputation for being loyal, hard-working and fair to my clients. I assumed all the contractors I hired in those early days would be the same. That was not the case. Although there may be more financial risk in hiring employees, there is far less risk to the company's reputation, the quality of service we provide to our clients and the company culture we want to create.

Turnover is one reason. A winning company culture takes time to cultivate and nurture. Turnover works against that. If you bring in contractors, you can tell them what the culture is, but if they are only going to be with you for a short time, they likely won't care.

However, culture does matter to an employee who plans to stay with the company long-term. In some instances, it's the primary reason people stay. They can make meaningful contributions to the company and feel supported and respected by like-minded team members. With employees, culture gets stronger over time. With contractors going through a revolving door, culture suffers.

To use a sports analogy, it's the difference between a professional team that has played together for many years versus an expansion team thrown together with players from a dozen different franchises. The former is sure to outplay the latter every time.

My conviction about growing a winning culture led me to take drastic action: I cut the company size in half, transitioned to an entirely employee-based team and slowly began to rebuild the company over the months and years that followed.

Thanks to a great group of people and a supportive, respectful company culture, we retain employees much longer than is typical in our industry. About 20-percent of our team has been together for a decade or more, and almost 40-percent has been together for five years or longer. It makes a difference in how we work and what we produce. Because our team members know the strengths and weaknesses of their colleagues, they work together seamlessly to turn out an excellent product for our clients.

A Flat Organizational Structure Will Only Take You so Far

When I worked alone, I had virtually no overhead. And since there was no one to share responsibilities with, I wore all the hats. I retained my aversion to overhead as I grew a team at InspiringApps. We didn't need an organizational chart, because everyone was a peer who reported directly to me. I was also still actively writing code on projects. I prided myself on my willingness to get my hands dirty and show that I wouldn't ask anyone to do anything I wasn't willing to do myself.

We managed to grow under that structure and create impressive solutions for larger and larger customers. In fact, we signed on one of our marquee clients, because I picked up the phone when they called one day to learn about the company. They were impressed that the president of the organization was accessible.

We have always been fortunate to have a steady stream of referral business, so I didn't have to spend much time selling, and we didn't have a dedicated salesperson. But I still had to balance my time between pressing development timelines, writing proposals and managing client relationships to bring in revenue to keep the wheels turning.

While the company was realizing the vision I had when I founded it, little did I know that my flat organization strategy was hampering our growth—and I was the bottleneck! I needed to define my role more clearly to set the company up for long-term success.

Having a flat organization makes sense when you're small, but there comes a point when it hinders growth. I realized that InspiringApps would never become a 100-person company with just one person managing everything. I also realized that InspiringApps could improve if we had people focused on areas of responsibility who had the autonomy and authority to make decisions that did not require my input.

I wasn't resistant to changing the organizational structure; I just needed the problem to become evident. Once I understood the need, my next challenge was what to do about it. I didn't know the solution or have a methodology to work from.

The answer to my dilemma came from the book *Traction: Get a Grip on Your Business* by Gino Wickman, creator of the Entrepreneurial Operating System, an organizational philosophy designed to help entrepreneurs like me grow a healthy company.

The book gave me the framework I needed to address my challenges. We "inflated" that flat org chart. There are at least three tiers now, whereas before, there were none. I formed a leadership team covering operations, marketing and art direction. On the development side, the largest group within the company, we now have team leads for iOS, Android and the web.

We're a couple of years into the transition and early progress has been fantastic. The people in managerial roles have more autonomy, can exercise their entrepreneurial muscles and work more as a team to propel the company forward.

Create 'Cool Stuff for Clients' or Build a 'Real' Business

Another professor once told me, "You aren't an entrepreneur until you sell your business." I disagree. I think an entrepreneur is someone who takes a personal financial risk and answers to customers rather than a boss. I met that criterion as an independent software developer, and I still meet it leading my company and employees today.

Chapter 1: **Brad Weber**

Many people have entrepreneurial characteristics, even if they aren't taking a personal financial risk. They are hard-working, resourceful, good problem solvers and willing to help beyond traditional job descriptions. I love to work with people like that, and I'm fortunate to do so at InspiringApps.

Because of our success, I hadn't looked critically at the business for over a decade. After proudly sharing what I thought was an admirable tale of success with a business advisor, he said, "So your business model is creating cool stuff for clients." That may appear to be a compliment, but it wasn't. The subtext was, "You haven't built a sustainable 'real' business." He was right.

His remarks felt like a gut punch, and I took exception to them initially. I was proud that I had two business degrees and had been in business for 25 years, but that quickly faded. I soon realized that even after a quarter century, I had not leveraged my business training the way I could or should. Now, I am grateful for the opportunity to build that real business. And I am happy to say that after more than 15 years of ups and downs (mostly ups), InspiringApps is thriving and positioned well for even more success in the years to come.

One word describes the difference between the "cool stuff for clients" and "real" business approaches: sustainability—building a company that can outlast me.

I carried my solo entrepreneur ways of doing business into InspiringApps. It was a flat organization because, for years, I was a one-person operation. I felt the company could not run without me. I was its "soul." Now, I want InspiringApps to sustain itself without requiring my daily contributions to survive.

Just before selling my first house, a realtor recommended small changes to make the property more attractive to prospective buyers. After making the changes, I was envious of the new owner who would benefit from the improvements and regretted not doing so for my own benefit sooner.

Working through *Traction* with my leadership team was the business equivalent to getting our house in order. We've made the company more valuable, which also makes it a better place for our team (and me) to work and enjoy the benefits of our efforts for a long time to come.

Conclusion

I love software development and entrepreneurship for many of the same reasons. Both provide the opportunity to create something beautiful, long-lasting and valuable from a blank canvas. There are risks and challenges, but none you can't overcome with hard work, ingenuity and resourcefulness. So, whether you are preparing to make your first mark or refining a masterpiece, remember that you hold the brush. Use your leadership skills to create something inspiring!

CHAPTER 2

FROM FLIPPING TIRES TO FLIPPING HOUSES

By **BROOKE SOUSA**

"Being the best means engineering your life so you never stop until you get what you want, and then you keep going until you get what's next. And then you go for even more."
–Tim Grover

In 2018, I was World's Strongest Woman and in 2019, I was named America's Strongest Woman. At the time, I just wanted to show my kids I could be a mom, a wife and still go after my own goals. I was able to build a six-figure business that focused on fitness, personal training and bodybuilding from the ground up on my own. My business was thriving. when suddenly in 2020, COVID-19 hit the world and my business hard. It forced me to quickly pivot, because I was facing losing everything I had worked so hard to build. My life as I knew it was on the line, and I refused to just let it all fall apart. I took what I had learned from competing, and I transferred it to creating a real estate business.

I created a pandemic-proof business using other people's money, which enabled me to invest in real estate. I realized I could use my knowledge and skills to create a successful business that would allow me to continue to support my family and upgrade our lifestyle. I am now in a place where I am able to use these skills to help others achieve their goals. No matter what life throws at you, you can always find a way to rise above and make the best of any situation. I am proud of how I could take negative situations and turn them into something positive.

I taught myself everything about how to rehab a house from HVAC, electric, plumbing, laying floors, foundation and the business side of it, too. It took me about 24 days to learn enough about how to do the work, and then I bought my first house. I started with flipping houses, and then I began to invest in rental properties to build a passive income. In just two years, I have grown my portfolio to over 100 properties. I'm now able to set a new example for my kids, showing them that no matter how difficult life may be, you can still win beyond your wildest dreams. It's been an incredible journey, and it's been very satisfying to see these houses go from unlivable to beautiful. I'm proud of what I've been able to achieve, and I'm grateful for the opportunity to do something I'm passionate about. I'm always looking for ways to improve the process, and I'm thrilled to see the impact I'm having on the community.

Every lesson and experience has brought me to a place where I can help others find success and reach their goals. I am now focused on passing on my knowledge and experience to others so they can avoid the same pitfalls I encountered. I am excited to continue to use my skills and knowledge and am grateful for the opportunity to make a real difference in people's lives.

I met a young man in Newark, Ohio, who was frustrated after the purchase of his first investment property. This kid was only 22 years old and had no idea what his next steps should be. By this time, I had purchased a lot of properties in the area and became known as the

Chapter 2: **Brooke Sousa**

Queen of Newark by locals. Someone contacted me and asked me to help this kid. I quickly realized that this was a property I had also bid on, so I was familiar with the issues surrounding it and the potential it had. I was happy to help him out and I offered to guide him through it. I was confident that with my expertise and the property, I could help him make the best decision for his future.

I was able to mentor the young man through the process, with the help of some local law enforcement officers, to remove the squatters. I helped him see the potential in the property and to take action that would result in a profit. That $63,000 property he wanted to give up on ended up making him a multi-millionaire in just a few months. He wanted to give up, but I coached him and now he is a multi-millionaire. That success story inspired me to continue helping people in similar situations. I founded a real estate investment company that grows based on the relationships we build and the people we help. My company has helped countless people achieve financial independence and achieve their dreams using real estate. I'm proud of the work I do and the impact I'm able to make in people's lives.

Business is a lot of work; few people talk about the downsides of it. No one talks about the 20th hour. That's the time when business owners are beyond stressed, stretched too thin, struggling to stay afloat, struggling to figure out the next step, struggling to make cash flow. That dark lonely night happens in everyone's success story, but the important thing is to be vulnerable and share the true experience with others. It's important to recognize when you're heading into the 20th hour and to ride through it. Get some perspective. It's important to prioritize tasks and focus on the things that will make a difference in the long run. It's important to remind yourself it is a part of the process.

If you're thinking about getting into this industry, I encourage you to take the plunge. It's not an easy field to break into, but it's one that's worth the work required. Don't waste your time or the time of others by thinking about it for too long—be committed to doing the work and being consistent. True success comes from going through the process with one's own hands, rather than relying on others or shortcuts.

Do your research, find out what you want to do, and who you are, and then talk to people who are already doing the work. Seeking out mentors and other people who are knowledgeable about the industry is a great way to help you get your footing. Whatever you do, make sure to stay consistent and determined. Don't let the fear of failure or the opinions of others stop you from reaching your goal. Do not give others power over your life or over your story. The more you push yourself, the closer you'll get to succeeding.

Make sure to be persistent and be willing to ask for help. Don't rob other people by not allowing them to help you in your own journey. Keeping up with the industry, reading relevant books, and attending workshops and seminars can help you stay ahead of the curve. By constantly learning and staying informed, you can increase your knowledge and find success in the industry. Don't be afraid to network and make connections—networking is part of any field. Knowing the right people can open doors and provide you with valuable advice and opportunities.

Ultimately, the key to any industry is hard work and dedication. You need to stay focused and dedicated, and never be afraid to take risks and learn from the mistakes you make along the way. With the right attitude and the right resources, you can find success in any industry. The most important thing to remember when it comes to networking is to be genuine. Don't just try to collect business cards and contact information—take the time to really get to know people and make meaningful relationships. Show interest in other people, and be willing to offer your own advice and expertise. Don't be afraid to ask questions and reach out to people you admire. Networking can be an invaluable tool for success, but only if you use it in a purposeful way.

In the last three years, I went from having no money to having $28 million in real estate. My success is possible for anyone who is willing to put in the work. It doesn't matter if you're a stay-at-home mom trying to start your own business, an unemployed young adult looking to start making money, a retired executive looking to start a new chapter in your life, or anyone else. With a vision and a plan, you can achieve anything you set your mind to. This is the perfect time to start living the life you've always dreamed of. With a plan, a vision and the willingness to be consistent, there's nothing you can't obtain. The most important thing to remember is that success doesn't happen overnight. It takes hard work and dedication to achieve the level of success I have achieved.

Every day I wake up, I'm reminded of the struggles I faced and the challenges I overcame. This reminds me of why I'm so successful, and why I'm so passionate about helping others achieve the same success. I'm proud to be able to share my story, and I'm proud to be able to help others achieve their goals. I'm a firm believer in the power of setting goals and reaching them. I'm also a believer in the power of taking action. When you have a goal in mind, it's important to take action, in order to make it a reality. This means you have to be consistent with your efforts, and put in the time and hard work required to achieve success. It's important to remember that success is not a linear journey, and there will be bumps in the road. With hard work and dedication, you can reach your goals and make your dreams a reality.

I hope my journey will inspire and encourage you to take your own journey. I want you to bet on yourself, live the life you want and reach your goals. No matter what obstacles may come your way, remember you can overcome them. You have the power to make your dreams come true. Believe in yourself, take risks and don't be afraid to fail. You will learn from your mistakes and become the best version of yourself. When you do, you'll find that all the hard work and dedication was worth it.

Don't be afraid to take the leap and follow your dreams. Life is full of surprises and you never know what might happen. But if you stay focused and keep working toward your goals, you'll be surprised at how far you can go. Life is an adventure, so give it your all and see where it takes you. With hard work and dedication, you can achieve anything you set your mind to. Take the plunge, have faith in yourself and never give up. You can make your dreams a reality.

CHAPTER 3

FIND THE BEST PRINT SERVICE PROVIDER TO LAUNCH A SUCCESSFUL FRANCHISE

By **BRYAN VIELHAUER**

You did it! All your hard work has paid off. You have built a successful business, with brand recognition and a loyal customer base; but now it's time for growth. Now it's time to take your business to the next level and start franchising. This big step as a business owner can be an extremely exciting and potentially lucrative journey that will take your business to new heights. You will start expanding into new markets, brand recognition will expand, and if all goes to plan, revenue will increase.

Over the course of this chapter, I aim to help you on your journey to become a successful franchisor, by pulling from my many years as a business owner working with successful franchisors of all sizes and industries. When I first started as a business owner, I relied heavily on the wisdom and lessons taught to me over the years, by trusted friends, family and mentors. As my Aunt Dot and Uncle Larry often professed, with hard work and education you can solve any problem. This lesson has been invaluable as I learned and grew my business alongside many of our customers.

To achieve your goals, you need to establish a solid foundation for growth. Before you can run, you must learn to walk. This requires finding knowledgeable partners who can help you build an infrastructure for sustainable growth. With the right partners, you can establish the necessary groundwork to achieve long-term success.

When first starting out, obvious partners often may include suppliers, lenders, realtors, lawyers and payroll. These partners help you get everything you need for your day-to-day business functions, find new locations, write out contracts and keep your staff paid. However, one of the most important, and often overlooked partners is a dedicated print service provider, or PSP.

What is a print service provider? This is a company that offers printing services to businesses. These services can include digital printing, offset printing and large format printing, among others. A PSP can also provide design and prepress services to assist clients in creating and preparing their files for printing. In the franchising world, a dependable PSP can help franchisors manage and maintain their brand, by producing consistent and high-quality branded materials like marketing collateral, signage and uniforms throughout all franchise locations.

As someone looking to franchise, you understand the value of your brand. Your brand has power; but left unchecked that power can be lost. And once it is lost, it is often difficult to get it back. A trusted PSP will work with you to make sure you control your branding every step of the way, as you grow your franchise. They understand that a new franchise is just as valuable as a franchise with 100 locations.

At Decal Impressions, we draw upon more than 50 years of industry expertise and more than 20 years of direct experience working with franchise systems to support new and existing franchises in managing their brand. As a service organization, it is our job to make sure the franchisor and the franchisees are set up for success.

My grandfather, Col. Frese, impressed upon me the importance of duty and service. This lesson continues to prove some of the best advice I have ever received, in both my personal and professional life. Although being of service is not always the easy road, it is the path that has allowed me, and Decal Impressions, to continue pushing ourselves and our customers from success to success. Through the dedicated efforts of our team, we have helped some of our customers grow from one location to hundreds across the country.

As you embark on your franchise journey, it's crucial to consider these factors when searching for a print service provider. These insights, gained through decades of experience working with franchise systems of varying sizes and industries, are key considerations for new franchisors seeking a knowledgeable and reliable PSP partner.

First, you will want to look for a company that has a proven track record of success. Do they understand how a franchise system operates? Can they provide you with insight as you go from one to five locations, from five to 150? Having a PSP that has experienced growth challenges at all levels, can help you navigate these hurdles as they arise.

What products and services can they offer? Can they only produce signs, or can they offer supplemental services like web design? When researching, don't focus only on what you need in the immediate future, but look at how they further support you down the road. Just because you only need uniforms and paper menus now, does not mean you won't need promotional items and signage in a few months or years. Remember, you want to look for a partner that can facilitate long-term growth.

Look for a PSP with long-term employee and customer retention. This proves their team is experienced, accountable and dependable. A PSP with long-term employee retention means they have experts in-house who will bring valuable knowledge to the table as your company expands. If they have long-term customer retention, it shows accountability to their customers. It shows that their customers know they can depend on their PSP when they need them most. We are fortunate to have many team members who have been here five, 10, and some well over 15 years.

When looking for a PSP, you want a partner that understands your potential. A partner that values your business at the beginning, who can utilize their knowledge and capabilities to help you establish a foundation for sustainable growth. For example, at Decal Impressions, we utilize our custom e-commerce portals to help franchisors scale their marketing capabilities as they on-board new franchisees. These custom e-commerce portals allow franchisees to order approved marketing, promotional and branded items with ease.

Imagine if you had to go to a different vendor every time you needed something. When this happens, franchisees often become lost, trying to order the wrong product from the wrong vendor, wasting time and generating frustration. By partnering with a PSP and centralizing ordering of business cards, signs, uniforms, marketing materials, coupons, promotional products, etc., it creates an easier and more efficient system. This centralized system enables franchisors to maintain control over their brand's message and maintain a consistent look and feel across all franchises. This in turn helps to increase brand awareness and recognition, which can lead to improved customer loyalty and repeat business. More importantly, this allows franchisees to focus on what they do best: running their business. This increases franchisee success, leading to overall franchise success.

Additionally, partnering with a PSP allows franchisors to stay ahead of industry trends and adopt new marketing strategies quickly. With the right partner, franchisors can experiment with new approaches to marketing and branding, while maintaining control over their brand identity. It can also lower the overhead cost for franchisees, as all orders will be placed through the same system.

Neglecting to implement a partnership with a PSP early, franchisors risk the threat of inconsistent branding and messaging, which can lead to a weakened franchise and ultimately harm the entire network of franchisees. This failure to employ strict branding rules from the beginning can lead to rogue franchisees, who may produce their own marketing materials, resulting in a diluted and inconsistent brand. This can confuse customers, weaken the franchisee's business and ultimately damage the overall reputation of the franchise. It is a slippery slope for franchise systems, and hard to climb back from.

Without a clear and effective system for producing branded materials, franchisees may struggle to market themselves effectively and efficiently. This can result in higher costs for individual franchisees, a lack of cohesion across the franchise network and an overall weakened marketing message.

In today's competitive business landscape, a franchise without strong brand control is at a significant disadvantage. It is critical for franchisors to recognize the threat of not partnering with a PSP and take proactive steps to ensure consistent branding and messaging across their entire network. By doing so, they can mitigate future pain points, and create a strong and cohesive brand identity that grows with the franchise. Remember, the best defense is a good offense. To achieve success at every turn, it's essential to maintain full control of your brand and create a nurturing environment that fosters growth.

As a business owner, you understand that in times of crisis, your ability to pivot and adapt quickly can make or break a business. And when a franchise system is involved, the stakes are even higher. That's why a strong PSP can be a critical ally in ensuring the survival and success of a franchise network.

At Decal Impressions, we understand this intimately. When the pandemic hit and franchise systems had to scramble to keep their locations operational under constantly changing guidelines, we were there to help. We worked closely with our franchise partners to create custom lines of social distancing graphics, tamper-proof decals and essential signage to ensure their franchisees could continue to operate safely and effectively. We know that in times of crisis, quick and deliberate action is essential to success. As a service provider, it made me extremely proud to know that through our efforts, we were helping our customers' businesses stay open, employees paid and families fed.

It is also important to have a partner that understands the value of customer service. You should look for a PSP that serves your business the way you expect your business to serve your customers.

Engaging with a PSP that does not adhere to brand guidelines, does not respond to customers (both you and franchisees) and does not meet deadlines is a recipe for disaster. With no accountability, you can expect to be left high and dry. Imagine a new product launch is scheduled to go live, but none of the signage or promotional products made it to your franchisees. Your new promotion is dead in the water. All that time, money and effort spent to create a revenue stream for your business was lost.

Although Artificial Intelligence, or AI, may be the wave of the future, you know a chatbot cannot handle every customer service request. A FAQ on the website does not answer every question. And communication can break down, even via email. It is crucial to have a PSP with a dedicated team to answer your call in a timely and professional manner, and can help stop a headache before it happens.

Having a PSP with a dedicated team that works in alignment with your brand's goals is paramount to a successful partnership. From graphic designers to account managers, having a unified front to support your growth can give you invaluable time to focus on the continued success of your franchise.

By utilizing resources, technology and industry knowledge, a true PSP partner will be a steward of the brand. In many cases, Decal Impressions works with franchisors as an outsourced marketing department, handling everything from design to production, and ultimately, fulfillment. We work to maintain consistent brand guidelines across all mediums, from web to print. This not only strengthens the partnership, but it also creates an environment of success for both parties.

As a business leader, it is my job to understand what will be best for my organization. As a service provider, it is my job to understand what will be best for my customers' organization. Sometimes, that can mean having some very tough conversations. Presenting our customers with honest information is not always what they want to hear, and on all accounts having to hear a customer is unhappy is very tough to hear. But through my experience, I have learned that being honest and having that conversation as soon as possible, builds trust, and clears the path for a long and successful partnership.

Partnering with a print service provider can help franchisors maintain brand consistency, control costs and gain expert insights, ultimately leading to sustainable franchise growth. By leveraging the strengths of a PSP, franchisors can focus on expanding their reach and growing their franchise, while a trusted partner handles the branding and marketing materials. Failing to partner with a PSP can lead to rogue franchisees, dilution of the brand and a weak brand image that negatively impacts sales and franchise growth. Don't let this happen to your franchise; explore the power of PSP partnerships and take control of your brand.

As you look to create your franchise, search for a print service provider that will help you lay the foundation to achieve sustainable growth—a partner that will be able to adapt and support your business as it grows and changes, whether that is adding in additional services or supporting hundreds of franchisees across the country. By implementing this key piece of infrastructure early, you will set up yourself and your franchise for long-term success.

CHAPTER 4

TRAVELING THE ROAD FROM CORPORATE TO ENTREPRENEUR

By **CARLTON MILLINDER**

The journey of an entrepreneur can sometimes be a difficult one, but it can also be incredibly rewarding. Entrepreneurship was not a journey I thought I would take, but I do remember watching my father's entrepreneurial experience in admiration. He was a great cook and owned a restaurant. He never read books or took classes about entrepreneurship, business development or owning a restaurant. He was able to defy all odds and open a successful restaurant with no industry experience or financial backing. Somehow, he was just able to flow into it, work hard and do well with it. His business created financial stability for my family growing up, so I always knew the benefits of being an entrepreneur.

"My greatest moments didn't come from my greatest moments. My greatest moments came from my greatest defeats. It was during my defeat that I had to find a way to get back up."
–Eric Thomas

My own entrepreneurial journey began unexpectedly after I was laid off from my corporate electrical engineering career. Getting laid off from a job can be tough on anyone. It's never easy to find out that you're no longer needed, and it can be even harder to figure out what to do next. When it happened to me, I was shocked and didn't know where to turn. I had to think outside of the box.

Looking back, getting laid off was the best thing that ever happened to me, because it forced me out of my comfort zone and into entrepreneurship. After I was laid off, I quickly realized that unemployment benefits were not enough to live on. Being in that position forced me to hustle, in order to make ends meet. I was at a crossroads, and one carried a lot more penalties than the other, so I started to drive for Uber and Lyft, while trying to figure out my next move.

Out of nowhere, a former classmate contacted me on Facebook and asked if I had any interest in travel. She had a business opportunity in the travel industry, which allowed me to have my own business. I knew I intended to travel more, and I have always been passionate about travel, constantly wanting to explore new destinations around the world. When she explained the opportunity to become a travel advisor, I jumped at the chance! I decided to take the plunge and jumped in with both feet. I knew this was an industry that required knowledge and patience. After all, it's all about building strong relationships, while helping people have the best possible experiences when they travel. I created a plan, set goals, put together strategies and worked hard to get started as soon as possible.

I joined a team of experienced and professional travel advisors who had worked in the industry for many years. I quickly realized this was going to be an amazing opportunity to learn from these professionals who could provide invaluable advice and support. Together, we discussed strategies, created marketing plans and shared our experiences with clients.

Chapter 4: **Carlton Millinder**

With their guidance, I learned the importance of the details, customer service and great communication. I studied hard to understand the travel industry and became an advisor in all aspects of it. I discovered that while booking flights and hotels was a key part of my job, there was much more to be done to make sure each client's experience exceeded their expectations. I wanted them to have the best vacation possible, without any problems or issues. As I was learning, I did a lot of research and had many conversations with suppliers to make sure my clients were getting the best deals available.

I am now proud to say that after much hard work and dedication, I have become an expert in the travel industry. My entrepreneurial journey has been a great success and I am now able to provide my clients with the highest quality of service and knowledge. I will never stop learning and growing in this industry, as it is constantly changing. I am excited to see what lies ahead for me in this ever-evolving business.

I quickly found I have a knack for helping my clients plan memorable vacation experiences. It's not just about booking flights and hotels; it's about creating an experience they'll never forget. My clients know I will always go the extra mile for them and create an experience based on their budget, as well as their vision for the trip. I am very patient with clients, because I know this industry is about building lasting relationships and caring for the people we help. At the end of the day, happy customers are what make this industry so rewarding. When customers come back to me for their next trip, I know I've done a good job.

My very first client was a blessing and a learning experience. She was a young lady who wanted to plan a vacation to Punta Cana for herself, her son and a few friends. This was a very unique, but great experience, because I had the chance to really learn the ropes of this agency and figure out my processes. I was able to work with different suppliers.

For her trip, I asked her to share her vision with me, including the activities she wanted to do, off and on the resort. After listening to her ideas, I came up with some additional ideas I thought her group would enjoy. I didn't want to insult her, but I also didn't want to scare her. I decided to give her a lower priced package option, a higher priced package option and one in the middle. I did make some mistakes along the way, but in the end, she returned from her trip completely satisfied with my work. Even better, she commented on my attention to detail and the care I put into finding her the best package within her budget.

When she returned from her trip, she told me, "you always thought about things outside of the things I was looking for." I said, "Yeah, that's what I was supposed to do, at least give you the options." I treat my clients the way I would want a travel advisor to treat me. I would want them to give me great options and a memorable experience, without feeling like I have to pinch pennies or sacrifice a good time.

This was a great experience and I am forever grateful for that first client. Since then, I have repeatedly applied my approach of providing options and working with my clients to tailor the perfect travel package for them. Whether it's a family cruise or an island destination getaway, I always strive to make sure my clients are getting the most out of their trip. My goal is to not only provide customers with options, but also ensure they feel like they can come back time and time again, if they need help planning their next vacation.

Chapter 4: **Carlton Millinder**

It was from this experience that my client strategy was born. I learned to provide them with multiple options, both lower-priced and higher-priced packages, so they can choose the one that fits their budget best, without feeling pressured or restricted. For each client, I take the initiative by talking with multiple suppliers and finding the best deals, just like I did with my first client. From that point on, I knew taking the time to listen to my clients and understand their vision was very important, in order to deliver a successful trip. It wasn't only about saving money, but also providing a valuable and memorable experience.

It's all part of being a travel advisor! Clients can expect detailed itineraries, personalized service and direct access to me at any point during their journey. They will also have peace of mind knowing their money is well spent, and they don't have to worry about any unexpected costs. I can't wait to continue on this amazing entrepreneurial journey! If you are looking for the perfect travel package, look no further! Let me help make your vacation dreams come true! The journey of being a travel advisor has been an incredible learning experience. With each client, I learn something new and find ways to improve my services. It's amazing how much you can accomplish when you put your mind to it and keep pushing forward.

I became an expert in finding the balance between quality and budget, as I could always find ways to optimize the trip, while making sure my clients were able to have the best time possible. I also started taking into account more than just the destination, such as flight times or connections, hotel amenities, local attractions and activities, etc. Since then, my agency has only grown, and I have been honored to serve countless clients, vendors and business partners.

Since that first client, my travel business has been an amazing journey and I have really enjoyed each client, vendor and business partner I've met along the way. The perks of being in the travel industry are endless: the obvious luxury of traveling to new and exciting places, interesting people you meet, but also building financial freedom. Establishing an additional stream of income doing something I love is extremely fulfilling. Financial freedom is something I have long desired and has now become a reality in my life. Creating an income not tied to a boss telling me what to do and how to do it is a dream come true.

I believe my success lies in the fact that I am able to provide service with an entrepreneurial mindset and an honest, witty personality. Each trip is unique and tailored specifically to the client's needs, and it has become my goal to make sure each one of them is fully satisfied in every aspect. With this mantra in mind, I have been able to create strong relationships with all of my clients, as well as our vendors, ultimately leading to long-term partnerships that benefit everyone involved. Being a travel advisor isn't just about booking flights or finding hotels; it's about creating memories for people that will last a lifetime! That's why I love what I do, and will continue to strive for excellence in the years to come.

My entrepreneurial journey has been one of growth and learning, both professionally and personally. It has been a challenge to stay on top of all the trends and changes in the industry, but also an amazing opportunity to meet wonderful people from all around the world! I am grateful for this experience and cannot wait for my next adventure.

Chapter 4: **Carlton Millinder**

In this business, I have encountered many challenges that have helped me grow and expand my travel agency. From unique requests to tight deadlines, each experience has made me stronger as a business provider. Travel is something that can change people's lives, even if it's just for one day. Seeing the joy on clients' faces when they return home with unforgettable memories is what truly makes the job worth it for me. Even when the work gets tough, I always remember why I am doing this—to share happiness with others and give them a chance to escape their everyday lives through travel.

When I think back to the beginning of my journey, it's hard for me to believe how far I have come. It all started with small steps of learning about the travel industry and taking on one task at a time. Every day, I grow in my knowledge of the travel industry and learn more about how to gain success as a travel advisor. It has been an amazing journey so far, teaching me about the importance of networking with people and forming strong relationships, in order to reach the end goal.

Through difficult times, I have still remained passionate about helping those who want to explore the world and contribute to their own ambitions. Moving forward, I am motivated by the potential of what travel can offer, and how I can give back to others through this field. My primary mission is to be able to support individuals in their own entrepreneurial endeavors. There is no greater feeling than being able to provide guidance and assistance as they strive for their dreams. Therefore, I continue learning methods on how I can better serve my clients and team members so we may find success, both professionally and personally.

For me and others who have taken on this endeavor, travel is more than just a business opportunity; it is a way of life. We are able to create our own paths, while discovering new cultures and experiences, all while helping people reach their goals. This endless journey has been filled with learning moments and plenty of rewarding experiences along the way. As I reflect on my triumphs thus far, I am constantly reminded of why I started this journey in the first place and why it continues to motivate me each day.

> *You cannot afford to live in the potential phase for the rest of your life; at some point, you have to unleash the potential and make your move."*
> **–Eric Thomas**

In conclusion, being a travel advisor has been an incredibly rewarding experience for me and I wouldn't trade it for anything. If you're considering a career change, I would highly recommend becoming an entrepreneur in the travel industry—it has opened up many doors for me and I'm looking forward to seeing where the road takes me next. If you love traveling as much as I do, and want to turn your passion for travel into a lucrative business, reach out to me. I can help you get started. It's time to begin your own entrepreneurial journey in the travel industry and make a whole new world of opportunities available to you. Together, we can make a difference in this world, one trip at a time. So join me on this entrepreneurial journey, and let's explore the world together.

CHAPTER 5

PUTTING KIDS FIRST: LEVERAGING PEDIATRIC TELEMEDICINE FOR A HEALTHIER FUTURE

By **CHELSEA JOHNSON**

The Case for Better Triage for Parents

I remember the exact moment I realized that telemedicine was the future of healthcare. It was 2016, and I was working the night shift in the community pediatric emergency room (ER). My next patient was a 4-year-old boy with complaints of fever. The pre-visit documentation noted the mom had called the nurse advice line earlier in the evening, because her son had a fever, a headache and neck pain. The nurse taking her call told her she had to go to the ER right away for evaluation, because her child could have meningitis—a potentially serious infection surrounding the brain. Upon arrival, the ER staff nurse already administered ibuprofen for pain and fever reduction, and then checked his vital signs.

When I walked into the room, I saw a tired, distraught mom sitting in the chair with three kids under six playing, climbing onto the exam table and pulling equipment off the wall. I was worried they were going to break something or injure themselves. Remaining calm, I proceeded with the evaluation and exam. Mom was becoming upset, because I was not appearing concerned as the nurse on the advice line had been. I explained: Your child is doing great! Meningitis is highly unlikely for all of these reasons, as I explained. The only way to confirm meningitis is to place a needle in his back and drain some spinal fluid, and then test it for viruses and bacteria. Mom shuddered a bit with this information. Ibuprofen is clearly improving your child's headache, neck pain and bringing down that fever. That's when I recognized that if I'd had the chance to talk to this mom after the triage nurse determined the patient needed an evaluation by a doctor, and had seen this patient before she'd come into the ER, I could have assessed the situation more expertly, and recommended the ibuprofen given at home. She didn't need the worry, the four-hour visit with three kids well past bedtime, or the impending ER bill … this was no emergency.

In my decades as a pediatrician, I've learned that parents often need peace of mind—they've heard horror stories, received well-intended advice and googled way too many symptoms. Parents want a trusted someone to reassure them that this headache or that cough won't develop into a life-threatening condition. Access to a telemedicine appointment with a trusted pediatrician could prevent unnecessary visits to urgent care centers and emergency rooms, which can come with long wait times and hefty fees. And yet, even in a post-pandemic landscape where telehealth is growing exponentially, pediatric telemedicine has been slower to catch on.

As an experienced physician and entrepreneur at the forefront of digital health, I am working to change the minds of healthcare organizations, insurance companies, patients, investors and other stakeholders. I know that pediatric telemedicine puts children and their families first, while allowing pediatricians the flexibility and autonomy they need to better care for patients.

Chapter 5: **Chelsea Johnson**

Blazing a Trail

I knew I would be a doctor when I was 12 years old. Living in a very small town in rural Nebraska, that year I attended a local "Reading in the Park" event, because reading was, and still is, a passion. There was a big tub, a horse tank actually, full of giveaway books under an enormous oak tree within the festival grounds. By the time I got there, a handful of books remained, including a biography about Elizabeth Blackwell, MD, the first woman doctor. This would be my first biography I'd read. I was captivated—here was somebody who had suffered much hardship to earn her medical degree, who had already paved the way for women to be doctors. From that point on, my entire young adult life was focused on medical school.

After several difficult decisions and a few setbacks, I earned a spot in the Rural Health Opportunities Program (RHOP) at Chadron State College, during my sophomore year. This program encouraged rural students to enter the medical field with the incentives of guaranteed admission and a financial aid package to return to rural Nebraska to practice medicine. I graduated with a degree in human biology and chemistry, and a spot at the University of Nebraska Medical Center. I was elated! So many students agonized about getting admitted to medical school. I was in and had no doubts about my ability to earn my medical degree.

Medical students must decide one of six areas of medicine to practice and submit applications for residencies—additional years of training in that area—after graduation. I knew I wanted to work with children early on, during my obstetrics and gynecology rotation. Every delivery I attended, I gravitated toward the warmer the baby was placed on once born. My pediatric rotations cemented my decision. I was accepted to a pediatric residency and spent three years honing my skills to be a pediatrician.

Following residency, I stayed at the teaching hospital, where I trained and continued working as an attending pediatrician—both caring for patients and teaching medical students and residents. After about 10 years, I felt that my career wasn't progressing. I transitioned roles within the same institution, not really making a name for myself or finding my place. It wasn't until years later, during a meeting with an executive coach, that I realized I was an "entrepreneur" in my own right, just in the wrong place. What I thought of as my succession of career failures was actual validation that I was someone who had ideas, and worked to create services that people would want.

During my career, I was an innovator, in a way. My roles involved doing new things and being (one of) the first physicians in that space. At my institution, I was the pioneer in general pediatricians working in subspecialty departments, while employed in pediatric hematology and oncology (blood and cancer). I was also a member of the physician team opening a new urgent care, where I participated in developing the policies and procedures, worked out the kinks in the patient care processes and was scheduling director for a number of years.

Fortune followed me, and I joined the physician team instrumental in transitioning another urgent care center to a community ER. Yes! That ER where I met the distraught mom worrying about her 4-year-old with fever. I began formulating ideas on how to triage care better. When I heard about a new opportunity to get involved in pediatric telemedicine within my organization, I jumped at the chance.

Leaning into Telemedicine

I had finally found my niche. I became Medical Director of our direct-to-patient telemedicine for the hospital's Medicaid population, developing policies and processes, hiring and training great physicians, and determined to deliver innovative care. I was excited to be doing work that I knew would help families and kids thrive. From the beginning, telemedicine faced resistance from doctors and hospital administrators.

The pushback from ER physicians who may have felt that access to telemedicine tread on their territory was surprising. I was frustrated that the program was not growing the way I wanted it to. I did not have decision-making authority to shift the program in the direction I envisioned.

Then COVID-19 hit, hospitals shut down and suddenly telemedicine became the hospital's number one priority. I finally felt that my effort and focus was paying off, and that my team and I were making a big difference in the lives of kids during a challenging time. However, the hospital threw me another curveball at the height of the pandemic. They had decided to decentralize telemedicine and they were eliminating my position. Did I want to go back to working in urgent care or ER again?

This was another pivotal moment in my career. I knew that the hospital was making this decision, which did not align with my passion and vision. Instead of taking resources away from telemedicine, we needed to be leaning in. This is where the future of medicine is, I thought. I left the institution where I'd built my career without an exit strategy.

A Shifting Digital Landscape

I knew I wanted to stay in telemedicine, but I still had a lot to learn about the business of medicine and the digital environment. After my experience of trying to go against the grain at a slow-to-change large academic hospital, I wanted a seat at the table, a voice in decision-making and an opportunity to learn more about providing digital health care. In those panicked first months, I applied for any telemedicine job I found. Most were not hiring pediatricians. One startup actually responded, yet told me that it wasn't focusing on pediatrics, only to call me a few weeks later with an offer to build the pediatric telemedicine program.

Working with an amazing collaborative pediatrician, we created policies, processes and training modules—from the bottom up. We hired, trained and supervised pediatricians for this kind of care. We worked with the app development team; the AI-driven symptoms checker development team; and the team of physicians seeing adult patients. We wrote patient care cards, did social media ads and wrote articles for digital journals and magazines. This was chat-based telemedicine, which connected patients (or parents) with a physician via real-time chat. The limitations of this model—and what I saw as a collision between digital health and social media, during a time of political upheaval and disinformation—soon became obvious to me. Because there was no trusted relationship developed between physicians and patients, and patients were not able to see physicians directly in the chat, a lot of verbal abuse occurred, especially when antibiotics were demanded and appropriately not prescribed. I felt that the company was not doing enough to protect physicians from harassment. After a particularly bad chat session, I gave my notice.

Chapter 5: **Chelsea Johnson**

Here I was again, without an exit strategy. But I was getting closer to finding the right fit. My next position, which required me to work with an investor and network of pediatric primary care practices to build a new pediatric telemedicine business, taught me so much about the intersection of medicine and the startup world. By this time, I was enrolled in an Executive MBA program, where I focused on understanding the partnership between the investment company and the telemedicine business. Not long after, equipped with years of clinical and telemedicine experience, as well as a growing understanding of how to reach my target audience and create revenue streams, I started my own company: Concierge Pediatric Care, LLC.

Putting People First at Concierge Pediatric Care, LLC

As my medical practice grows and scales, I am creating a culture that empowers and protects physicians. As a former employed pediatrician myself, I know first-hand that medical leadership has failed its physicians significantly during the pandemic and its aftermath. Because so many healthcare leaders did not understand how to lead through crisis and change, they did not take care of employees during COVID. Too many physicians are now leaving medicine or are retiring early. And too many are doing side gigs, trying to find another career. We have not been valued for our years of education, experience and expertise, undertaking an accumulating workload, and increasing barriers to delivering high-quality care. We are not compensated appropriately; additionally, much of the work is unpaid. We are not given the space, time or freedom to relax and to step away. We are burned out, fed up, quietly quitting, while regretting our career choices and succumbing to suicide at an alarming rate.

I believe that the success of a medical business depends on taking care of your people—your employees and your patients. The heart of healthcare is relationships. The core being the doctor-patient relationship. "When the leader creates an environment in which people feel that someone has their back, they will do extraordinary things," Simon Sinek said. "Let us all be the leaders we wish we had."

My vision for this company is offering a valued compensation, flexibility, autonomy, a seat at the table and a safe environment in which to express ideas and concerns. Because, as my favorite inspirational speaker shares, "When a leader embraces their responsibility to care for people instead of caring for numbers, then people will follow, solve problems and see to it that that leader's vision comes to life the right way, a stable way and not the expedient way." I believe that the telehealth model, because of its built-in accessibility and versatility, makes this kind of inclusive culture possible.

The Future of Pediatric Medicine

We know that pediatric telemedicine works. Eighty-percent of my telemedicine visits can be resolved with a diagnosis, treatment plan and a good night's sleep for parents. With tools like digital otoscopes and stethoscopes, over 90-percent of visits resolve with an extended virtual exam. In publication after publication, over 80-percent of patients having had a telemedicine visit are very highly satisfied with the care received, and looking forward to their next telemedicine visit. And yet, pediatric telemedicine has been slower to grow than its adult counterpart, because parents are hesitant to seek help from an unknown entity, especially because children are much more likely than adults to have established relationships with primary care doctors. I understand the need for a trusted physician, which is why I carefully vet the pediatricians I hire, and give them the tools to build the doctor/patient relationship in the digital realm. Not only can pediatric telemedicine keep kids healthier, by providing immediate quality care and eliminating unnecessary urgent care visits, it can also create new opportunities for connection, or "touch points," between doctors and patients.

Let me share this delightful story. Back when I worked in telemedicine at an academic children's hospital, I oversaw a pilot program in which pediatric orthopedic surgeons had telemedicine video visits with their patients following spinal surgery. This is a significant surgery that makes it impractical and sometimes painful to load a child into a car for a one, two or three-hour ride to the hospital. I helped facilitate these visits to ensure the physician and family had seamless connectivity with the virtual visit. Following a memorable visit, I was struck by the surgeon's delight. He spoke so highly of the experience, because he could not only evaluate the child's wounds easily, but also he got to see the child's family environment. For example, how the child's bedroom was set up to accommodate his post-surgery recovery. The surgeon felt that this intimate window into the lives of his families, not possible during an in-clinic visit, gave him new insight, and helped him to better treat patients in recovery.

And pediatric telemedicine reverberates beyond visits from home. For example, the use of telemedicine in schools has the potential to keep kids in school and parents at work, thus decreasing the amount of time and money wasted on unnecessary doctor visits while combating chronic absenteeism, a problem with 20-percent of the school-aged population. I believe that pediatricians are the best people to speak on behalf of children. Therefore, in order to elevate how we treat kids, we need to see more pediatricians on school boards; consultants to school administrators on health policy, education and healthcare accessibility; state and federal task forces and committees, where child health and welfare are at stake; and other groups who influence and create policy.

It all comes down to taking care of people. If pediatricians are given the support they need to care for kids, children and families will thrive. Pediatric telehealth is not only the future of medicine, it's a chance for us to invest in the future of our kids.

CHAPTER 6

TANGIBLE ASSETS YOU CAN HOLD

By **COLLIN PLUME**

Precious metals are often overlooked in favor of more publicized investments. However, they offer a unique opportunity for investors to diversify and potentially reap the rewards of their distinct characteristics. Gold and silver have historically been deployed by savvy investors as a tool to increase portfolio efficiency and reduce risk. Stocks are only shares, crypto is purely digital and real estate is obviously not transportable. Precious metals are tangible assets that provide ownership and control, allowing a person the ability to take it anywhere and use it as they please. Investing in these types of assets can help cushion performance drawdowns during times of market volatility. The important thing to remember is that having someone in your corner with their finger on the pulse of the market trends is key.

In many cases, a person's mind jumps to jewelry when thinking of gold and silver, because that is where we mostly see it out in the world. Jewelry is gold's most obvious use and represents a large amount of the demand. However, the world of precious metals goes much deeper than a bangle. The quality between a gold or silver piece of jewelry is vastly different from an investment in precious metals bearing the same name. Physical gold and silver, acquired as an investment, is held to far higher standards, similar to precious metals used in industry. Something that is often overlooked is that both of these precious metals are essential in our modern society in countless vital applications. That's a big reason why these specific investments react differently to the ebb and flow of the market, versus other tried and true investment strategies. Our clients are investing in a physical asset, something real. They aren't putting their assets into intangible situations.

Our investors have the option to physically possess their investment, which isn't possible in many other industries. They also have the option to have it housed at our depository. One advantage of precious metals is that they hold value no matter where or when you are—they will always be valuable and in demand. While I personally invest in real estate, I cannot move my property around with me as I please. However, I can do that with my precious metal investments. There is an element of freedom that exists when you have the option to hold your assets that don't exist elsewhere.

Precious Metal's Value in Industry

Investing in gold or silver can be an effective strategy for those looking to protect their savings, while taking advantage of long-term growth opportunities. The continued developments in tech and medicine create further demand for precious metals.

Gold has become an increasingly important material in the electronics sector. Most smart phones and laptops contain a small, yet crucial amount of gold. It's essential in most electronics as well as medical robotic equipment. Demand for gold from this sector continues to rise with newly emerging technologies.

Gold is a crucial component of the most advanced technology. From medical implants to aerospace engineering, gold plays an important role in many industries, due to its electrical and thermal conductivity, corrosion resistance, malleability and excellent ductility. The electronics industry alone uses about 300 tonnes of newly mined gold each year.

Silver also has thousands of industrial uses. It is increasingly being recognized as a necessary component for the transition to renewable energy. As global leaders have made it a priority to find alternatives to traditional energy sources, the demand for silver is projected to skyrocket from the already substantial 55-million ounces per year. It has the highest electrical conductivity of any metal. Through the past 10 years, the solar photovoltaic and electrical vehicle sectors have been in constant demand for silver.

Precious metals are essential to modern society in countless applications. They can provide investors with both security and returns due to the fact that they are necessary, finite and unable to be substituted or replicated.

Dollar/ Inflation/ Recession

Currently, we are in year one of a major recession. Inflation is palpable and widely recognized. Getting in front of this early trend from an investment standpoint is invaluable. We are already seeing indicators that gold and silver are poised to increase in value, in the same way they have over previous recession periods. Contrary to market predictions in the media saying otherwise, in 2022, gold proved to be the best-performing asset in its class and the best store of value.

Inflation affects investments significantly. Gold and silver, as investments, are historically proven to be among the most reliable and stable of assets. These precious metals have increased in value when other investments have tanked during previous recession periods. The last big recession was in the early 1980s. During that time, gold and silver held their value and increased over a five-year period, while other investment avenues proved unstable.

Gold has been used as a store of value for centuries, and remains an important asset. It's a highly valued investment due to its dual role as a commodity and a currency. It has intrinsic value that is independent of other currencies. Historically, gold prices have been inversely related to the U.S. dollar. When the dollar appreciates, gold prices drop. When the dollar depreciates, gold prices rise. This makes gold an attractive hedge against inflation and market volatility.

The U.S. dollar has faced some serious challenges lately. The Federal Reserve's aggressive rate hikes and high inflation leads to a lack of confidence in the dollar. This has resulted in investors turning to gold as an alternative asset. I expect this trend to continue. Investors must be prepared for changes in the market and have strategies in place to manage risk. It's important to understand that currency markets can be volatile and influenced by a number of factors. When a portfolio has a variety of investments, including precious metals, risk is more easily managed and investors are better able to take advantage of potential opportunities to protect their investments as a whole.

Chapter 6: **Collin Plume**

Why investors are Reverting Back to Old-School Investments

Investors have begun to return to a more rational and value-based approach to investing. This shift is necessitated by a number of factors, including the pandemic, unmanageable inflation and the current recession. Many previously reliable markets have become unpredictable and volatile.

Investing in precious metals eliminates counterparty risk. Gold and silver serve as global currencies that hold significant value around the world. As an asset, they are not subject to government control. Precious metals are a finite resource and unlike cash, they can't be created at will. Gold is an investment that will always hold value.

Everyone noticed what happened this past year with regards to crypto investments–if you don't hold it, you don't own it. Our business is about physical assets. Recently, crypto was being compared to gold, based on the short-lived upturn in the value of select cryptocurrencies. In under one year, those crypto values ballooned and then fell drastically. This is only one example of asset volatility that investors in precious metals do not experience. The longevity and stability of an investment are of utmost importance. Gold and silver have always retained their unrivaled strength in the market.

The economy has an ebb and flow. Recession periods are inevitable and smart investors are prepared for these situations. The current economic recession presents an opportunity for investors to diversify their portfolios and protect their wealth. Precious metals, such as gold and silver, historically have been strong investments during times of economic downturn. They also have shown to hold their value spanning decades, through numerous economic highs and lows.

As a diverse investor, I've used my experience to shape Noble Gold into something I'd choose to invest in, regardless of my connections to the industry. My journey in investing is similar to anyone who is curating their portfolio. It's important for many investors, including myself, to pass wealth down through generations. Investments like real estate are fantastic and are smart to have in a diverse portfolio. However, structures don't last forever and require a significant amount of upkeep over time. When you're dealing with precious metals, the quality of gold that you invest in now will still be of the same quality 200 years from now.

Precious Metal Investment Strategies

Direct Ownership or Home Delivery

Investing in precious metals allows investors the option to own their assets directly in the form of bullion or coins. Owning physical gold and silver is particularly attractive to those who wish to maintain complete control over their investment. It can be shipped safely, directly to the home, or housed in our depository. Clients have the peace of mind that I personally inventory each piece of their investment at the depository—they only need to request it be sent to them at any time. Physically having precious metals in your possession allows freedom that few other assets provide. Investors are able to travel anywhere with their investment and can be sure it will hold high value wherever they go.

IRAs

Oftentimes, when it comes time for a person to take advantage of their IRA, they would rather roll their investments over into a gold IRA than cash out. Investors have the opportunity to take their distribution in gold, silver, platinum or palladium. Rather than exchanging a growing investment for depreciating cash, their asset remains an investment of which they can take possession. Another advantageous element in this process is when moving your investment from one qualified account to another, there are no tax penalties. Converting an IRA to precious metals allows for a significant increase in personal control over one's own money, compared to other types of investments.

Mix it Up

A diversified basket of precious metals offers the most advantages when it comes to choosing whether to invest in gold, silver, platinum or palladium. This allows investors to spread out their risk, while taking advantage of the unique characteristics inherent in each metal. It provides exposure to both non-cyclical and cyclical drivers across all four metals, providing more consistent returns, compared to investing in any single metal alone. With new tech being developed every day, each type of precious metal will continue to be necessary for various applications due to its unique properties. Diversifying will allow investors to take advantage of the emerging technology that uses them.

Reduce Risk by Owning Your Investment

Noble Gold deals with physical precious metal investments, because of the increased control and decreased risk associated with actually owning your assets. While that is not the only way to invest in precious metals, there are advantages that don't apply to other types of investments. Because gold stocks don't mimic the prices of gold bullion, they provide less diversification to an investment portfolio. If there is a stock market crash, any investments in a gold mine or manufacturer will suffer. Meanwhile, the prices of physical gold will increase. When you are the owner of your investment, you aren't subject to the same ever-changing variables. Additionally, we provide a high level of transparency that has become increasingly hard to find. Investors who have control over their assets and are well-informed can expect to get profitable returns. We are passionate about facilitating those opportunities for our clients.

CHAPTER 7

THE RELUCTANT ENTREPRENEUR

By **CURT MAIER**

I have enjoyed three distinct careers, beginning as a professional military officer for my first five years. After that, I was a Fortune 300 creature for 20 years, starting as a sales guy, moving up to sales management, business management and general management. Then I was a country manager in Malaysia. When I returned to headquarters, I had various assignments running global businesses, where I ended up as a mergers and acquisitions general manager.

My third career, which has been the most satisfying, has been as an entrepreneur and small business owner. But the transition from corporate guy to entrepreneur was not a smooth one. It all started when I left the military in the mid 1980s. There was no such thing as a transition plan back then. Nowadays, they have transition assistance programs to help prepare you for leaving the military. When I left in 1984, they looked at me, and said, "Don't let the door hit you on the way out."

When I got out of the Navy, my plan was to get a job with the biggest, baddest Fortune 500 company I could. I put my myself in the hands of a headhunter, who scheduled interviews with all the usual suspects: Dow Chemical, Hewlett Packard, Texas Instruments, etc. I ended up choosing one that I didn't even know existed: Air Products and Chemicals. They make industrial gases used in manufacturing processes—from food freezers to NASA to hospitals.

What I learned very well was how to progress through the layers of corporate management. As my college degree from Notre Dame was in engineering, the company also paid for my MBA, which enabled me to get promoted within the corporation. I did well enough that they tapped me to get into mergers and acquisitions, where I learned the buy side, versus the sell side, where I am now.

At that stage of my life, my wife and I realized that with two young kids, we needed to do something different. I was in Beijing one week and then she was in Germany. And how does that work with kids? I'm old school. I thought we had enough money and maybe my wife would want to stay at home, because our youngest daughter was entering kindergarten. But I knew my wife liked her professional life.

So, one Sunday morning, I said, "Honey, why don't you consider either staying at home, or maybe using your CPA knowledge and experience to run your own shop? Fall is coming, kids are starting school, and our lives are crazy. We need to start thinking about this."

She replied, "I agree with you. We need to consider something here. But what did you tell me Friday night when I picked you up at the airport?" I looked at her, and asked what she was talking about. She replied, "Let me quote you. You said you just made another owner a millionaire."

I had been in the Mid-Atlantic, where we bought a company for $9 million dollars that was worth only eight and the owner was now a multi-millionaire. I looked at my wife and said, "What's your point? That's what I do for a living."

Then, she said something very prophetic. She said, "What's the difference between those owners and you?"

I looked at her and said, "Hey, where is this going? I'm doing really well. You know I'm a corporate guy. I am what I am."

She followed that up with, "I don't think you like your job much anymore." I thought, what? Then she continued. "Do you really like competing with everyone for the next rung up the ladder, and going to off-site diversity seminars, etc.?" I told her that we're in the same boat. We're corporate creatures who are paid a lot of money. We have golden handcuffs. It is what it is. Do I like it? No, I don't like all of it, any more than you do. But I'm successful.

She continued, "Well, there's a difference. You're running a P&L in a publicly traded company. You must have enormous pressure that you keep inside. I agree, we need some flexibility. But why don't I remain the W-2 to secure the compensation and benefits, which will enable you to become an entrepreneur and control your destiny."

I was very uncomfortable with this discussion. I looked at my watch and said, "Honey, I got a tee time at nine o'clock. We'll talk about this later."

On the way to the golf course, I thought, that it didn't go the way I imagined. I was just planting a seed with my wife. After I finished my round of golf at the club, I asked a friend if my wife was crazy. He looked around, and said, "How long have you been a member here?" I told him that it was about six years. He asked, "How many of these guys work any harder than you?" I told him not many. I'm lucky to get one round on the weekend. These guys are playing every day.

He said, "You're right. How many of these guys are any smarter than you?" That was a little more difficult. I looked around. That guy owns a law firm. That one owns a printing business. These are all entrepreneurs. I don't know who's smarter than me.

He continued, "Look, I know you're running a quarter-billion dollar business and none of these guys are any smarter than you. My answer to your question about your wife being crazy is, no. On the contrary, you are the luckiest guy in the world."

I responded, "Excuse me?"

Then, he let me have it. "She's exactly right. You're wasting your time. You're making shareholders wealthy, not yourself. Do you understand how lucky you are? You're very fortunate … you have a green light."

That night, I went online looking at businesses for sale. I was in Allentown, Pa., about an hour north of Philadelphia, which is where my company was headquartered. I noticed some healthcare businesses for sale for $2 to $3 million, where the owner was taking home $400,000 to $600,000 a year, and the light bulb went on. They're the same as the guys I've been buying out. They're no smarter than me. What they've done is they've taken a risk, and they control their life.

But because of my conservative, risk averse nature, I'm not jumping up and down yet. The next weekend, I saw my friend at the club, and he said, "Do yourself a favor. Sign a nondisclosure agreement and go meet with one of these business owners. You're smart. You can determine if the numbers are good. But also, ask the guy what he does all day. Try to put yourself in his position and ask yourself if you could see yourself doing that. Or even better." So, I did.

Chapter 7: **Curt Maier**

A week later, I met the owner of a business. I realized he had been working maybe six hours a week. He lives 60-miles away and didn't even commute. He paid a woman to run the business. He wasn't greedy; he was taking home $300,000 a year and paying her $70,000. I knew I could do that business in my sleep. You would think I'd be excited.

That night, my wife and I talked about the meeting, but I didn't look happy. She asked, "What's the matter?" I looked at her, and said very quietly, "I'm scared. What if I fail? I would let you down. I would let my family down. And I would lose whatever money I invested."

She helped me get really clear on my worst-case scenario, which came down to: If I failed, I would just go back to working for the man again. We had plenty of money coming in to cover all our expenses. She made a lot of sense, but I was still not excited.

The following week, my company initiated headcount reductions to save money and increase profitability. Given that we had just completed a major $165-million purchase of a regional healthcare company, which came with significant merger and acquisition management expertise, my position was eliminated. This enabled me to enjoy a rather lucrative early retirement package, which provided me with the capital to fund my pursuit of a business.

I call myself The Reluctant Entrepreneur, because I was quite satisfied with my career, yet I realized the opportunity to own my own business would enable me to make even more money, enjoy the flexibility I craved by being the owner, and give me the luxury to focus on those aspects of the business I enjoyed the most.

My strength was primarily in sales and marketing, knowing I could hire an operational team to run whatever business I chose to purchase. With my early retirement severance package softening the blow, I started looking for a business to acquire. I couldn't find anything that didn't have something wrong with it. That's when a friend said, "You should consider a franchise."

I immediately reacted, "No way! I've run a global business. I don't need help." But he insisted I check it out. So, I shifted my search and ultimately, I found a franchise business in the senior healthcare space. And in 2005, I decided to pull the trigger. I invested about $400,000. I hired and trained staff. I negotiated a lease on the building. It took about a year and a half to reach break-even, and I was nervous every day, because I was tapping a line of credit to meet payroll. Eventually, I replaced my corporate income, and I was able to hire someone to run the business. I became an absentee owner, and it was hugely successful.

In 2007, my wife got an offer from a global corporation to take a high-level position in Seattle. When she asked what I thought about it, I told her we should go and that it's a great opportunity for her, and kids are still young. Let's get out of Allentown.

So, in 2007, we moved to Seattle, and I became Mr. Mom, driving the kids to private school, violin lessons, and swim team practice and meets. I still owned a business, so I had my pride. About four years later, in 2011, I got a call from a former employee who was asking me for a recommendation for a job in the industrial gas industry. I told him my story and suggested he do what I did.

After I shared all the details, he said, "Curt, it sounds like I should buy your business." By the end of 2011, I sold the business to him.

Chapter 7: **Curt Maier**

It was such a pleasurable thing. I helped him get financing. I helped him transfer operating licenses. I helped get the lease transferred. I was basically working as a business broker to help him acquire my business. I made sure the staff was well taken care of, and that the transition went smoothly. Then, on the flight home, I wondered what I would do next. I realized there are people out there like me who need help selling their businesses. I thought, I want to be a business broker.

I found a franchisor of business brokerage called Murphy Business Sales and they trained me how to do it. I took over the territory on the East side of Seattle, got my real estate license and built a great business. I also helped transitioning Veterans coming out of the Army, Air Forceand Navy locally at Joint Base Lewis McChord and several Naval Bases in the Puget Sound region. I knew 90-percent of them would get jobs, but 10-percent were capable of owning a business. I helped them get funding, introduced them to business professionals and assisted them in overcoming any obstacles in buying a franchise.

In 2016, after my youngest left for college in the fall, I sold that business to one of my agents. A year and a half later, feeling well entrenched in my retirement, I was very surprised by an offer from a friend who owns IBA, a business brokerage with which I had done several deals. He started by telling me that I still had too much tread on my tires.

I told him I was never working for anybody ever again. But he made me an offer I couldn't refuse. Instead of having a job, I'm paid to schmooze. They pay me to leverage my network, which is substantial, to find deals on the sell side for their dozen brokers. My one caveat was that I wanted to continue my passion in franchising by offering buyers that alternative, especially helping Veterans. He agreed, and that's where I am now.

Money no longer motivates me. It hasn't for a long time. It may sound corny, but I really enjoy helping people buy and sell their businesses. The entrepreneurial journey may not be for everyone, but I'm sure glad I took the leap. It's had a huge impact on my life and the lives of people I help.

CHAPTER 8

LIFE LESSONS AND LEGACY

By **CYNTHIA GALLARDO**

Legacy is not just what you leave behind!

After 15 years of working in corporate America, I was let go. It was a huge blow professionally. I had always been the one empowering others in achieving their goals. So, I had never been the one on the other end of this dreaded work experience. It was like I was in a dark abyss with no hint of light peeking through the slim shadows to light the way out. My husband had never seen me in this state of mind before. I was experiencing a state of depression, triggered by this nightmare. We decided a change of scenery would be a great way to become more clear-headed, and determine my next steps and our next steps. We decided on Niagara Falls, N.Y.

This was my turning point—my defining moment.

I made every effort to think of all the positive things in my life. And since I have always been a positive person, filled with determination, I fell into the comfort of my family history. Throughout my life, I have always known that our family, and what it stands for, establishes our reputation. When I look back at the earliest memories of my family, legacy started there and continued with my grandparents.

I lost them at a young age. I wish I would have written down their lessons learned and their thoughts about life. Their decisions impacted everyone in our family—the great, the good and the bad. This is what I want people to realize. Value your legacy. Write it down. Make wise decisions.

My parents are also a huge inspiration to me and they have had a tremendous impact on my life. They created a strong foundation for me, based on the four pillars of life that I had been and continue to actively live. They have created a sense of tradition that can be passed on from generation to generation. Not only can a person save themselves, utilizing valued ideals and principles to create their own legacy, but also one for the generations to follow.

My pillars, for example, include four life attributes: physical, mental, emotional and spiritual. I live each day with the goal to live and leave a lasting emotional legacy with my ethics and beliefs that I pass onto my own child and family members. Spiritually, I strive to pass on my faith and what I hold dear. I would like for my emotional resilience to be another offering that can inspire determination.

I am the oldest of seven girls. Our family is deeply rooted in our love for one another. There have been differences; yet we know love is the common thread that weaves our family together. My father instilled in me the value of integrity and fortitude. My mom echoed my father and supported me with the same strong foundation. They were my cheerleaders, and they still are to this day. The same applies to each of my sisters. Because of my parent's legacy of mental fortitude and emotional support, and the values they instilled in us, my sisters and I are all professionals. We are my parent's legacy and it's pretty amazing. While I am internally motivated, I have had external environmental factors as well that have driven my sense of purpose. The combination of the two has led to the unique perspective of how we preserve memories, share and inspire future generations, as well as documenting accomplishments and expressing our pride in the mental stamina to keep going.

Since I was a young child, I have always given my best. I live by a certain creed that does not permit excuses. Results—not excuses. I graduated magna cum laude as an undergraduate. I have always been a problem-solver and solution-maker. That's why when I was let go from my professional career, I felt like a failure. It was like a fog that overshadows your brain. Going to Niagara Falls allowed me to reflect and focus on how I was going to move forward.

At that time, I had two life challenges: My career, and my desire to start a family, which seemed as though it was never going to happen. Both hung in the balance, until I gained clarity.

Birth of a New Legacy

When I reflect back on these various stages of my life, I have gained new perspectives. In particular, I appreciate the many opportunities that have opened up for me and allowed me to reinforce another Gallardo Creed—leaving every interaction with a net positive. For every negative experience, I leave two positive solutions, resulting in a better experience and outcome. I apply this concept in everything I do.

I came up with this concept, because as I reflected on my goals, there seemed to be a constant, positive result when I used this approach. When I found myself in opportunities to coach others, I always expressed the benefits of being the best versions of themselves, and using this net positive perspective. It has been so rewarding to see mentees always finding ways to create solutions, by offering multiple positive alternatives. I attribute my attitude and methods utilized back to my parents.

As a lifelong learner and this passion for the lessons I learned through my own heritage, I went back to school and received my Juris Doctorate. I decided to focus on estate planning and entrepreneurship. I had a way to combine my skill-sets. I could educate on living one's legacy along with protecting and preserving their legacy.

After our respite in New York, my husband and I knew our previous desire to be entrepreneurs was something we were going to actively pursue. While this seemed a bit scary, my husband and I launched a new business. We launched a commercial cleaning business, as a Jani-King Franchise. As a synergistic partnership, we have surrounded ourselves with business owners who have been there and done that. These business owners knew our business and utilized a trusted business model. We even received a franchise-of-the-year award after the second year. We are very proud of that accomplishment. To this day, we have continued with our commercial cleaning business, and have since then, expanded into other areas of entrepreneurship. Together, we were determined to create our own history—our own legacy.

When I read the *7 Habits of Highly Effective People*, by Steven Covey, it made a huge impact on me. I was working in customer service and attending graduate school at the time, and the lessons I gleaned from this book were invaluable. Synergy really was the highlight for me. First-hand awareness of what bringing individuals together, in order to create or deliver something other than our individual selves could not do, yielded tremendous business growth.

As a result of the positive gain, everything we do in our organizations is based on synergy and connections. Our whole is so much greater when multiple people are committed and share the same vision. I can do a lot by myself, but when I think about how much more we can accomplish together, as a team, the possibilities are truly endless. In business circles, we always talk about the power of one, but to make it greater, we need to work with other individuals. This reminded me of my family, because we are so much stronger together.

The other challenge I faced was that I wanted to start my own personal legacy, by creating a family. My husband and I struggled with infertility and this greatly impacted our lives. But, as I have said before, I am a solution-maker and a problem-solver. I felt strongly that I wanted to pass down the valuable life lessons of my parents and grandparents before me, and leave a lasting legacy. We chose a foster-to-adopt pathway to parenthood. Our son was our baby the first day he came to our home. What a realization that we have this blessing to share our lives and contribute to future generations. I recognized more connection to synergy, by becoming a mother. I also realized my son was *our* family blueprint of the future, in lieu of DNA, his DNA and our DNA. DNA, plus synergy, equals legacy.

Leave a Lasting Legacy

My personal goal and hope is to inspire others to live and leave a lasting legacy. We can forge new pathways to success and fulfillment, simultaneously as teams and individuals, by embracing the combined effect of holistically and authentically working together. I never thought I would be an entrepreneur. My husband and I wanted flexibility to focus on the things we love.

Live and leave a lasting legacy! I believe this has become my authentic motto. Legacy is about what you are doing now, and not just what you are going to leave to your beneficiaries.

This has been a bit of a full circle experience for me. I know I will continue to expand and grow. But it all starts with you. And it also starts with me. We are our own secret sauce in our families and in our businesses. No one else has our story.

Remember me as your leading legacy lawyer!

CHAPTER 9

THE OBSERVATIONIST: SUCCESS IN BUSINESS AND LIFE—IT'S ALL ABOUT PEOPLE THROUGH THE LENS OF A BUSINESS LEADER AND PROFESSIONAL MAGICIAN

By **DAVID REICH**

I learned my first magic trick when I was 12 years old. By 13, on an hourly basis, I was making more than my dad, but he had to drive me to all the birthday parties!

Fast forward a little bit, and I found myself following the traditional path of, "go to school, get a job," where I earned degrees in computer science and business. However, I never lost my love for magic and making people smile. A few years down the road, I was looking at what I was doing with my life as a business leader, with a sideline as a performer. I decided it was not a choice. I figured out how to make them not only coexist, but combine them to become a master of both, using each to make me even better at the other, becoming more successful than either one alone! I put magic into every class, keynote, speaking and business interaction, and every magic show has messages that will change your life.

I am someone who enjoys business and technology, building resilient and high-performing teams, while helping people do and be more than they ever thought possible. And I'm someone who also loves the art of magical performance. I get totally jazzed by making people smile, laugh, look and say, "Oh no, he di-int!" And in the process, celebrate the experience of those incredible moments of revelation that they'll take with them for the rest of their lives.

I took lessons from my business experiences, magicians such as Penn and Teller, and even comedians such as George Carlin, to develop to where I am today. Carlin had a wonderful way of observing the world, and through his humor, made people see things in different ways that entertained and enlightened them. Penn and Teller, for example, strategically divulge some secrets of magic, and I do the same. We do that to enhance the audience experience—not just to show how smart or cool we are, but for a specific purpose.

As a business leader, I saw the spectrum of personalities, dynamics and cultures across large and small organizations around the world. These different personalities and motivations that each brought to the table gave me insight into who I am and where I wanted to go.

I'm here to share these secrets of magic and business with you, not for you to say, "That's cool," but as a speaker, teacher, coach and performer, for you to be entertained, educated and enlightened.

"Well, how did I get here?"
–David Byrne, Talking Heads

I grew through the ranks of computer programming, team leadership and management by solving business problems with big, expensive toys. I developed as a business and people leader, and experienced expanding impacts on people and across businesses, leading teams from 3-300, as well as technology and product portfolios from startup to $250 million. I was more than a mentor; I evolved into a sought-after coach. A mentor has the right answers. A coach has the right questions. And using my lens of a magician, I ask insightful questions that help people not just accomplish tasks, but also grow in the process.

As a performer, I always knew I was not the David Copperfield type, doing stage shows with large illusions. I also knew I was not the spooky mysterious type. And while I tell funny stories in my speaking engagements and performances, I'm not the comedy magician who makes things appear out of silly places. What I *did* realize was that I can use my skills as a performer to leverage who I am, to deliver experiences that people not only have fun with, not only learn from, but as a result, open their eyes to things they would've never noticed before. And most importantly, whether seeing me in a pure entertainment venue, as part of a course, a conference or organizational gathering, people remember these experiences and inspiration. When I get emails or run into people who have experienced my work and tell me how I positively impacted their lives … *that* is what drives me.

That is how I became **The Observationist.** The next question I had to solve was how to realize this vision. A vision without a plan is just a dream. And a plan without action is just good intentions.

In thinking about this idea and how to bring it to life, I went back to a fundamental idea I learned as I was maturing as a magician, and I apply it to business and everything in life. It's deceptively simple. One word.

Why?

As a performer, I wanted to know why people should watch me. Why do I turn my wrist that way when I am holding a coin in my hand? Why am I using these specific words when I want a spectator to stand in a specific place, or the audience to act a certain way? And the biggest why: I'm a business leader and a magician. Why should these people be paying attention to me? It's not about who *I* am, but what I can do *for them*.

Recent business trends have been focusing on, "the five whys." In other words, before you decide or settle on some significant strategic direction, you should be asking yourself the question why, at least five times, to unfold the rationale for a project in the first place. And in doing so, unleash the power of insight into *your* audience to think about why they should consider what you are offering in the first place—whether it be an idea to a team, a product, strategic direction or any type of communication.

Once you sort out the whys—and this is often even more time consuming than the project execution itself—you have confidence in knowing you're doing the right things, for the right people, for the right reasons.

Know Thyself—and Own up to Things!

Just as important as knowing the whys, you also need to play to your strengths. What are they? What are your weaknesses? Should you even work on overcoming those weaknesses? Or are they not terribly critical, and you can do even better focusing more on your strengths? All this introspection is vital for success and fulfillment in everything you do.

Chapter 9: **David Reich**

Whether business, sports or being a professional magician, the first question you must look at is, "Who am I?" A mentor of mine calls it, "finding your sacred purpose." This is probably the hardest thing to do. It's also important to remember that this is not a lifelong commitment. Analysis paralysis gets the best of all of us. As another business mentor, Tom Peters, once told me, "Purposefully pick a direction and run like crazy at it. With your eyes open. And if you need to change course, do it! But don't stop! Keep running **towards** a destination." Think, find your purpose, go for it. Change as you grow, but keep moving toward something.

In the development of my vision and plans, and the exploration of my whys, I wanted to know who I was and how to realize my vision. I know I love all the different types of magic performances–traditional magic with cards and coins in a close-up setting; mentalism, which is essentially impossible feats with the mind; everything from influencing decisions, to mind reading, making things float, bending silverware, and so on. I was also very intrigued by the power of the mind and delved into hypnosis. It's incredible how powerful the human mind is, and that we can manifest things physically with our minds. I also know my personality and while I can be the party magician, the spooky guy, the serious guy or the comedy guy, I don't identify with any of them, but instead, bits of ALL of them. It took me a long time to design a balance of all these elements, combine that with *my* strengths and skills, along with the business leader elements of *my* personality, in order to get to the successes I experience today.

Knowing one's self is critical to any type of personal and organizational success. The personal side is obvious. As an organizational leader, whether it be a team of three, a company of thousands, a group of people getting together to brainstorm, a single customer or an auditorium full of people to hear you speak—these all are your **audience.** They are the receivers or collaborators of any messages you wish to convey. Regardless of who or how many they are, it is important, née **critical**, to know what **motivates them**. As I have coached many executives, speakers, leaders and even people preparing for job interviews, "Just because you have the need to say it, does not mean they need to hear it."

Finally, a humility check: It's not about you. It's about *your audience*. First, last and always. What can you do for them? That's what they want, and why they are listening to you.

> *"All the great speakers were bad speakers at first."*
> **–Ralph Waldo Emerson**

Knowing your audience is only two-thirds of the battle. The other one-third is often the hardest: Your communication. Some people are naturals, and they just "got it." Most, however, need to work on it.

My entrée to public speaking is pretty funny. In college, I was asked to teach a computer class to juniors and seniors while I was a sophomore. I walked into the room, 8 a.m., on the first day of classes, and it was standing room only, even though I got there 30 mins early. I was so intimidated, I put down my bag and went to the bathroom. I gathered my composure and remembered: They are here to hear me, because I know what I'm talking about. And they are here because *they need to know* what I'm talking about. (Why are they here, and why am I here?) A few years later, I was a radio DJ and had to learn how to communicate to people I could not see! That, too, was an enlightening experience.

Here's a secret. You're better than you think. Just do it. You *will* make mistakes; be open to constructive criticism. Record and (yes, while often cringeworthy) watch yourself. Watch others. You'll notice they're not quite as wonderful as you thought, and you'll say, "I can do that!" Focus. Solicit feedback and practice. You will get better. Know yourself; play to your strengths and either sidestep or fix the weaknesses. You'll never be good at everything. Don't try.

> *"Rapport is the ultimate tool for*
> *producing results with other people."*
> **– Tony Robbins**

In this time of email, texting, social media, TikTok and other bite-sized, superficial forms of communication, mastering the art of rapport makes you an unstoppable force.

To be trusted, to be believed, to be valued—you need to establish rapport. Sometimes it's with an audience of five, sometimes with 5,000. Try this one out, "Hi, I'm Dave. I'm a magician. May I borrow your $20 bill for something cool?" Really???? Any time you are working with people who don't know you, you need to gain rapport. Otherwise you're just a TV advertisement. This is the critical ingredient to all effective communication. Attempts at rapport are why oftentimes public speakers start off with a joke. Then again, how many times have you heard one of those and rolled your eyes? You can see those canned, disingenuous jokes a mile away. Attempt to build rapport? A swing and a miss!

Here is the secret to building rapport: Be authentic, candid and vulnerable. These elements will cause people to *want* to listen to you, it will get them on your side, and they will want you to succeed. Tell a brief, but real story. Make it fun. You want people to relate to *you*, so just be you! If it's slightly embarrassing (note my teaching story), but is relevant to the talk, class or meeting topic, so what? You want people to feel close to you.

Here's another secret: This is sometimes why a magician or mentalist will mess something up on purpose, in order to develop a connection with the audience. After that, they're on the performer's side. They *want* that magic to happen! *Aside:* while it *is* a technique that performers use, you're never really going to know if they messed up, messed up on purpose or only want you to *think* they messed up. This is how we really have fun with audiences … but I digress …

Whatever you do, be authentic, candid, and vulnerable. And whatever you do to achieve this, make it relevant–relevant to the event, topic, group dynamic or whatever the situation calls for. Too often I see speakers who tell the same stories regardless of the audience. That shows they don't care about the audience, but instead about what *they* have to say. Situational awareness—a skill critical to mentalists—is also a skill developed over time, through attention to people and observation! Notice how what you say is being received, and if needed, modify your delivery on the fly. That is the holy grail of communication. That is how you build rapport, and when done right, even the worst cynics can't help but cheer for you.

We are all performers. We do what we do, and we want people to listen. As a magical performer, I want them to look where I want them to look, do what I guide them to do and see what I want them to see (or not!). In business, we want people to listen to what we say, buy what we sell, and as leaders, have teams do what we want them to do (and be happy to do it). This only scratches the surface of the ways the combination of these skills and arts can make one greater than the sum of the parts.

I'm not saying to go out and learn to do card tricks. By examining how magicians do what we do, how we understand audiences and use that knowledge to motivate and engage them, you can apply those principles to anything in business, and in life.

We go through our lives in patterns. It's human nature. We're creatures of habit and routine. People miss what's right in front of their eyes. That is only one of the tools magicians use to perform seemingly impossible things. That is how master communicators get people to see things as they want. Whether you are the speaker or the listener, by truly observing yourself and the people you interact with, your life and the lives of whoever you're talking to become richer.

That is how you become a master at whatever you desire, and have people want to be with and do with you. The Observationist can help you, your teams, students, sales forces and leadership teams do just that. Learn more about yourself and about how we can all be Obervationists, at **www.davidreich.com**. And hey, check out my TedX talk while you're there!

CHAPTER 10

UNDERSTANDING THE GRIEF CAUSED BY CAREER TRANSITIONS

By **DIANA STEPHENS**

If the COVID-19 pandemic has taught us anything, it is that the only thing that is constant is change. The entire planet has experienced a profound shift of consciousness. For a few months, everything came to a standstill. This time offered us space to go within and think. There were all sorts of transitions that arose from the pandemic, from the overworked front-line responders to the people who could easily transfer to working from home. Others had their jobs evaporate overnight. Many people had time to reflect on what matters most and they moved to new locations, clustered closer to their families, or changed careers altogether. This pandemic transition and its long-term effects merit further study. The number of transitions caused by the pandemic are too numerous to list in this article, but the overarching theme is that we had plenty of time to pause, reflect, and look at our lives and what really matters to us.

Transitions Are Not One Size Fits All

A transition looks very different to someone who has spent 25 years of their career with one company than to an employee just starting their career, maybe two years in. The older person finds their life upended overnight. They might have a mortgage on their house, two to three kids (maybe in college), car payments—how are they going to manage without the income or the health insurance? Layer on top of that uncertainty the technological advances that have occurred in the past 25 years, and that person has a lot to learn.

Not all transitions are created equally. Some are minor changes and others are momentous and feel like the world is caving in on us. My experience with change was the latter. I was dealing with job loss while caring for my mother with Alzheimer's, eventually moving her into a care facility. During some of my job transitions, I also dealt with personal health issues and continuing financial strain.

Life Disruptors versus Life Quakes

In his book, *Life Is in the Transitions: Mastering Change at Any Age,* Bruce Feiler makes the distinction between life *disruptors* and life quakes. He defines a disruptor as an "event or experience that interrupts the everyday flow of one's life." He writes, "Many disruptors, like having or adopting a child, or starting a new job are not necessarily negative, but they can still be disruptive. Even the typically negative life events like losing a spouse or being terminated can become the catalysts for reinvention. Disruptors are deviations from daily life."

Additionally, he defines life *quakes* as, "events that upend our lives exponentially more than everyday disruptors. Life *quakes* involve a fundamental shift in the meaning, purpose, or direction of a person's life. It is a forceful burst of change in one's life that leads to a period of upheaval, transition, and renewal." A health diagnosis, job loss, divorce, or death of a loved one can all be considered life quakes. But it is really how we classify these events in our lives, and how much change comes as a result. Some people move through a divorce or health issue quickly and put it behind them and move on. For others, it is a defining moment that shifts their lives. Nevertheless, both life disruptors and life quakes can be the catalyst for transitions.

Job Loss and Transitions

The subject of job loss is one that I am all too familiar with, having experienced five downsizings in a 10-year span from February 2004 to May 2014. I experienced job loss every other year for 10 years. Two of the layoffs were due to division closings, and the other three were due to eliminating my position during a corporate reorganization. Each of these job losses had a profound effect on my life, both spiritually and financially.

As I went through each of these downsizings, sometimes I had an outplacement structure and sometimes not. I found that the outplacement arena was not a safe haven for sharing the range of emotions I was feeling. I also participated in various job search work teams, and none of them addressed the emotional side of the job search, nor helped to give me solace for what I was feeling. The focus was all about numbers on the board, interviews, networking calls, and resume critiques. These all are important tactical steps; however, they do not help with the emotional support needed to navigate through this uncertain time.

Spiritual Changes and Awareness

Nevertheless, spiritually these events helped cause a profound shift in my consciousness, helping me become more mindful and embark on a much deeper and inward-facing spiritual journey. I explored all types of modalities to find emotional solace and attempt to get to the root of, "why is this happening to me?" I delved into spiritual reading and found Buddhist teachings very enlightening. I created a quiet space in my home for meditation. I actively journalled about my experiences, feelings, and thoughts.

I learned about the law of attraction and set an intention for the vision of the new position I wanted. I have maintained this practice all these years, and still actively use these supportive spiritual measures. I believe strongly that each person should tailor mindfulness practices to their own beliefs and lifestyles. Different modalities appeal to different people. In this chapter, I will present some thoughts on how to navigate through grief during a transition.

The first step during a job transition, whether involuntary or voluntary, is to pause and understand that this life changing event will cause a sense of loss. Even if one does not like their job and considers it a stress relief to not be going to work anymore, this event is still ranked in the top 10 of life-changing stressors. Because of this change, it is important to take time to reflect and process through the change and understand the impact on one's life. This step is crucial before moving on.

Seven Types of Loss

Humans have a natural resistance to change. Change can be a most unwelcome visitor. In their article, *The Hidden Perils of Unresolved Grief,* Charles Dhanaraj and George Kohlrieser write, "At the most fundamental levels the experience of grief is one such example of a resistance to change."

Chapter 10: **Diana Stephens**

There are many conflicting emotions brought on by a shift in a familiar routine. McKinsey outlines seven losses that occur at the time of a job elimination. One tends to feel many of these losses at this time. These losses include:

1. **Loss of Attachment:** This includes the question, "Who am I connected to?" A job loss causes a break in connection with the familiar. Daily routines are disrupted. There is a loss of community in not being able to see colleagues on a regular basis.

2. **Loss of Territory:** This includes the question, "Where do I belong?" A job loss causes an instability in belonging. Once part of a team structure, leaving the familiar disrupts the "normal" one had been used to.

3. **Loss of Structure:** This includes the question, "What is my role?" The role is eliminated; thus, there is a loss of feeling involved and valued. The question arises, how does one regain the feeling of involvement and being a valued contributor?

4. **Loss of Identity:** This includes the question, "Who am I?" This life event causes one to re-evaluate who they are, their values and goals. Are one's values changing? Have old beliefs fallen away and are new thoughts more important? This is especially true as one ages and approaches later chapters of their career.

5. **Loss of Future:** This includes the question, "Where am I going?" This event offers the chance to change direction.

The question becomes, what direction do I want to go, or should I go? Transitions give the opportunity to ponder this question in great depth and detail.

6. **Loss of Meaning:** This includes the question, "What is the point?" One re-evaluates their life's purpose during a job loss. Loss of meaning can contribute to a sense of being lost, not knowing where to turn next. All of a sudden as the situation shifts, one starts to think of deeper probing questions about what next adventure would best be suited to find a greater clarity around purpose.

7. **Loss of Control:** This includes the statement, "I feel overwhelmed." One feels out of control with the job loss. Disruptions, especially ones related to security, can paralyze people. The feeling of being out of control can lead to grief and depression.

In our society, the word "grief" is typically associated with the deep sorrow of losing a loved one. However, there are other life circumstances that can produce profound sorrow and grief. One is the loss of employment. The loss of a job is quite stressful, and the event itself can set off a cycle of grief. When one loses their job, they lose a community of colleagues with whom they have interacted on a regular basis. There is also a loss of familiar routine as well as an economic impact.

The economic impact for most people can be the most devastating. It is important to understand that this can cause sorrow and grief in one's life. Grief is a normal human response to such a life event and should not be taken lightly or left unattended. However, given the right mindfulness, grief can also be managed, reconciled, and overcome.

In his book, *Unattended Sorrow—Recovering from Loss and Reviving the Heart,* Stephen Levine writes, "Nothing is more natural than grief, no emotion more common to our daily experience. It's an innate response to a loss in a world where everything is impermanent." If grief is left unattended and the subsequent feelings are not acknowledged and processed, the inaction can cause a multitude of emotional and physical side effects.

These side effects can include disturbed sleep, lowered energy, loss of self-confidence, loss of social interaction, loss of appetite, and the risk of leaning toward addiction. Levine writes, "Unresolved grief is like a low-grade fever. It flows in peaks and valleys. Sometimes it spikes into almost overwhelming afflictive emotions; at other times it lies almost dormant, nearly comatose, just beneath the surface, until a shadow crosses the heart and releases it." Clearly, Levine brings to light the emotional and physical consequences of holding in sorrow. Taking the time to understand and process grief is of paramount importance to one's well-being.

In order for one to move through the sorrow and grief of a job loss, it is crucial to understand the five stages of grief. One of the most well-known books on this topic is *On Grief and Grieving* by Dr. Elisabeth Kubler-Ross and David Kessler.

In this book, Dr. Kubler-Ross defines the five stages of grief as:

- **Denial**
- **Anger**

- **Bargaining**
- **Depression**
- **Acceptance**

These five stages, "are part of a framework that makes up our learning to live with what we have lost. They are tools to help us frame and identify what we may be feeling; however, they are not stops on a linear timeline in grief. Not everyone goes through all of them or goes in a prescribed order," they write.

Understanding the five stages of grief can enable one to process loss and move forward with their life. Knowing that one is moving through the stages can give hope to a traumatic situation. One can feel that they are moving forward one step at a time each day or every week. It is important to acknowledge and process grief. A good understanding of what one is feeling emotionally will help to make that person stronger as they move through the stages of this transition.

Only once one has reached the acceptance stage can they begin to look at new resources to help them on the next leg of their life story. Losing a job is like having something abruptly taken away, never to return. It is a shock to the system. Coping with grief helps to set the stage for the healing process and the next stage of the journey.

If you would like to know more about how my company can help you through this process, please contact me via my website. I look forward to sharing the tools to build a solid foundation to stabilize you through your various life stages.

CHAPTER 11

THE MINDSET OF "GET TO" RATHER THAN "HAVE TO" IN YOUR CAREER JOURNEY

By **GREG JOHNSON**

In my line of work, I see people in different stages of their careers, many of whom get stuck and struggle with how to move to the next level, next stage or next career path. While some people cannot escape their conditioned mindset, many others enjoy the excitement and challenge of pushing themselves into a mindset of opportunity and empowerment. I am an Executive Coach with *Above The Rim* Executive Coaching, and I help professionals play their career *Above The Rim*.

I have a unique perspective and set of skills that I use with my clients in order to help them understand a different way of thinking about career changes. I am driven to help professionals create a paradigm shift in how they approach their careers. I want to empower clients to take control of their career destiny and to play their careers *Above The Rim* by leveraging the most innovative and powerful career management tools and strategies available anywhere.

A vast majority of professionals "exist" in their career. They are surviving, not thriving. They may have had a dream, but they have learned to "settle." They have stopped pushing the envelope and instead do what is comfortable.

As an executive coach, I ask:
- What are you thirsty for?
- What are you learning to take your career to a higher level?
- What can you do in the next 12 months that will stretch you?

One of the things I love about my work as a career and executive coach is that I work with so many exceptionally intelligent and gifted professionals. By remaining curious while working with them, I continue to learn ways to improve my programs. I am also constantly following thought leaders in various industries to see how they are doing things and I'm always looking for ways to take my practice to a higher level. My programs are consistently evolving. What gets me out of bed each morning is the excitement of the journey. Everyday, **I get to** experience new people and new things.

I like to remind my clients that the career is not a destination; it is a journey. For me, the biggest part of the career journey is the people we get to engage with and learn more about every single day. I am so thankful for all of the wonderful people I have been able to meet and work with. Not only do I have an opportunity to work with wonderful professionals, and positively impact their careers, but I also get to learn from them and am myself positively impacted.

I strive each day to teach the value of the **get to** mentality versus the **have to** mindset. I want people to feel like they **get to** do their job: They **get to** learn more about their industry and they **get to** be challenged to grow, either in their current career journey or when they move into a new career. As an entrepreneur, it is a similar mindset,

Chapter 11: **Greg Johnson**

where we desire to experience new things and to take an uncommon path. This path includes curiosity and wanting to learn about people who are part of the journey.

Throughout my career, I have been blessed with many fantastic opportunities. In 2008, the company I worked with relocated from California to New Jersey. It was at this time that I hired a career coach to help me determine my next chapter, since I didn't want to move my family across the country. In the process of working with this coach, I started to help some of my friends who were going through transitions. I will never forget the feelings of excitement and wanting to do more, as I helped my friends uncover their passions and discover the next leg of their career journey.

I have so many fond memories of my career over the years. I think the thing I am most proud of is the journey I have been on, the unexpected adventures I have experienced, the success I have achieved and the relationships I have forged along the way. I am also humbled by the impact I have had on people and the oh-so-great impact they have had on me.

If you had described my career to me when I was in high school or college, I would have never believed it possible. I had ideas about what I wanted to do, but more importantly, I had a deep desire to experience new things. From creating my own internship opportunity while in college, when I built the Japanese business clientele of a local hotel, to leveraging the relationships I made with Japanese businessmen while working at the hotel, to launching my post-collegiate career in Japan. Traveling on this journey enabled me to broaden my horizons and instilled in me an insatiable curiosity of what I could do.

There have been wonderful peaks and deep valleys all along the way. The one constant throughout my career has been relationships. More than business success, relationships are where our legacy is built.

I believe it is my constant quest to learn, to explore that shapes my career, brings me success and sets me apart from others.

Some of the people who have most influenced my philosophies of success are professional athletes. How they approach their careers offers valuable lessons that are applicable to achieving success in the corporate world.

One athlete who I have an immense amount of admiration for is Los Angeles Laker legend Kobe Bryant. During his career he harnessed the qualities of the great players who came before him, always seeking to draw on their success to become a better player.

Early in his career, he dedicated himself to learning from the greats who came before him. He was always identifying skills he wanted to improve. He sought out the best and would train under them. As his career progressed, he also mentored young people coming into the league after him. He was constantly mentoring up and mentoring down.

His "Mamba Mentality" and the words he said to his daughters expressed it all. Bryant discussed how he hoped to pass his work ethic along to his girls during his jersey retirement night in December 2017.

Chapter 11: **Greg Johnson**

"You guys know that if you do the work, you work hard enough, dreams come true," he said to Natalia, Capri and Gianna. (The event was recorded and clips were posted on social media.) "You all know that, we all know that. But hopefully what you get tonight is the understanding that those times when you get up early and you work hard, those times you stay up late and you work hard, those times when you don't feel like working—you're too tired, you don't want to push yourself—but you do it anyway … that is actually the dream.

"It's not the destination, it's the journey," he continued. "And, if you guys can understand that, what you'll see happen is that you don't accomplish your dreams. Your dreams won't come true. Something greater will and if you guys can understand that, then I'm doing my job as a father. Thank you guys so much and mamba out."

His post-basketball player career was also inspiring. His short film, *Dear Basketball,* won an Academy Award in 2018. And he continued to inspire others. He wrote books that were *New York Times* bestsellers. His legacy is extremely powerful, because he had a **get to** mentality for everything he did.

When I meet with a client who is lost in their path and unsure of their next steps, but is still curious and willing to consider the **get to** mentality, this is when I start working with them on the strategies to give them a road map for the next leg of their journey. I work with them to help them discover what they want to do, where they want to do it and why they want to do it. Then we flesh out the strategy that I call Plan A, Plan B and Plan WOW. Leveraging this strategy allows my clients to focus on their research and branding, creating a more efficient and effective job search.

Plan A

This is the primary target industry and function. It is their concept of their ideal job based on their skills, aptitude and passions.

Plan B

This is the secondary target industry and function. It may not be the Dream Job, but it is a good path, as it still leverages their skills, aptitude and passions.

Plan WOW

This is completely off the radar from Plan A and Plan B. It is discovered through networking driven by strategic curiosity and the **get to** mentality to thrive. When learning about and cultivating relationships with people outside of our focused search, in our discussions with them, it is here that our wheels start spinning and the excitement of something new begins to flourish.

I would say, about 60-percent of my clients land in their Plan A or Plan B, but about 30-percent land in their Plan WOW. Seeing so many people absolutely thrive in the next leg of their journey is why I love coaching.

I find it curious that more people don't think of using a career coach to help them move to the next level in their career. Highly successful musicians, athletes and actors all use coaches. Why shouldn't business professionals who do not want to settle also use a coach?

Most professionals are specialists in what they do, whether they are an engineer, a systems analyst or marketing executive. But they're

Chapter 11: **Greg Johnson**

not specialists in managing their career. They put their nose to the grindstone and they focus completely on their daily tasks. They get caught up in the daily grind, and when the storm hits, they have no idea what to do next. My job is to help them through not only the rough patches when the bottom falls out beneath them, but also in the good times. During both good and bad times, people can find new ways to look at their jobs, career path and enhance and expand their views on what they bring to the table.

How Society Changes Our Mentality

The pandemic significantly altered the way everyone does business. I have used this "chaos" as an opportunity to refine how I deliver my coaching. Just before the pandemic, in 2019, I started leveraging Zoom to facilitate one-on-one coaching sessions, as well as deliver career management webinars. Once the pandemic hit, I went fully remote, and launched brand-new online career management webinars.

In 2022, I began the initiative to take many of my existing webinars, and convert them to on-demand self-paced learning modules to create greater access to my material. My immediate goal is to take this work and further my program offerings to help professionals play their career *Above The Rim* through the new programs I am launching in 2023.

Society is always changing. It is safe to say that this change has created chaos in our economy and in the marketplace. As Sun Tzu, the great Chinese military strategist said centuries ago, "In the midst of chaos, there is opportunity." I think this serves to deepen my passion to help clients discover opportunity in this ever-changing landscape.

Many people hesitate to use a coach, because they think they should be able to do it on their own. Others expect coaches to have a magic bullet and want the coach to do the work for them. Society often squeezes our innate curiosity out of us. By the time many professionals are mid-career, they have lost their curiosity and are jaded in their thoughts of their careers. They believe jobs are **have to,** rather than **get to.**

I am honored and excited to do the work I **get to** do. I am humbled by the impact I get to have on others and the impact I get to receive from others. I love when I **get to** experience light bulb moments with clients as they discover the next leg of their journey.

One thing I can relay to others about being successful in business, is to engage with other professionals, and to constantly learn things you can bring to your own practice. It is also important to set boundaries and to say no to some things. Identify the most important things that need to be accomplished and schedule time to complete them. Set boundaries for when you are working and when you are playing. Plan time to do things with your family on purpose. Stay curious and stay thirsty.

CHAPTER 12

MODERNIZE OR DIE: 8 PRINCIPLES FOR DOING BUSINESS THE WAY YOUR CUSTOMERS WANT

By **JASON KENNEDY**

"Modernize or die" may seem like a blunt title for this chapter, but it is a mantra every business and industry should take to heart. Failure to modernize is a death knell your customers will ring until you accept your need to change. That mantra certainly holds true for my industry, motorsports.

I have run a high-performance driving school for many years. We rent road course racetracks, and teach sports car owners to drive them the way they were built to be driven. Our instructor network spans the United States, and we run more than 30 events annually.

My background is in corporate IT, so I'm heavily into technology. I realized that while there is software for just about every other industry, however, none was purpose-built for motorsports. There was nothing racetracks or racing event operators could use that encompassed all the different aspects of online ticketing, point-of-sale, communications and marketing—everything available is piecemeal.

I also learned that drag strips were especially behind the times, even by motorsports standards. Today, many track owners work solely with paper and cash at the gate.

Track owners, particularly those who have been around a long time, complain that younger people don't get into the sport. They want to, but they don't want to deal with cash and paper, or stand in line for two or three hours to enter an event.

Younger people want to purchase tickets online, in advance, scan their phones at the gate, and be on their way quickly and efficiently. They don't carry cash. If that's the only way you do business, you physically can't work with them.

It's time for racetrack owners, racing event organizers and you to learn that doing business the way your customers want—using technology—is the key to survival long term. It is also the compelling force that drove me to start my software company, Trackside Systems, and why I am on a mission to modernize the entire motorsports industry.

8 Modernize or Die Principles

Practically every consumer-facing industry has adopted modern ways of doing things. You can order fast food from a kiosk or an app, and have it ready at the counter or drive-through window.

Go to any outdoor entertainment venue—concert, water park, theme park, zoo or aquarium. Nobody expects to walk in and pay cash at the gate. Air travel has been that way for a long time. You can't just show up with a handful of cash and buy a ticket.

Chapter 12: **Jason Kennedy**

Some venues may still allow you to pay at the gate, but you may not be able to get in right away. They might say, "We're full until three o'clock, so you can buy a ticket to enter then." However, if you bought online, you would have already had your ticket for 10 a.m. when you arrived.

When a track owner tells me that their customer base won't go online, I always ask, "Do you think they travel by air or ever go to a concert or an amusement park?" If they've done any of those things, they've been forced to transact online.

With that in mind, here are eight principles I learned through my time devoted to modernizing motorsports, each of which can be applied to any industry or business, including yours.

1. Be Your Own First Customer

I have a strong belief that you should be your own first customer. Here's why:

During my technology career, I saw a lot of failed software projects. The reason was that the developers did not work in the industry they were building the software for. They couldn't get to that nuanced, detailed level of what it takes to make the software highly effective.

When I started Trackside, I can't tell you how many hours I worked the front gate at racetracks, just to observe and learn how they do business. I needed to put in the time to really understand what the customer experience looks like, learn how they do business and identify where I could add value or improvements.

2. Be the One to Solve the Problem

Sometimes, instead of hoping someone else will take care of a problem, you should do it. That's entrepreneurial thinking. I had assumed someone would come along and modernize motorsports, only to conclude that I was that "someone." As a result, more and more tracks are modernizing to use digital technology, instead of doing business the old-school way with cash at the gate.

3. See Your Business Through Your Customer's Lens

Early on with our driving school events, I saw how much better the experience was when our customers registered online. We got the payment upfront and collected the necessary details to run the event, instead of spending hours and hours tracking who paid and who didn't. It also eliminated the guesswork of preparing for the event and wondering how many people would show up. We also had their contact information to send important pre-event details so they could better prepare.

That is looking through your customer's lens. If I'm a customer used to digital experiences in other industries, and I come to a racetrack that only accepts cash, what's going through my mind? I'm likely saying, "Oh my gosh, this is so out of date and clunky, and takes forever." Do you really want that to be the first impression your customers have?

4. Do Business the Way Your Customers Want You to

What's happening in other industries, such as retail, restaurants, concerts and other entertainment sectors, sets the expectations with consumers for how everything should operate. Meeting their expectations is critical if you want to attract new customers to your business, and retain your existing ones.

If I had a dollar every time a track owner told me how hard it was to attract young people into racing, I'd have a lot of dollars. What will happen when you refuse to accept the way prospective customers want to do business? You eliminate an entire audience.

5. Foster Customer Loyalty

Countless consumer-facing industries offer loyalty programs. I can earn loyalty points if I buy my coffee at Dunkin' or Starbucks. After earning enough points, I get a coupon for a free cup of coffee or other product. It's an incentive to keep coming back. Customers expect that.

Trackside brings these capabilities to racetracks. Customers get points for each dollar spent. After so many points, they get a coupon to use toward a ticket purchase. (The track owner can set these parameters.)

Encouraging customer loyalty is necessary in this highly-competitive modern age, but it's nearly impossible without a digital system. I've heard track owners say they tried using punch cards, and people would make knockoffs or lose the cards. When you use electronic systems, all those problems go away.

6. Your Email List is Gold

A customer email list can become as valuable as gold. On the other hand, if you fail to collect your customers' email addresses, you will struggle to reach your market. Building an email list also eliminates manual work on the backside for the event organizer.

Trackside systematically and automatically collects this information when the customer purchases their ticket or racer registration.

This feature allows track owners to market to their ever-growing email list perpetually to keep filling up events and selling tickets. That is the exact strategy we used to grow our high-performance driving school from one or two events per year to more than 30, along with the coinciding exponential revenue growth. With the diminished organic reach of social media, building an email list is critically important and can save you a lot in advertising spending.

7. Make Decisions with Data

Most racetracks depend on sponsors to meet their financial needs for the year. What do sponsors want? Data. They want to know how many people their names were put in front of, how many tickets are sold at certain events and what the most popular events are. That information helps them decide which events to sponsor. If a racetrack owner or event organizer can attract more people from farther away, they can get a regional or national sponsor, instead of just local.

Sponsors are scrutinizing events more every year to ensure they receive the most value for their dollar. Companies are also trimming marketing and advertising budgets, which means the limited sponsorship dollars available go to the people with the best data.

Having hard data isn't only about attracting sponsors. It also lets you know what is going on in your business. Most track owners have no idea; they're guessing. They might try to count cars in the parking lot or people in the stands, but they don't have real hard numbers, until they use a software system to track that information. Trackside provides intelligent analytics to put all this information at the fingertips of track owners.

8. Don't Overlook Cash Flow

What will your cash flow look like if you only accept cash on the day of the event? Probably not good, I assure you.

We run our high-performance driving program during the summer months—May through September. However, our biggest sales occur from January through March, because we're pre-selling the upcoming season. That frees up capital to reinvest in our program, and we don't suffer from a long dry spell with no cash flow.

From a pure cash-flow perspective, online transactions open a whole new world for a business. Event organizers can sell more tickets, because they give people additional buying time. They aren't subject to the whims of a customer who says they don't feel like going on the day of the event. Their ticket is bought, whether they go or not.

Modernization First Steps

Find the Right Software for Your Business

One of the first steps to modernization that you need to take is to find the software system best suited for your business. For example, Trackside may not be the perfect fit for every racetrack, just as no single software solution is right for every restaurant—coffee shops may need one type, while fine dining needs another.

Some business owners think they must go 100-percent digital and upend everything they're doing. That can be a psychological barrier to entry. Instead, plan on making incremental changes to improve efficiency and reduce friction for you and the customer.

Conduct a Customer Survey

We conduct a customer survey every year in both of our businesses. Collecting customer feedback is instrumental in helping us prioritize changes.

It doesn't have to be a long survey either; a single question can get you valuable feedback. For example, we ask, "If you could change one thing about doing business with us, what would it be?"

Examine Your Process

Take a step back and look at everything you do daily to run your business. What information would help you make better decisions? What decisions are difficult, because you don't have good data or information? What tedious, manual tasks could you automate?

One benefit of using technology is that it gives you more time to work on your business, not just in it. For example, a racetrack owner could spend time on maintenance and repair, or find ways to improve the facility, instead of fighting with different pieces of software in the office. Think about what you could do with your business if you only had more time.

Conclusion

The Norwegian politician Erna Solberg said, "We have to dare to modernize to get room to maneuver for the priorities of the future."

She may have been talking about politics in Norway, but her statement holds true for motorsports and just about every other industry. If we fail to modernize, if we choose not to do business the way our customers want and expect, we may as well write our epitaph, for we will eventually die.

Chapter 12: **Jason Kennedy**

It doesn't have to be that way. Put these eight principles into action and watch your business thrive.

CHAPTER 13

ACTIVATING THE POWER OF AUTHENTIC LEADERSHIP

By **JENNIFER A. INGRAM**

"Authenticity is a collection of choices that we have to make every day. It's about the choice to show up and be real. The choice to be honest. The choice to let our true selves be seen."
–Brené Brown

It is not our current title, role or status that tells the story of who we are. There are a number of factors that shape and inform our worldview—or as I often refer to it, our lens. The collective experiences, lessons, skills, education and observations that shape our lens are not just our own, but also those inherited across generations. The cycle of socialization serves as a framework to more deeply understand just how much conditioning is out of our control, which heavily contributes to and influences individual development.

Our lens is a collection of imprints, informed by the past and present; made physical through dimensions of identity and proximate through experiences; shaped by stories of who and what we can or can't be with social conditions and popular culture; imposed by narratives and stereotypes conveyed by members of our family, community, workplace, schools and the media to name a few. Our lenses are complex constructs that contain the blueprint of our values, ideas and opinions about ourselves and the world around us; as such, it is foundational to uncover deeper knowledge about ourselves and in our relationships with others, in order to operate from a space of authenticity.

The pursuit of living and leading a life of authenticity is not for everyone, for a myriad of reasons. The process of deepening understanding and the interconnectedness of our intersectional identities, the lenses we use to view and experience the world, and the environments in which we navigate can be overwhelming. Unlike a singular training that introduces a new skill, committing to a journey of authenticity is a lifestyle shift, riddled with inquiry and curiosity, impacting every aspect of life.

It's also important to acknowledge the acts of bravery, vulnerability and courage it takes to willingly open up, explore and share parts of ourselves that make up who we are, beyond what we do, in uncontrolled environments. It can also be daunting to unearth or share triggers that are connected to past traumas or less than positive experiences; however, consciously or unconsciously, those triggers will show up. The difference is the ability to see and manage them, and hopefully share with others specific things they can do to avoid re-traumatization and be thoughtful in ways they engage.

Further, as a society, we have long prioritized physical health with a lesser emphasis on mental health and wellbeing. Through authentically sharing triumphs and struggles alike, one can inherently model practices that address the importance of health and wellbeing, and also promote the same within others.

Chapter 13: **Jennifer A. Ingram**

The Tax of Authenticity and the Cost of Covering

For all the benefits, it's important to note very little in life is free—and that includes authenticity. I describe the expense in two ways—the tax of authenticity, and the cost of covering. In recent years, there has been a growing body of research published that explores the often harmful and normalized cultures that disproportionately and negatively impact experiences of folx from marginalized communities or identities who may be underrepresented in the groups.

The tax of authenticity is an acknowledgement and choice to embrace the risk associated with displaying authenticity in the presence of uncertainty. It's often shared within organizations and teams that there's a desire for folx to bring their whole selves into a space, or that there's a desire to generate a culture that is inclusive—with little framing around what that actually means, or inadequate skills and resourcing to provide appropriate levels of safety and support. Much like the certainty of life, death and taxes you can expect a tax, but the amount is to be determined.

The tax of authenticity is accrued and felt through the expenditure of mental and physical energy navigating the invisible structures and norms that require calibration to dose the right amounts of authenticity, in order to mitigate negative unintended consequences. To maintain experiences of safety and reduce harm, it's imperative to determine the amount of tax you are capable of or willing to pay, in order to preserve individual wellbeing.

Covering is a term that accompanies a body of research published by Catalyst that references the act of "covering" stigmatized parts of identity to fit in. In this context, what I describe as the cost of covering is the opposite of the tax of authenticity. In determining what it costs to not take the risk, and instead, to withhold authenticity. Displaying high amounts of vulnerability and authenticity in spaces that lack reciprocal acknowledgement, humility and self or social management displayed by others, can make it seem that it's safer to cover or assimilate. The cost of covering varies, but might include barriers to others getting to know you and establishing meaningful relationships; establishing trusting relationships; or differentiating yourself from other technical experts or practitioners. While the cost might seem insignificant or minor in isolation, they are often the limiting conditions that impact someone's trajectory.

Finding the balance between the tax of authenticity and the cost of covering is one that is deeply individualized and depends on personal goals, thresholds for risk and reserves for resiliency. One practical step is to gain clarity on the things that are within and outside of your control. Observe the presence or degrees of safety by seeing the behaviors or actions that get rewarded—and those that are not. Work to balance the cost and tax appropriately, while honoring the threshold of risk and safety. Outside of organizations, it's important to maintain a clear understanding of who you truly are and to seek out spaces where you can safely and authentically lead.

"Authentic leaders inspire us to engage with each other in powerful dreams that make the impossible possible. We are called on to persevere despite failure and pursue a purpose beyond the paycheck. This is at the core of innovation. It requires aligning the dreams of each individual to the broader dream of the organization."
–Henna Inam

Chapter 13: **Jennifer A. Ingram**

The word "leadership" is one that is frequently used, but seldom examined and defined to the extent that fully encapsulates its relevance. As used in this text, leadership isn't just about titles and assignments. Anyone can be a leader. It encompasses a set of values, skills and abilities that facilitate the progress of a collective toward a shared target. In my opinion, leadership is defined as the ability to engage and inspire others toward a common goal. This includes leading yourself.

There is great beauty in the freedom of self-expression, from a space that allows our inherent lights and gifts to be illuminated. Expressing from this space gives us a greater appreciation of ourselves, while also honoring the wholeness of others. It is through this exchange that we are able to more deeply see and genuinely interact with others around us. This approach of more conscious awareness also increases the ability to identify individual biases, and trace their roots and origins, while we work to mitigate and manage them. To be effective, I have the belief that it's also necessary to maintain a degree of self and social awareness—by being aware of yourself, your lens and expanding to be inclusive of how you understand others.

"I've learned that people will forget what you said, people will forget what you did, but people will never forget how you made them feel."
–Maya Angelou

How do you make people feel? What lasting impact does your brand leave? Within the business that you run, the department you lead, the team you coach—what differentiates you from others? As an executive and an entrepreneur, I've learned a lot of lessons and have worn many different hats. I have identified that authentic leadership has been a key differentiating factor, and it has served as one of the greatest contributors to my success. However, it wasn't until I moved beyond the "what" I was doing and committed to living and leading authentically that I saw my effectiveness as a leader that inspires increase exponentially.

So often we discuss tactics to facilitate the inclusion and belonging of others absent the role and accountability that leaders possess. I openly share stories of who I am, my lived experiences, lessons passed down across generations, and instances of tragedy and triumph to model the invitation for others. Leaders often set out to empower others, but end up minimizing the inherent power that is already present within. Instead, I invite you to inspire others to live into their power by creating spaces and conditions that are more inclusive, accessible, and promote distributed authority.

People are seeking a deeper connection with substance and meaning. Authentic leadership wasn't something I set out to learn or model. I became more authentic in my leadership after seeing the positive impact on others and their experiences of inclusion and belonging. Are there risks? Absolutely. But for me, the tax of authenticity far exceeds the cost of covering. Leading authentically and sharing with others has become a practice aligned with my purpose—making each moment worth it, if I'm able to model and teach others practices that positively impact the lives of others.

Authentic leaders set the tone, give permission and establish expectations that uniqueness and differences are valued. They create and maintain cultures that are healthy, demand mutual respect and center people. Leaders do this consciously and unconsciously all the time. It becomes present in the decisions that are made, the erosive behaviors that are tolerated, the comments that go unacknowledged and those who are embraced.

Chapter 13: **Jennifer A. Ingram**

The added layer of complexity beyond the items above are the social dynamics and hierarchy present, identities of the individuals and the individuals at the receiving end. Authentic leaders who aren't actively managing the diversity on their teams and prioritizing safety run the risk of being tone deaf, perpetuating minimizing behaviors or worse, benignly endorsing harm. There are many attributes that differentiate good and bad, or effective and ineffective leaders. Beyond the functional fulfillment of the task, it's not always what is done, but how.

There are more than 7.8 billion people in the world, but there is only one you. To harness the power of authentic leadership, there must be a genuine desire and willingness to be brave and share you. In my experience, leaders often get stuck in the what and how, and fall short of living into the expansive opportunity presented in the why and how. Gifted in the why and how are things like why it's important and how culture and conditions are created and maintained; why it's important to see uniqueness and the strategies of how diversity is managed; or how accountability for experiences, positive or not, are owned. Leadership has always come with responsibility, but it is amplified for those who commit to a path of authentic leadership. Authentic leaders must strive to create an atmosphere that acknowledges, recognizes and celebrates the voices, perspectives and experiences to be valued and embraced. This is a pathway to achieve inclusion, belonging and accessibility.

There's an old saying, to gain a friend you have to first show yourself to be friendly. Leaders who show themselves authentically are also likely to display empathy, openness, trustworthiness and care or concern for others. Authentic leadership is a journey, not a destination, where one is in pursuit of becoming more open, accountable and possessing a deeper understanding of the gaps between our lenses—the environment and the lenses of others.

I hope to inspire, encourage, compel and challenge others to utilize their power in ways that are more open and expansive. The purpose of this chapter is to offer my opinions and views on the importance and power of authentic leadership, as well as how to achieve it. It is my sincere hope that you, the reader, will accept my challenge to implement authentic leadership in your assigned positions of power and in your daily life. To be an authentic leader, you must be vulnerageous—vulnerable and courageous—by engaging with humility, and by walking boldly and with integrity.

To truly live in more inclusive and equitable communities, where members experience belonging, it will require developing relationships that are mutually beneficial and expand our collective knowledge. I am eager to continue this conversation and facilitate a paradigm shift that elevates the relevance of authentic leadership. This includes, but is not limited to, engaging with more individuals, organizations and communities, in order to foster deeper connections between various stakeholders and new opportunities for collaboration.

Within your networks, keep talking and exploring the concepts covered. Seek out others committed to leading authentically, and identify strategies to support the changes you wish to see within your sphere of influence. My wish for you is that you will continue to calibrate your lens, seeking ways to enhance your ability to engage with others in more authentic ways. I hope you feel inspired to take what's been discussed in this chapter, and harness your power, allowing YOU to differentiate your brand, by creating a value proposition that is truly one in a million.

CHAPTER 14

FROM STRATEGY TO EXECUTION: HOW A FULL-SERVICE MARKETING AGENCY CAN BOOST YOUR BUSINESS

By **JENNIFER JOHNS SUTTON**

I spent 25 years in the marketing industry, prior to opening my own agency. Those years were spent working at various advertising agencies and marketing firms. I was working on big established global brands and smaller or startup brands—overall helping companies of various sizes, industries and types across numerous industries grow and thrive through effective marketing and advertising strategies. I was doing very well in marketing, when suddenly, the recession of 2008 devastated the country and created a ripple effect throughout the marketing and creative industry. At that time, many agencies closed their doors or cut staff dramatically.

When recovery started to happen, there was a shift in the needs of brands and companies, and how they were responding to marketing agencies. The Chief Marketing Officers (CMOs) were now unexpectedly responsible for every single touchpoint, from product marketing, to people strategies, to processes to physical presence. Hence, there was more pressure put on account planners and strategists within the agency to prioritize based on specific clients' goals and objectives, with limited resources they might have in their time to generate sales, improve margins or get more share of wallet within their current customers.

Despite the economic downturn, I saw an opportunity to start my own business. I had the experience, knowledge and passion to make it a success, and I was determined to make it work. So I used my savings to start my own marketing agency, and never looked back.

Over the years, I've helped many companies reach their goals through successful marketing campaigns, and I'm very proud of my accomplishments. I saw a need in the industry for something new that could meet the new needs of business owners and marketing executives. I ventured out on my own in 2013, and founded Bright+CO, a full-service marketing and advertising agency that was founded on the idea that an agency could serve the business community in a better way.

Our mission at Bright+Co is to be the most innovative, dedicated and productive marketing and communications firm, providing growth companies with a level of thinking and integrated solutions that surpasses their highest expectations. And our motto is, "We work hard so our clients don't have to."

We work with a number of different clients, from established companies to startups, to ensure their goals are not only met, but also exceeded. We understand that each client is unique and has different needs, providing tailored solutions to fit each individual situation. We strive to create marketing and communications campaigns that are as unique as our clients and their products. Our team of experts work relentlessly to create and execute dynamic, creative and effective campaigns. Our ultimate aim is to drive results that exceed our clients' expectations, and our team is committed to delivering on that promise.

Marketing is Both Art and Science

My background is in research design, understanding buyers attitudes and perceptions, as well as media consumption behaviors. I use data to properly plan and buy media, which then evolved into me developing brand strategies and integrated marketing communications (IMC) planning.

The data is the foundation of a strong marketing plan, as well as having a strong understanding of the digital landscape, including social and how to use it to help reach target audiences. I am also well-versed in traditional media, such as radio, television, print and outdoor.

I believe in the power of storytelling with media to create a brand experience that resonates with consumers. I also use data-driven insights to understand how consumers are engaging with the brand, and adjust my strategies accordingly. My goal is to create an effective marketing strategy that will help the brand achieve its goals, whether that be increasing sales, building brand awareness or driving website traffic.

After years of working with some of the best creative minds out there, I began to understand, appreciate and respect the art side of marketing. I realized that this is what it really takes to create a great brand identity—a great story, impactful visuals—and turning those powerful assets into great brand campaigns.

I quickly became known as a brand strategist. By paying attention and really honing in on proven methods and processes for developing strong and enduring brands, I created success for my clients. I combined my unique ability to dot-connect, integrate and act as a true catalyst and changemaker, in order to ensure the goals set were met. This helped companies grow and scale. And that's where the real magic occurs—when the science of marketing is seamlessly combined with the art of marketing.

Fractional Marketing

Marketing has become extraordinarily complex. There are thousands of tactics to choose from, along with thousands of tools and technologies to support marketing efforts. And many companies have fractionalized their marketing efforts—hiring companies to do social, digital ads or PR. Then they wonder why they aren't achieving their goals, or maybe why their CEO is pressuring them to generate more, better results.

That's where a model like ours comes in, because we are solution-agnostic and media conversant. This means, we aren't selling a templated solution. We look at holistic solutions that drive better results. We find that most businesses prefer fractional support, because it's the most effective way to achieve the results for their company. We are big picture, strategic thinkers that operate as a fractional Chief Marketing Officer (CMO) for companies.

It starts with creating a strong brand strategy, and brand storytelling—not just content marketing. People confuse content marketing to be the same as brand storytelling. However, they are not the same. Brand storytelling is creating a series of plot points to build an emotional connection between a brand and its target audience. It's a summary of your company's history, mission, purpose and values, with a narrative structure that brings it to life.

Content marketing can channel brand stories, but not all content marketing is brand storytelling. Content marketing involves creating educational or promotional content to attract new customers, engage existing ones and increase brand loyalty. It is just one channel for telling your brand story. Brand storytelling tools and techniques are used to create branded content that speaks to the values and vision of your company, and generates an emotional response. Brand storytelling explains your values and engages with potential customers who share them. Then we can determine how best to deploy those stories—in social, advertising, events or on a website. Specifically with social media or paid media—there is the added complexity of using the platforms and buying tools to execute on those plans.

Outsourcing Marketing

Outsourcing all of that fractional just makes better business sense. One full-time employee works 1,880 hours annually to perform their defined tasks. This is based on them working 40 hours a week, minus 10 national holidays, four weeks of vacations and two-weeks of sick or emergency time.

Finding great marketing people in different and complex disciplines is often difficult, coupled with the overhead expense of the tools or technology to equip for these roles. Or having to figure out how to fill 1,800 hours of time with someone internally who may not have the experience or disciplined methods for getting results. Or if you manage those people—are you equipped or have the time to evaluate their work and provide guidance on a daily basis to keep them productive?

We take that headache away and manage toward the activities and results CEOs want and need from marketing. No more having the pressure to fill those 1,880 hours or play oversight in task management, working around vacation schedules or having to train or conduct performance reviews. We take all that pain away. This means less risk and less overhead cost to the company.

For the price of one or two full-time employees, a business can hire a team of specialists who understand brand building and brand storytelling, at a Chief Marketing Officer (CMO) level, and at a tactical level for a fraction of the cost. This addition to the team would be able to work on the activities that generate results. By outsourcing, there is no need to pay for training, insurance, employment taxes, vacation time, etc.

Bright+CO in Action: Case Study

We worked with a high-end winery out of Napa Valley. They needed a new website combining all seven brands within one website architecture, with a focus on maintaining each brand's unique story. We also needed to create new e-commerce flexibility and fluidity, in order to increase sales and support upselling/cross promoting products.

The results:

- 16-percent decrease in bounce rate and 35-percent decrease in exit rate

- 10-percent decrease in mobile bounce rate
- 29-percent increase in the ecommerce conversion rate of the site
- 48-percent increase in ecommerce revenue

This same winery also challenged us with the question: How do we expand and transform historic basic digital approach into a full funnel, results driven success across the full brand portfolio? Our solution was to expand beyond lower funnel-only tactics and social-only placements, re-evaluate all strategic targeting and create a collaborative agency/client environment, where performance is closely monitored, results are shared and learnings are understood.

The results:

- Generated close to $400k in revenue from ROAS optimized tactics in under four months, which outperformed previous ROAS benchmarks by almost six times
- Outperformed previous CTR benchmarks by 50-percent

Tactical Implementation

Bright+CO fills the marketing gap experienced by many business owners and executives, by combining fractional marketing, outsourcing and integration services as a cost-effective tactical solution that helps them effectively reach their audience and expand their brands. We can execute at the tactical level. We are strategists, dot-connectors, program creators and storytellers—bringing proven disciplines to the process that allows for better collaboration, innovation and creativity to generate meaningful results.

We understand that brands are only successful if they address an unmet need. For us, that need was adopting a scalable service model with access to a high caliber, vetted and experienced team, combined with proven methods and systems for building better brands, better integrated marketing communications plans and better digital footprints.

We believe the only way to achieve this is through a comprehensive, integrated approach that is customized for each individual brand. That's why we have developed a comprehensive suite of services to meet the needs of brands of all sizes. From strategy and creative services to digital marketing and analytics, our team of experts is ready to help you find the right solution for your brand. With our help, you can be sure your brand will stand out and make an impact in the digital space.

In a complex and ever-changing industry like marketing, everyone is looking for illumination—some kind of short cut or magic template to success, which really doesn't exist. Marketing has become extraordinarily complex. Consumer behaviors have changed. Media has changed. Social media is complex—more complex than most realize. Media planning and buying, especially in digital, is more complex than most realize. But the creation of a strong brand foundation has not. It just takes work and experience to get it done right. And tactics cannot be in silos, in order to be truly effective.

Planning marketing and communication strategies, selecting the right tactics and building budgets can be overwhelming. We are that guiding light—the sense-makers. To accomplish measurable, remarkable things with our brand partners, Bright+CO has developed a uniquely effective approach to smarter marketing. And we maintain an agnostic mindset and invest in a data-driven culture. It's in our DNA—and in our name.

We leverage data, curiosity and expertise to solve complex problems and tell brand stories, creative ideas and tactical solutions that disrupt, delight, engage and resonate. No silos. No egos. No guesses or assumptions. We transform real insights into action. We offer services that scale, data that delivers and tools that simplify. The result? Better ROAS (return on ad spend). Better ROMI (return on marketing investment). And better ROI (return on investment). We work hard so our clients and ultimately their clients don't have to.

10 Reasons Why Outsourcing your Marketing Makes Sense

1. **Expertise:** A full-service marketing agency has a team of experts in various areas of marketing, allowing you to benefit from their collective knowledge and experience—working together to focus on the activities that generate best results.

2. **Cost-effective:** Outsourcing your marketing to an agency can be more cost-effective than hiring an in-house team, as you only pay for the services you need, and don't need to deal with overhead, oversight and performance management.

3. **Time-saving:** By outsourcing your marketing, you can focus on other aspects of your business, while the agency handles all your marketing needs.

4. **Access to technology:** A full-service agency has access to the latest marketing tools and technologies, which can help improve your marketing campaigns.

5. **Flexibility:** With a full-service agency, you can scale your marketing efforts up or down as needed, depending on your business needs.

6. **Objectivity:** An outside agency can provide a fresh perspective on your marketing strategy, helping you to see things from a different angle. A full-service agency like ours is solutions agnostic, so we look at problems objectively and not try to force one service, because that's the only thing we sell.

7. **Measurable results:** A full-service agency can provide detailed analytics and reports on the performance of your marketing campaigns, allowing you to measure the results of your investment.

8. **Customized solutions:** A full-service agency can tailor their services to meet your specific marketing objectives, ensuring your marketing efforts are aligned with your business goals.

9. **Competitive advantage:** By outsourcing your marketing to a full-service agency, you can gain a competitive advantage over your competitors, who may not be using professional marketing services.

10. **Peace of mind:** With a full-service agency handling your marketing, you can rest assured that your marketing campaigns are in good hands, allowing you to focus on other areas of your business.

Conclusion

We are a one-stop shop for branding, marketing, public relations and advertising solutions, integrated in a way that brings better, tangible results. If you are a company that is ready to see results, let's discuss your marketing strategy. We will not have an outdated conversation, but instead a new concept that will actually get you what you want.

At our agency, we create marketing strategies that are tailored to your company's needs. We make sure our clients get the best results in the most efficient way possible.

We understand that the marketing landscape is ever changing, so we constantly stay up-to-date with the latest technology and trends. Our team of professionals are dedicated to ensuring that your business gets the exposure it needs to grow and succeed. We are confident that our creative approach and innovative marketing strategies will help your business reach its full potential.

If you are a company that is ready to see results, let's discuss your marketing strategy. Schedule a free consultation today.

CHAPTER 15

SMALL BUSINESSES, COMMUNITY CORNERSTONES

By JESSICA Z. BRANDENBURG

It's been said a million times to "find your passion," or "do what you love and it won't feel like work." And people who say these things, I'm guessing, have experienced their ah-ha moment. It took me decades to figure that one out. It was more of a chain reaction of removing my own blockers.

My first blocker was that this passion was directly tied to entrepreneurship, and because of my childhood, when I chose my life path, all I knew is what I didn't want to do—work for myself. When I was one year old, my parents left their stable teaching jobs and opened a men's clothing store in Madison, Wis. My dad was a music teacher and worked at two different stores in the summertime.

Reflecting back, in my adult life, I can see that he always held onto the passion of teaching and music, but what I have held onto was the stress of "the store" as we called it in my family of four.

I am very appreciative that the store was successful enough that both my sister and I were able to go to college without any loans. Also with it being a family business, I started to work at a very young age and gleaned the importance of a strong work ethic and a semi-monthly paycheck.

A few years after graduating from Valparaiso University, I started working in technology and loved the innovation, foraging a new way to run businesses. Most of my career was working for a medium-sized business with big name customers. My natural inclination is to create order, organization and work with tangible data and numbers.

I held various operations positions, first on the consulting side until, in 2013, I migrated to the services side of SaaS (Software as a Service). And as the industry matured, I turned my attention to customer success. The shift in software companies was due the fact that they realized a lot of time and effort was going into obtaining new customers, but there needed to be a focus on retaining existing customers.

I always used the analogy of "trying to fill the bathtub with the drain open." For 13 years, I worked for two different sales enablement companies and I liked my work. The happiest moments were when I was creating new processes and spearheading change.

Blocker number two was that I didn't like to talk about work. I've made very good friends at various companies over the years, and because work is so ingrained in our lives, it does often come up. It is the networking aspect, the explaining of what my work entails that was painful to me. For years, I knew that this was always a direct result of every family dinner conversation topic was, "the store."

Tech has not been without its heartburn. I survived the dot-com burst. My company was delisted from the New York Stock Exchange, and we went from over 10,000 employees to 126. However, my number came up in July 2022, and I found myself unemployed for the first time in my life. I did not panic, immediately, as I had a solid background in SaaS customer success operations. In a downturn economy, you need to hold onto your existing customer base, so an organization is even more reliant on customer success.

However, there was this lack of excitement in reading director roles for customer success and enablement. I had the experience and I knew exactly what the role entailed, but reading the job descriptions suddenly seemed like a bland chicken dinner.

A woman named Patrice Darby reached out to me on LinkedIn and quickly evangelized me—she has vision, passion, grit, empathy and a great sense of humor. We clicked. I did an about-face on all of those beliefs that I held onto for decades, as I joined an honest to goodness start-up. The zinger is that that platform is for entrepreneurs. This was truly a pivotal point in my life.

In forging this new path, I became an independent consultant to advise during a critical path for the platform. Not only is the start-up new, and I am now working for myself, I have new responsibilities, such as paying my own taxes and healthcare. However, the biggest surprise to me has been that I suddenly love talking about work. I love that the company mission is to make a difference in black and brown communities, by closing the economic gap, and by strengthening the success for entrepreneurs.

This was not a new mission for me, but ties into how life evolves to show us our path. Being a Chicagoian, I witness the inequity each and every day. For me, the most painful one is in the winter riding the L (elevated train) and seeing school children in too thin of jackets for the winter, where I am dressed head to toe in the warmest gear. I've also witnessed, first-hand, being a female in technology. Especially in the beginning, it was truly a male dominated industry.

It was during a work volunteer day that I was exposed to a STEM based public school, Chicago Technical Academy. I loved the thought of giving support to diverse girls who had an interest in the same field that I enjoyed, ensuring that there were more opportunities for females and females of color in tech.

I joined the committee for a fundraising event for the Young Women's Leadership Society, called Little Black Dress Night in 2017. The impetus of the committee is a program in the spring, with mainly corporate sponsorship, bringing together successful leaders, participating in a panel discussion on how they achieved the success.

Over the years, one theme is constant—nobody followed a straight path. This is a good lesson for the girls, because they do not have enough mentors in their daily lives. Another important aspect of the evening spring event is networking—a first-hand exposure, similar to what they will experience in a corporate setting.

Every year, even during the COVID virtual meetings, I walk away with new knowledge and awe of the accomplishments of the panelists, and the dreams of these young girls, who have their sights on going to college and what life will look like after graduation. From a post-poll perspective, it is always the stories from the girls who are the audience's favorite portion of the evening.

My involvement in ChiTech also gives a first-hand view into a world of families who are only a few miles away from me, but so very different. Of these students, a majority rely on free lunches, which disappeared on a dime during the pandemic. Remote learning was conducted on cell phones, as many homes do not have internet access. Everyone struggled during this time, and although I did not

Chapter 15: **Jessica Z. Brandenburg**

have children to tend to, my white friends, who all were able to work from home, were also able to pay for additional support, such as tutoring. I would have done the same, because we want the best for our children and know how important education is.

The easiest years for obtaining corporate sponsorship for LBDN was the year after George Floyd's death. In 2023, it is more challenging, due to the threat of a recession, and like everything else, inflation is making the cost of the food and beverage higher.

In 2022, I went with a friend to a fundraiser for a Catholic high school for the school's diversity program. The amount of money that was raised during an end of evening auction was unbelievable. Paddles were going up at all of the circular tables in the packed gym, the fast talking auctioneer securing donations for various fun and different activities for up to $10k. This too, was a very different exposure for me, but what truly stuck with me that night was the difference in the level and participation in giving between a Chicago public school and a Catholic one, which are a 10 minute walk from each other.

I worry about the divide that our future holds, when one side faces so many constant obstacles, and another that has more opportunities.

My mother has many health issues and I am often asked if she would move to Chicago to be closer to me since my father has passed away. The simple answer is no, because Madison is her home. It's a simple concept to understand. However, in impoverished areas, the sign of success is when you leave. Why cannot we lift up communities that have had decades of struggles and neglect?

One of the huge barriers for these black and brown communities is a lack of access to capital. The ripple effects are immense and cause communities to crumble. The annual difference in wealth flows to White families and Black families is about $330 billion. More than 75-percent of the difference stems from differences in return on investment, cost of debt and intergenerational transfers.

When it comes to financial services, Black Americans and other people of color face inequities across the board, including lower access to financial institutions in their communities, lower approval rates, and less availability and participation across a range of financial products and services, according to McKinsey.com.

In 2021, small businesses owned by people of color were more likely to apply for financing than White-owned firms, but were about half as likely to get all the funding they requested, according to a Federal Reserve survey. While Black-owned businesses in the U.S. have grown significantly in recent years, they still make up a small share of firms and revenue in the country, according to a Pew Research Center analysis of Census Bureau data. The data says, in 2020, Black adults comprised 12.4-percent of the overall U.S. population, however, only three-percent of business ownership.

There are countless articles and studies trying to get at the root of inequality in the United States. One of the most interesting is from the Brookings Institute and the relationship to yelp reviews, such as, "In Black-majority neighborhoods, poorly rated establishments grow at roughly the same low rate as highly rated establishments—and both perform worse than poorly rated businesses in neighborhoods, which are less than one-percent Black. When all factors are included, the full model of our research suggests a 0.2 percentage point gap between businesses in non-Black-majority neighborhoods and Black-majority neighborhoods, amounting to $1.3 billion in unrealized revenue each year. This gap jumps to $3.9 billion when comparing highly-rated businesses in Black-majority neighborhoods with highly-rated businesses in other neighborhoods."

The words "underserved communities," means everything from having better street lighting to making communities safer and jobs in neighborhoods, not a 30-plus minute bus ride away. The heart of the American dream is the opportunity to succeed, to provide food and shelter for family members, education for children, hope for a better life, and freedom of opportunity. What I hope I am changing, is creating gray neighborhoods, because we will all flourish.

A study published in 2008, from two professors from the University of California, Santa Cruz, outline the barriers to successful minority businesses and at the end summarize findings as, "Clearly, improving access to capital for minority entrepreneurs is important, especially in light of the striking wealth inequality that exists in the United States. However, increasing opportunities for the acquisition of human capital and business human capital should also be viewed as vital goals for minority business development. In particular, governmental programs providing mentoring, internships or apprenticeship-type training may help to reduce historical inequalities in business performance. These policies may serve as a substitute for the lack of opportunities to work in family businesses for some disadvantaged groups. The potential benefits may be large, because simply increasing the number and average employment of minority businesses by only 10-percent would result in the creation of one-million new jobs for minorities."

"The best help you can get is someone who genuinely cares and knows how to help you get what you don't even know you want."
–Richie Norton

Here are some ideas of how to be more inclusive in our everyday lives:

- If you participate in social media, try to diversify your feed.

- Be conscious about supporting black owned businesses.

- Follow different podcasts (Some of My Best Friends Are, is one of my favorites).

- Volunteer! Find a local small business development center on sbg.gov.

As Americans, we all share a common bond—our humanity. We may come from different backgrounds and have different perspectives, but at the end of the day, we are all connected by our shared goal of making a better tomorrow. Despite our differences, there is much that unifies us. We each have unique strengths and talents that can be used to benefit our communities, if we work together. By pooling our resources and combining our talents with others, we can create a better world for everyone.

Working at a start-up is one of the most rewarding and fulfilling experiences I have had. Not even being six months in, I know this role is a game changer for me. I enjoy all of the different aspects (hats) that I get to wear, but the most joyful experience is making an impact and being part of something bigger. The feeling of accomplishment that comes from knowing that I'm making a difference is unparalleled. I am a part of an amazing team, which is a rewarding experience, especially when the team is significantly smaller than the ones with which I am used to working.

I also have a deeper appreciation for communities—caring deeply about the places where we live, and helping those around us form connections and providing support. I am working on making my circles of connections bigger, because helping just one more person a day has a profound impact over a lifetime. It is a perfect infinity circle, because everytime you help someone, you also receive benefits—learning, new relationships and a greater sense of purpose, which all lead to a feeling of enjoyment.

Everyone has their stories and celebrated successes. For me, it is what I have spent half my life running away from, and I have now embraced it as my sweet spot. My work mantra is to find something that brings you joy.

Resources:
- *https://www.sba.gov/*
- *https://www.mckinsey.com/industries/financial-services/our-insights/the-role-of-financial-services-in-improving-racial-equity-in-the-us*
- *https://www.fedsmallbusiness.org/survey/2022/2022-report-on-firms-owned-by-people-of-color?mod=ANLink*
- *https://www.pewresearch.org/fact-tank/2023/02/21/a-look-at-black-owned-businesses-in-the-u-s/#:~:text=Despite%20this%20growth%2C%20businesses%20majority,from%20classifiable%20companies%20that%20year*
- *https://www.brookings.edu/research/five-star-reviews-one-star-profits-the-devaluation-of-businesses-in-black-communities/*
- *https://npc.umich.edu/publications/policy_briefs/brief12/*

CHAPTER 16

BECOME A FULL-TIME FEMINIST AND CHANGE THE WORLD

By **JESSICA NAVA**

Feminism. What does this word mean to you? What emotions does it bring to the surface? Feminism is a word that carries a lot of emotions, from all sections of society. For me, it is a powerful and important word. Feminism is about equal opportunity. Feminism for me is not the man or woman picking up the bill. It's not the man opening the door. I'm still, and always will be, a feminine woman. I want to be treated like a woman and respected like a woman.

But when it comes to work, pay, education and politics ... I want equal representation and, more importantly, equal opportunity. Diversity, Equity, Inclusion and Belonging (DEIB) has been at the forefront of my personal and professional life for many years. That is why I decided to take a career-changing opportunity, leaving a corporate tech job to become the Chief Growth Officer at The Moxie Exchange, home of the Everyday Inclusion app.

When I think of those in history who define my most perfect version of feminism, at the top of my list is the late Associate Supreme Court Justice, Ruth Bader Ginsberg (March 15, 1933–Sept. 18, 2020). RBG had no fear in standing up for what was equal and right. My favorite case is Charles E. Moritz v. Commissioner of Internal Revenue

(Nov. 22, 1972). Case 469 F.2d 466 held that discrimination on the basis of sex constitutes a violation of the Equal Protection Clause of the United States Constitution. Equal opportunity is not just about equal rights for women; it's about equal human rights.

So let's dig into the word "feminism"—what it means and what is behind it. The word feminism often conjures a visual of women burning their bras. While bra-burning was part of the movement needed during the 1960s, feminism is so much more than that now. We need to look beyond what has long been considered acceptable and aspire to become so much more for everyone—creating true equality for education, income, political representation and social standing. There is an amazing book and TED talk called, "We Should All Be Feminists," by Chimamanda Ngozi Adichie. It breaks down what feminism is perceived as, such as bra burning. That perception of feminism needs to die, because that's not what it is anymore.

The reality for many women is that they are responsible for many of the day-to-day tasks in their lives and households. Personally, I'm busy being a mom, a house cleaner, a cook, a chef, a caretaker … you get the idea. So just by our very own nature as women, we're phenomenal at getting all of those things done. But those responsibilities have had a negative impact on how quickly we've been able to drive the feminist movement.

Enough is enough. Now is the time to step up and take action. We all need to create a world where true equality is at the forefront in all leaders' minds. We CAN create a better world for our daughters, as well as those who are under-represented and need their voices heard.

Chapter 16: **Jessica Nava**

That's exactly what we're doing with Everyday Inclusion, and why I joined a mission-driven organization. I'm excited to marry my personal experience with the mission-driven work of my career. I feel like everything I've done in my life has led me to this point. I have three teenage children, and when I think about the world they are going to inherit, I know what I'm doing is right and important. However, it is important to note that it is not only about women's rights; it's about everyone's rights.

Four Necessary Changes to Business Environments

There are four important elements of my journey with DEIB and Everyday Inclusion that I would like to share with you. Below are each of these aspects of what I like to bring each of these to the forefront of the conversation, when corporations are looking to understand the necessary concerns of their employees. Business leaders and corporate officers have a unique ability to create change in their companies. At Everyday Inclusion, we look at the analytics provided by employees and evaluate how companies are responding to their concerns, both good and bad. It is up to the leaders of those organizations to create change.

1. ***Never judge a book by its cover.***

    - I may, in my own unconscious bias, see a white cis-gen boomer man. But I have no idea if that person comes from a low-income or single-mother household, or what his religious beliefs are. It's about getting to know people, in order to see people for who they are, not what we perceive them to be.

- Our employees are an amazing resource and wealth of knowledge, so we should listen when they voice concerns. If we're not allowing people to show up as themselves, we need to work on that.

- As we continue to hire more diverse teams, we need to be willing and able to help employees be truly authentic.

- Ask questions when you don't know the answers or you don't understand where the employees are coming from.

2. **Create a safe space for all employees.**

- Everyone deserves to be treated with human kindness and respect, bottom line. We have no idea what is happening with other people, especially in the workplace. We have no idea where people have come from or what they are currently going through. People wrongfully assume diversity is race, gender or sexual orientation. It is so much more than that. Humans are the beautiful intersection of their religion, their mental health and their abilities … plus race, gender and sexual orientation.

- Instead of making assumptions, we as business leaders need to make the changes that are necessary for everyone to succeed.

- Meet employees where they are at in their learning journey. Allow them the privacy to learn and grow and create a safe space that allows for mistakes to be made.

3. Activate allies.

- We can do nothing alone, without leaders, decision makers who can actually move the needle for us. These leaders need to embody what allyship looks like.

- Allies are important to those who are unheard. We need you to learn to use your privilege for those who are unheard or unseen.

- The under-represented section of the workforce cannot make changes alone. Until we sit in the boardroom or the executive team leadership room, we need you to think about the underrepresented and what they need.

4. Find your own voice.

- My leadership motto is: Ensure that every voice is heard, including my own. There are so many of us who are scared to speak up for fear of retribution.

- Business leaders should create an atmosphere where everyone is heard, truly heard. But more importantly, we should create a space where everyone feels safe to express who they are and what they need to thrive in the company.

- By allowing employees to have their voices heard, we will all feel more comfortable in the company and will work harder for the greater good.

By utilizing these four elements within your company to create an inclusive business space, all employees and the company atmosphere will thrive.

How My Career Path in Sales Lead Me to The Moxie Exchange

Think about the women or minorities on your teams. How does it feel to be the only? I worked in corporate sales and as a business development executive for 23-plus years and know firsthand that sales is not an easy job. But it was even harder being the only woman in the room.

The global percentage of women in executive ranks, according to international accounting firm Grant Thornton, shows that the numbers have "remained above the 30-percent tipping required to precipitate significant change for the second year in a row. The proportion of women in senior management has increased from 31-percent to 32-percent in 2022 and never dipped below the first record." Add to that another frightening statistic: The global percentage of women in B2B sales, as stated by chief.com, shows that "women hold only one-third of B2B sales roles, according to the Bureau of Labor Statistics, despite representing 47-percent of business majors with bachelor's degrees."

While these numbers are not encouraging, they are the reality of where we are today. Too many women hesitate before going into sales or leadership, because these are male-dominated fields. Yet women can be wildly successful in these fields due to some of our natural skills as communicators, listeners and community-builders. Women have an innate ability to connect with people and allow a safe space to open up and talk. The corporate world has not always allowed space for women to lead. If you decide to take the leap into sales, which I highly recommend, you should start by developing a mentor or sponsor right away, in order to learn quickly what you should and shouldn't be doing, and to learn more quickly from your mistakes.

I picked sales and leadership for a few reasons:
- Career potential and growth
- Earning potential
- Freedom and flexibility
- To learn companies and people's stories
- To help companies with solutions

How can you have success in a sales role? Keep in mind these few things you need to know when embarking on the sales path:

- It will be grueling. Accept it, own it and move on.

- Be a sponge. Know that in the beginning you need to be HUMBLE and learn from others. You will not know it all, you will never know it all, and that's part of the fun in sales.

- Sales is a team sport! Learn to recognize others for the win, call out their input and support, and down the line you will get 10 times the support others are getting.

- Build a community of other like-minded individuals you don't work with and network, learn and grow from them.

I didn't always have a strong voice. As a mother of three teenage children who are mixed race, I have finally found my voice. It may shake sometimes, but I am thankful for the women before me who have blazed the trail. There is a saying: Rosa Parks (Feb. 4, 1913–Oct.

24, 2005) sat, so Ruby Bridges (Sept. 8, 1954) could walk, so Kamala Harris (Oct. 20, 1964) could run. All of these women, and so many more, did what was necessary at the time to push the needle forward for others. And that is what I am trying to do with my career at The Moxie Exchange.

Five years from now, I hope the Everyday Inclusion app is being used by 10 million people. And I hope that I'm recognized as a thought leader in this space and whatever that looks like. For the naysayers out there who do not believe in DEIB or moving the country forward in the business sphere, I would like to say to you: What if it was your daughter? What if it was your wife? How would your perspective change? Consider how their inclusion, or lack thereof, impacts you.

It is our job as business leaders to make business personal. We will drive change in DEIB, one person at a time. I'm not asking people to agree with everything someone else says. I'm asking them to treat that person in a way that makes them feel included. That's it. You don't have to agree with them or their lifestyle, but we still have to treat people well.

My call to action is for both men and women. Be allies. Let's support women and the feminist movement, because it's vital for our success as a society. I'm not asking for preferential treatment, but instead equality for more than 50-percent of our global population. Let's all take ownership for our actions, in how we show up and how we treat others—because some day, it may be your wife, your daughter or your granddaughter who is being left out of the business equation.

I'm betting my whole career on it. When I think about the tens of millions of lives we are going to impact with Everyday Inclusion, I choose to focus on being a champion for the unheard voices around the globe.

Have relentless curiosity. Listen, learn, grow and ask questions. Take a leap of faith in something you completely believe in and know is right. Every human being deserves to feel included and belong exactly where they are. Imagine a world where everyone feels like they're included and belong for who they are. Let's be that world.

Resources:
- *https://www.grantthornton.global/en/insights/articles/women-in-business-2022-global-and-regional-findings/*
- *https://chief.com/articles/women-in-sales*

CHAPTER 17

REDEFINING SUCCESS

By **JOSEPH FANNIN**

As a leader, I always try to keep an open mind. I value my team and I respect them. I'm intentional about leading by example. Many of our employees are working hard on high ladders, and they have to take safety training. Even after their training, they have to be confident enough to complete the job with excellence and in a timely manner. My team knows I'm not going to ask them to do something I wouldn't do. I also stand behind them and their work. I support them, as needed, and I've even shown up and helped them on projects. I'm not afraid to get my hands dirty, even though I've been out of the field for a few years.

It's important for my employees to trust me. They know I'm honest, and they know I have their best interests at heart. I'm loyal to them, just as much as I am to my clients. More than anything, I listen to and implement changes based on employee feedback. I'm not so stuck in doing jobs in a certain way that I can't take an employee's suggestions into consideration. If something works well, and it's efficient, great. But if there's a better way to do something, I'm all for it. I think that's what my team respects most about me.

On Friday mornings, we have our company meeting and tacos. We've been meeting like this for some time now. It's a chance for me to hear what my employees need in the field, or what we can buy to make their jobs more efficient. If I can do something or buy something to make their jobs easier, or help them complete jobs faster, I'm all ears. My goal is to build a team that exceeds my skill-set, as there are many industry leaders who have paved the way for me.

In the past 10 years, I have learned valuable lessons in life and business. Not only through pushing myself past mental blocks, but also in times of tribulations and success. If I was going to give advice to young entrepreneurs, or those who aspire to take an idea and build something from it, I would say there is no better time than now.

Our passions toward an idea can quickly pass by. I've had many ideas over the years, many of which have passed by without action. Inspiration to make a move is the pivotal moment to execute. It is time to dive in and give 110-percent. Take notes. Put your ideas down, "on paper, on purpose." You have 75-percent more likelihood to achieve the goals you write down. Hold yourself accountable. Make a SWOT analysis (strengths, weaknesses, opportunities, threats). Put the ball in motion, and watch how the snowball grows larger with the momentum and potential for success.

One of the best moments of my entrepreneurial voyage was when I hired my first business coach, John Russell of The Russell Consulting Group based in Austin, Texas. John was laid-back, but a genius businessman. The first task assigned to me was to write two obituaries. The first was to write one as if I died suddenly today. The second was as if I had died in 30 years. This was a staggering and odd task. After a week or so of procrastination, I finally sat down and started to type what I thought people would say about me, my accomplishments, the memories they had of me and who I was as a young father. It was the hardest thing I had ever contemplated.

Chapter 17: **Joseph Fannin**

The second obituary was much easier than the first. It was a manifesto. An intentional syllabus of my future. A way to write down what I wanted to be. What did I want to achieve, be remembered for and what was my legacy? In kindergarten, many of us desired to be a fireman or doctor when the teacher asked, "What do you want to be when you grow up?"

In the short time after writing these obituaries, I met with John to go over the assignment. He quickly dialed in on my why. It was in this moment that I felt my own passion was confused and distracted by the menial tasks of the day-to-day business. I was off course. I was lost. I was spinning the wheels of a two-wheel drive truck, trying to climb a mountain. John was quick to assess and point me onto a focused path. There were many conversations John and I had where I would catch my tongue and realize I was the biggest mountain in the way. I was the reason I felt stuck. I was the factor that was holding the business back. It was my fear of failure, my misunderstanding of business, and the desire to have everything perfect that was holding me back from the success I desired.

One day, I told John, "I can't afford an office or space to work out of. I'm stuck working out of my home."

Quickly, John retorted. "How do you know? Have you looked? How much are they? What are the lease terms? Do you have a real estate agent you could talk to?"

Instantly, I had to put my foot in my mouth. I did not look. I did not know what the cost or terms were, but I was certain I couldn't afford it. I say this to highlight the mountain, this proverbial mountain, that I had projected in the path of my business. I had put chains on my future for no reason at all!

In the time of working with John, I had many moments of humility. I felt empowered. I knew my self-limiting beliefs were the obstacle, not the things I was unsure about. Overall, my time pursuing self-development, business coaching and research has paid dividends in my personal fulfillment—but also has been an inspiration to those around me.

There are a few books I would recommend starting with as an aspiring entrepreneur. *The E-Myth,* by Michael Gerber is a staple for businesses, which was another task John assigned me. I was naïve for many years, until I finally read it. There are so many common struggles depicted in Michael's book, which was published in 1995 and later revised. I was shocked reading this book. I realized I had made many natural mistakes that most business owners make. In the beginning, I felt I could do everything—sales, marketing, production, advertising and administration. I was going to do it all.

Unfortunately, this is a fatal error many of us assume is the small business' destiny. After taking a step back, reflecting on the past and what potential was in the future, it came to me that I was only good at certain aspects of business. I should not be doing things I despise or don't have a desire to do. A client of mine, who was a college professor, once told me, "If you can pay someone less to do the things that you're not good at, while making more money doing the things you are great at, why would you struggle to learn how to do it?"

In the next few years, after reading more about business and my industry, I concluded that I had to delegate, which was a hard task to swallow. I had to let go of my desire to control all of the many aspects of business that I was not passionate about. I did not possess the

Chapter 17: **Joseph Fannin**

desire to be great at bookkeeping, but I did have a passion to lead and do the best I could to take my opportunities and to pay it forward to those around me. This was an epiphany for me, a self-realization of my talent and determination. I finally had a why! At first, I was driven to create something I was inspired to do. I desired a challenge and the why was evolving into something that I was led to be. In that moment, I found the sole reason why I enjoyed the entrepreneurial journey.

As a passionate leader, I quickly became obsessed with pushing my knowledge and understanding of business, but also as a mentor. If I could elevate my potential, and as a byproduct, inspire my team to push themselves to achieve their goals, it would be the fulfillment of my why. In a reflection of the years since I had this epiphany, it has become more apparent that I am not just a boss, friend or mentor. I am an example of potential and putting everything I can to pay it forward.

After a short break without a business coach, I came across a leader in the industry who had an inspiring story. Brandon Vaughn's dad had a window cleaning company for more than 30 years—until he came down sick. While Brandon tried to start a couple of companies, he already had some setbacks and failures. When his dad was no longer able to keep working, he stepped in and took his dad's company over in Portland.

Within five years, he went from being a one-man show to having over 40 employees, more than 20 trucks on the road and generating more than $4.5 million in four locations. After selling the business, Brandon worked with another guy named Josh Latimer. Together, they built a business coaching program, "Conquer" that I was a part of for a year and a half. These guys have truly taken their skill-sets and poured them into other people like me. I learned that I didn't have to reinvent the wheel. These men have inspired me to not only produce great, quality work—but also the importance of valuing people and relationships over revenue.

As a creative entrepreneur who is devoted to changing our industry for the employees' and customers' benefit, I am most thankful for the opportunities I am blessed with, including being able to work for myself, creating careers for others and inspiring young minds to be their best. I would like to inspire young minds to take the leap and bet on themselves. I came from humble beginnings and a poor family. I always thought of myself as less fortunate.

It took me a long time to realize my why. I noticed that I enjoyed creating opportunities for others. I strive to be the one who others can count on. When I look back and see all of the mouths I helped to feed, and all of the customers' lives I've been able to touch, I realize this is so much more than a job. It was then that I realized success looks different for everyone.

I believe I found success early on, which was setting out to create something I could ultimately be proud of. I set out to create something that I can say I dedicated my all to. When I felt like giving up, I got back up and kept hustling. Success is our own finish line. We get to define it. Sometimes, we reach it sooner than we expect. And, sometimes, we have to move it closer. I have paid it forward and I'm always willing to think outside of the box. I take myself seriously, but I also strive to have fun. Always bet on yourself. Do your research and educate yourself. Follow your gut and instinct. Be humble and lead with passion. Never stop learning and surround yourself with those who you admire and aspire to be like.

Chapter 17: **Joseph Fannin**

The pros definitely outweigh the cons in terms of business degrees, education and understanding. However, that is not a reason to hold back on inspiration. I had the fire to start something from nothing, with a skill-set, some tools and very little money. If there is one thing I can attest to, it's that betting on yourself will be the best return on investment you will ever experience. No one else will bet on you and go all in on a maybe.

If you are passionate about the journey, and not fixated on being stuck in a closed-minded box, push yourself past those mental mountains, surround yourself with those you aspire to be like and you will be blessed with bountiful returns. Failure is not a roadblock; it is the stepping-stone to greatness. It should not be a hindering factor. Be willing to risk taking something from nothing and doing great things. We as humans have a desperation of validation, but also an inherent envy to be as "successful" as others. If you can take that desire and manifest it into your passion and ideas for business, you will see the unbarred possibilities grow exponentially.

In conclusion, I aspire to motivate those who have a passion to be a creative entrepreneur, to drive into the fog of their dreams, and chase their desires to innovate and start something wonderful. Bet on yourself, put your best foot forward, and do not look back—except to reflect on where you were when you started, and to see how much you have accomplished!

CHAPTER 18

WANT TO WIN? LEAD AND BUILD A GREAT TEAM!

By **KEITH ANGELL**

I've been fortunate over my 30-year career to intersect with some of the smartest venture capital, private equity and large corporation leaders in the global technology markets. I've worked with and learned from outstanding individuals from Kleiner Perkins, Greylock, Norwest, Silver Lake, HIG, Mill Point Capital, Exxon and IBM.

I've served as a C-Suite executive or Board Director for 12 high-growth technology companies over the last three decades, and been engaged with numerous IPO, sale processes, and merger and acquisition efforts. Over all these different terrains, there have been a number of factors that correlate to the ultimate success of an enterprise, to the equity value creation of technology firms. But there is one element that far surpasses all others as the strongest correlation to "winning".

I was golfing with the managing partner at a major private equity firm a number of years ago. While a neighbor and club friend, he was also an extremely successful professional who had made dozens of portfolio acquisitions, and turned almost all into successful companies that brought outsized returns to him and his PE firm. As we settled for post-round refreshments, I asked Scott what the secrets to his many company successes were. His answer, without hesitation, affirmed my own viewpoint: "The absolute strongest correlation to building great companies is the leadership team. Find the right CEO that creates a winning team, and everything else will follow."

I reflected on Scott's wisdom and my own experiences to that point in my career. I had seen every type of CEO and corporate leader, from command and control zealots, to laissez faire "visionary" dreamers. I had worked with exceptional IQ and low EQ managers, and vice versa. But when I categorized these various individuals by the results they drove, the reality of the correlation became quite clear. Indeed, the key to enterprise success hinged on the leader, generally the Chairman or CEO of an endeavor, and the team he or she built. In fact, no other factor—the market, the competition, the value proposition, the paradigm shift or any other—held a candle to the outsized light of what a great leader, and an engaged and aligned team can achieve.

Let's start with great leaders. What does it mean to lead? I most appreciate the Thought Leaders definition of leadership. They say that to LEAD means to Listen, Empathize, Add value and Delight. Clearly, this means a strong leader must have both a high IQ and EQ, and he or she must be focused on adding value throughout the stakeholder chain—from employees to customers to shareholders. To delight those same stakeholders means to focus on the key satisfaction elements like employee retention and net promoter scores. Let me highlight a few examples.

I began my career in the Management Development Program at Exxon Corporation—then the most valuable company in the world—where senior leadership had developed and utilized one of the

Chapter 18: **Keith Angell**

premier training techniques available. Like General Electric, Procter & Gamble and a few others, Exxon cycled high potential, emerging talent into 18-month positions, where they were given a chance to sink or swim, managing bigger and more complex parts of the organization across different corporate sectors.

The training developed multiple competencies required to succeed as a leader, both in experiential management skills and softer leadership techniques. But perhaps most importantly, the MDP trainees were exposed to some of the brightest leaders at Exxon, who welcomed the chance to teach these young charges. Recalling the dozen or so vice presidents and senior executives with whom I worked, two key leaders stand tallest among the list. Both had savvy management skills and high intelligence, but both were most consequential, because of their exceptional emotional intelligence.

That high EQ allowed them to listen effectively to their constituencies, empathize with their management teams, build confident, caring and committed alignment, and overachieve on a consistent basis. For them, leadership meant crafting the right strategy with great tactical execution. That tactical progress was only achieved through buy-in by all the leader's team of the vision for an aligned future state. From that training and those powerful examples, I learned the critical importance of complete vision alignment and commitment for executing a tactical plan. Further, I studied how to combine insightful analytic skills with softer listening and team-building competence.

I have tried to take that listening mantra to heart in my career. I encourage open and frank discussions in all my executive meetings. Further, I dedicate hours every week to having one-on-one conversations with teammates all over the world beyond my direct reports. I ask my human resources teams to schedule 15- or 20-minute appointments for me with contributors from every department. At Pythian, that meant meeting employees working from 30 different countries with time zones all over the globe. But by doing that every week over three years, I was able to have over 600 valuable discourses understanding ways that teammates thought we could improve as a company and innovation areas where we might invest.

Midway through my career, I had similar learning experiences at IBM Corporation, then the most valuable technology company in the world. I had the good fortune to serve selectively on the IBM Strategy Committee, where both Sam Palmisano and Ginni Rometty presided when they were CEOs. I noted their strengths and weaknesses in leading the firm, and their direct reports as IBM navigated the choppy waters of technological disruption in the 2005 to 2014 timeframe.

My takeaways? Both showed tremendous proclivity to see the future state required to win, but one was much better at aligning their leadership teams to execute on that vision. Building winning teams is more than just producing a strategy and announcing a vision. Winning teams require alignment and team commitment, and that is only achievable through buy-in and ardent confidence.

When I took over as the CEO of Velocity Technology in the mid-2010s, the company was hemorrhaging cash and on its way to bankruptcy. Unbeknownst to ownership, the founder had leveraged a series of acquisitions to hide the intrinsically poor operating performance and core financial results. I remember getting to week three of my CEO tenure when the new CFO and I discovered that the company literally would not have the cash to make payroll at the end of the coming month. Within a week, I was forced to lay off almost 100 people and introduced a series of severe cost-cutting actions. But that reduction in force gave me the opportunity to reset the entire senior leadership team structure at the company, to promote high performers and remove old school thinkers loyal to an old paradigm.

It also gave me the chance to promote a diverse set of respected managers who, I had come to know over my first month, were the ones who could turn the ship around and execute on an aligned vision for the firm. Within that first year, I restructured the SLT to consist of ethnic and cultural diversity from around the globe. Within three years, we turned a company losing $1 million per month into an enterprise generating $2 million of cash every month, and worth half a billion dollars. I listened and added value as a leader, but more importantly, put the right team in place to execute a new vision. What really made that transition work was good leadership, but an even better TEAM.

Building a great team may be the most important task of any CEO. There are many well-known acronyms around TEAM, including, "Together Everyone Achieves More" and "Trust, Energy, Attitude and Motivation." While these certainly resonate, personally, I have adopted a slightly more tactical, "Transparency, Expertise, Alignment and Measurement," as the key elements of a strong team. Let me explain.

I took over as CEO of Pythian Services in early 2020, just as the pandemic was hitting the technology services market hardest. I had been serving on the board since a private equity firm had carved out a neglected division and had put together a value creation plan, based on an investment thesis focused on the immense opportunities in the data and analytics services market.

After a quick tuck in acquisition, I had a number of chess moves to make, in order to assemble the best possible team of senior leaders to take the company forward. I prioritized bringing together the most diverse group of talent that would align to our vision of "unlocking the power of data," and believed wholeheartedly in transparent, accountable and measurable management philosophies.

I promoted four key women to executive positions and increased their equity shares. I gradually eliminated holdovers and naysayers, and low performance individuals. The SLT became 40-percent gender diverse and 50-percent multinational. And over the next three years, revenues, margins and EBITDA all doubled. By putting the best experts in place and aligning on a vision and strategy, we created a vehicle for tactical execution that outperformed the market, even during the Great Resignation, increasing interest rates, high inflation and a banking crisis.

That team absolutely bought in on a transparent and collaborative working environment, on furthering their own expertise in their respective areas of responsibility, on vision alignment and on measuring the key performance indicators for the business. That core group, consisting of some of the best performers with whom I have ever worked, tripled the value of the invested capital in under three years, and helped create one of the leading data and analytics companies in the entire world.

Bill Gates calls this type of leadership and teamwork a "transformational leadership style." He believes that this TLS will inspire and empower employees, encourage open communication, allow leaders to act as a mentor and role model, and encourage a vision-oriented environment. I agree that exceptional leaders who follow the tenets listed above will absolutely inspire and empower others. And that building high expertise teams aligned around a future vision will overachieve any other peer group.

As a Board Director, I have come across a number of CEO and Senior Leadership Team dynamics. In the private equity and venture capital business, that combined team is essentially where you place your financial bet. In any case where a CEO change has been warranted, the investing or owning entity has never said they changed too early; in fact, the opposite is always true. If owners don't believe they have the right leader in place, they need to make the change as quickly as possible.

I have served on the Investment Committee of a venture capital fund for five years. The focus of that fund has been to leverage detailed analytics in all the investments, and the IC uses an algorithm to determine the quality of the investment. Every investment opportunity is carefully and persistently worked against key criteria, and those criteria and their relevant scores are analyzed for an ultimate decision. Chief among those measurement criteria is a full assessment of the CEO. That criterion is algorithmically the most important criteria in the entire decision matrix. CEO IQ, EQ, prior success and transformation leadership scores clearly correlate to the return on investment for this industry. A low reading there automatically disqualifies the opportunity. Leadership and team building are clearly paramount to success.

When I mentor young people, I lead them through a five-session course that includes training on personal leadership and their responsibility to add skills and experiences in their lifelong journey to create value. In the first hour, I focus on the traits of leadership and how those traits—Listen, Empathize, Add value and Delight—are critical to the success of any relationship. In the same first orientation, I stress how "success requires a village", and how any individual can build an aligned team around them as their "board of directors" or "board of advisors." Even for young professionals and emerging talent, all of these principles ring true.

If you want to win, LEAD and build great TEAMS.

CHAPTER 19

LIFE AND BUSINESS LESSONS FROM A CEO & DAD OF SEVEN

By **KEVIN M. CAMPBELL**

After nearly 30 years in the tech industry, I now run a successful enterprise data management Company, Syniti, that helps the world's largest global organizations achieve success with their digital transformation initiatives. I also happen to be the lucky father of seven amazing kids.

Below are five lessons I'd like to share with you:

1. Prioritization is critical—but balance is in the eye of the beholder.

I have seven kids, ranging in age from pre-teens to college, all with very different needs, passions and motivations. I'm also the CEO of a fast-growing, global data company where speed is of the essence. The projects we work on for our large clients are very complex and mission-critical to their success. That doesn't always add up to having a lot of time, or creating the most harmonious and balanced life.

I wish I could tell you there is a magic formula to create a perfect balance in your life—there isn't. What works for me is understanding what's most critical for me to handle as a CEO and as a dad—open lines of communication and working when I can, not necessarily during "normal" working hours.

Figure out the best schedule for your needs—what works for you and your family, as well as you and your business. There's no one-size fits all answer. Maybe you're a morning person—getting up extra early is the right way to start tackling the daily email deluge, or carving out time to work on a project before anyone else is online. Perhaps you're a night person and your creative juices are flowing when everyone else is snoozing. Figuring out your needs schedule-wise will guide everything else.

In life, and in business, you can't be everything to everyone. You can't possibly do it all, especially not on your own. Identify those big rocks, such as what's absolutely the most important meeting for me to be in? What thing will truly move the needle for our business? What event coming up for my kids means the most to them? The reality is, I can't be in every meeting with a prospective customer, and I can't make every single one of my kids' events. It's just not possible—with seven kids and a 24/7 business, there are just not enough hours in the day.

What I can do is make the decision with my kids or my team, or look at past experiences to determine: How important is this and what will it mean if I'm not there?

This is where communication is just as important as having a great work and life support system. A great example is when my kids had a field day race. I worked with my assistant to move around non-critical meetings so I could sneak out and watch my twins dominate a crossed-leg relay race.

Just remember: What works for you, won't necessarily work for someone else. I'm okay working when I can, even if that means answering emails while watching soccer practice on a Sunday morning. That's not always true for my team and employees. So be clear that you're working when you can, but don't expect they do the same.

I learned the hard way that choosing the ways we prioritize is important, and those are different for each kid, as well as for Syniti. Your values drive what you choose to prioritize. Identifying your values and understanding why they are important to you helps you make decisions that are memorable and meaningful.

2. People are the key to creating and sustaining success.
This was one of the harder lessons for me as I'm an operations guy at heart. I was all about the process, getting things optimized to be most efficient—and yes, I have a Six Sigma certification. I was very blessed to work for the legendary investor, Ray Dalio. It wasn't always fun, but I learned a lot from him. He always used to say, "It's about the WHO, Kevin."

The first fifteen times he said that to me, I didn't understand, and not just because I know "The Who" is a band. However, eventually I figured out there are many routine tasks you can put a process around, but at the end of the day, it's about the people. It's who you put in a specific position that makes the biggest difference and is the biggest indicator of success.

Seeking to understand individuals and what drives them, is a concept that works for my kids as well as my employees. My oldest daughter is hugely driven, and she's very hard on herself. She's studying to be a lawyer right now and we are past the point where I can help with her schoolwork. However, what I can do is listen, talk her through these tough moments, remind her that I'll love her no matter what and emphasize that it will all work out. On the other hand, I have a couple of boys who, if they call and say, "I'm going to fail out of school," then I need to start digging and figure out what's going on.

My kids, just like my employees, ask for and need help in different ways. Understanding those different personalities and what drives each of them makes a huge difference. Learn about them personally, and connect with what matters to them. Different people require different motivation—as well as different motivation over time. Some are super competitive and do better with a hard push, some do better with logic, some do better with encouragement, but ultimately, everyone wants to know you care.

I always say the job of the CEO, or any leader, is to get more out of your people than you think is possible, and especially, more than they think is possible. That's the only time I feel great and like I've succeeded.

The other thing to look out for is that 10-percent of the people cause 90-percent of the challenges. Whether it's that one crazy supplier or that one coach who's a pain in the neck, you just have to get past those situations. Some people are just going to be a problem, no matter what you do. Don't wait to address these issues.

3. Mentors matter—have one, be one and be sure to give back.

Some of the most meaningful relationships I have are with my mentors. My earliest mentor was my dad. I learned my work ethic and got my interest in business from him. I like to joke that when you're twelve, that's the only time in life when you know everything. The rest of life is a journey of realizing how little you know, as well as how much you have to learn and grow. Career-wise, I'm really fortunate to have some amazing professional mentors.

The chairman of my current company, Bill Green, has been my boss at different times over 35 years. He taught me how to drive change by figuring out what you can do to move the needle. It's never about changing dozens of little things. You need to figure out the two or three most important behavior changes and put the right people in the right positions.

Syniti also has a great board of directors. As you can see from our website, we have the board of a $10 billion dollar company, not a $200 million dollar company. The feedback I get from board members when they express why they are willing to join us is because I listen. Many CEOs want to present and convince, versus getting feedback and guidance from the vast experience within their board. I consider myself fortunate to be able to learn from the people on my board, to call them up and say, "Hey, I've got this tough problem. What do you think?" Of course, none of them will give me the answer, but they give me ideas to think about. That's the value of having mentors.

It is important to remember that mentorship goes two ways. Too many of us are far too busy. If someone asks me for a quick 15 minutes of coaching, I will find the time to talk. They might not like my advice or want to take it, but I'm always happy to spend time with people, sharing with them what worked for me. It's important to not give people the "answer," but instead to provide opportunities to expand their thinking and consider other options. Taking that time to connect reinforces a culture of approachability and reciprocity. That's how you build networks and get good people on your team.

4. *Your toughest clients are your best clients.*

Contrary to many people's opinions, your best clients are the toughest ones. One of my first big, complex manufacturing enterprise resource planning software implementations developed a bug just as we were getting to the end of development. A weekly process that was supposed to take 12 hours, was taking over 70 hours to run. And this client was not happy.

We looked at every option to fix the problem, but the logic just wasn't working. It was looking like an unsolvable problem. The solution was to send me, along with the smartest guy from our client's company, to Chicago for three months in order to rewrite the software and make it work. It ended up being some of the best work I've ever done in my life. It was tough, detailed work and I was away from my family. However, we finally solved the problem no one else was able to solve. And until recently, most aerospace and defense companies ran that same software we wrote sitting side by side, morning to night, for three months.

The people who push you and say the traditional answer isn't good enough, or it's never been done before–those are the people who really drive innovation and creativity. The best way to learn and grow is to spend time with people who have real problems to solve. Even when you come from differing points of view, spending hours debating over how to address a problem can result in deep learning.

You can also apply this in your own life. There have been times in my life when I thought, how am I ever going to get out of this problem? Whether it's a financial problem, something falls apart, or everything breaks in threes, somehow you always figure it out. Those tough spots build resiliency. And the relationships you build in tough times are the ones that stay with you forever.

5. It's lonely at the top.

When I am asked for advice or my opinion, I always offer a strong point of view. When you have a strong point of view, you need to have people around you with whom you have long-term relationships. These are the people who will tell you what you don't want to hear, but most likely, need to hear.

I surround myself with people who get me, my style and how I like to work. However, it is important to have those people who push you and who challenge your viewpoint. I always have a paid coach who is not an employee, not a friend and not a family member. I pay them to give it to me straight and direct. Over time, I have to decide if that advice is good or bad.

Every few years, I review whether I'm getting the right advice from the right mix and amount of people. Are they willing to tell me what I might not be considering?

Ultimately though, when you're the CEO, the final decision rests with you. When your board wants X from you in the next year, and your team only thinks you can do Y, who makes the final decision? You, and you alone. That can be a lonely place, so it's important to have a trusted group of advisors, as well as to always prioritize your mental health (and that of those around you). Take time to rest and recharge, and to reach out for help. There's still too much stigma around mental health—it affects all of us.

Patience, empathy, communication and adaptability are skills I've worked to gain over my career and my life. They've helped me raise seven incredible kids, and build strong and long-lasting relationships with my employees, my mentors and my customers.

You get to decide what life lessons you apply to your business. Make them memorable.

CHAPTER 20

THE POWER OF BEHAVIORAL SCIENCE TO IMPROVE LEADERSHIP

By **KURT NELSON**

Great leadership is more than just deciphering the market, managing the company's finances and making great strategic choices. It requires a deep understanding and ability to lead people. As a behavioral scientist with more than 25 years of studying and working in the field of human motivation and engagement, I research why people do what they do. My company, the Lantern Group, is tasked with understanding what drives employee behavior and engagement. Our experience and research in this field has shown that leaders often do not understand the deep and complex motivations behind their employee's behavior, which can lead to programs and initiatives not having the effect that was expected or intended.

At its core, the Lantern Group is a behavioral change and communication agency. We work strategically with organizations to bring applied behavioral science insights into the company, and develop programs and strategies to help motivate and engage employees long term. These interventions include everything from total rewards design, manager training and employee communication, to bringing behavioral science education to the leadership team, so leaders can better understand the people they work with or those who work for them. We help leaders understand how their behaviors, their words and their programs will impact their employees—oftentimes, in ways they don't necessarily understand or think about.

Effective leadership requires that you understand the human dynamics that impact what you're trying to achieve. Leaders, by definition, have followers. With followers, a key part of a leader's role comes with making sure that their followers are engaged, motivated and inspired. The way a leader acts or reacts to certain situations, the things that they focus on and the words that leader says, must provide guidance and inspiration—even in times of correction. If leaders don't fully understand the impact of their words and/or their actions have on their team, they cannot ensure that they are maximizing how the team is performing. This can literally make or break your dream team.

Understanding how to set, communicate and assign goals is also a key aspect of being a great leader. Goals can be powerful motivators—if they are done right. For most leaders, it's about making sure you have set large keystone goals for your team that will drive the business forward, but also helping to break down those large goals into smaller milestone goals that are actionable.

This is the big piece: If the goals are too large, your team may be inspired overall, but those goals won't drive action. Large goals can also frustrate team members, because the goal seems so far out of reach that employees become discouraged and stall. On the contrary, if the goals are too small, your employees may know what to do, but they won't have any higher motivation to do them. The sweet spot between the two extremes is to create "Goldilocks" goals. With Goldilocks goals, you translate those bigger keystone goals into smaller manageable goals that are not too large or not too small.

Chapter 20: **Kurt Nelson**

Good leaders think about what is required from the perspective of their employees.

As a leader, one of the hardest parts of motivation is crafting goals that fall into this Goldilocks zone. Behavioral science can help craft these Goldilocks goals by giving us insight on how we, as humans, are motivated and engaged. As mentioned before, if a goal seems too easy, it won't have a strong motivational pull. But if the goal seems too difficult, it can actually be a demotivator. One of the most effective ways to get your goals to the Goldilocks zone is by collaborating with employees to actually create the strategic goals and break those goals down. People naturally support what they help to create.

Gaining buy-in by giving employees a part in building the goal is tapping into a psychological trick called the IKEA Effect. Basically, it's the concept that people feel stronger about a piece of IKEA furniture, because they had to build it. Because they had to spend a few hours putting the piece of furniture together, they feel a sense of ownership once it's completed. Studies show that, when we feel ownership, we are more attuned to it. We value it higher, and we will keep it longer. Goals are the same way. If people help create or build their own goals, they are going to buy into those goals more. They're going to put more effort into those goals. They're going to stay on them longer, and they're going to be more likely to achieve them.

However, it is important to understand that our brains often like to fool us in this regard. When we ask people what will motivate them, or when we think about what motivates us, our brains are wired to give us an answer that is easy, and one that fits with social norms and our self-identity. The trouble is that research shows these easy answers often are not what really drives behavior. As leaders, we have to walk a thin tightrope of providing key directional goals that actually drive the right behaviors, and allowing input by our teams on their goals to gain alignment. How do you get them to be engaged each day and to stay engaged with those same goals over time? That is the question every leader must ask themselves.

Another critical element of motivation is understanding how goals actually motivate people. Goals, by their nature, drive motivation in a predictable way. Motivation typically starts out high, dips in the middle, and then becomes high again, once we get close to the finish line. Behavioral scientists call this the Goal Gradient Theory.

For example, let's say you want to lose 20 pounds. When you first set that goal, your motivation will be relatively high. Near the end of the goal, your motivation is high, as well. However, there is often a dip in motivation in the middle of your weight loss. This "Middle Problem" can derail many people from achieving their goals. As a leader, you need to understand and beware of that problem. This is one reason why setting smaller milestone goals within the larger goal is effective. It reduces the dip in the middle and brings the uptick that is associated with finishing the goal closer. Employees are able to celebrate the success of achieving smaller goals, instead of waiting until they've attained the larger goal.

Another way of overcoming the middle problem is to tap into how our brains perceive goal progress. We know that if people think they're closer to the goal, they will work harder. Psychologists have shown that this progress can be illusionary and still drive motivation. A study conducted by Ran Kivitz shows this illusionary goal progress effect. The study was conducted with over 10,000 coffee buyers,

Chapter 20: **Kurt Nelson**

where the researchers gave half of the group a punch card that allowed them to get a free coffee after 10 punches. The other half of the people received a punch card that had 12 holes to punch before getting their free drink; yet, the card had two holes pre-punched. The results were fascinating! They showed that it took roughly 15 days for the persons holding the 10-hole punch card to buy enough drinks to redeem their card. However, it only took 12 days for the people holding the 12-hole punch card. Notice that both groups had to buy 10 coffees no matter what. But our brain tricks us into thinking we have already made progress toward our goal when we see two holes already punched. This progress gets us through the middle faster, thus changing our behavior.

This leads me to another aspect of motivation. We are motivated by a sense of progress. This is called the Progress Principle. If we feel that we are making progress, even if it's a tiny bit of progress, it activates reward pathways in our brain and provides us with a motivational kick. However, if we see ourselves moving backward, or even just staying put, that can actually be demotivating. It is important for leaders to understand this to ensure you are not unwittingly demotivating your team. Think about how you communicate to your team—particularly if your team may not be performing well. Do you berate them for how much they haven't done? Or do you show them how much progress they have made? While it is easy to show disappointment, it is harder to redirect your words and actions to provide your team with something they can latch onto, in order to increase their engagement.

In addition to goals and progress, leaders need to understand some of the basic tenets of employee motivation. We can think of this very simply: We are human beings, not robots. We are motivated by a wide range of desires and needs.

One model that helps simplify these various needs is the Four Drive Model of Employee Motivation, developed by Nitin Noria and Paul Lawrence, of Harvard. They show that there are four underlying drivers of employee motivation: the drive to acquire and achieve; bond and belong; comprehend and challenge; and define and defend. To be an effective leader, it is important that you understand and leverage all four of these drives.

The drive to acquire and achieve taps into our desire to obtain and keep resources. In organizations, this speaks to the pay we receive, our bonuses, the awards and the accolades—all of which provide motivation to perform. As leaders, we tap into this drive by ensuring that we correctly align rewards with behaviors, and recognize the behaviors we want to see repeated. The second drive is our need to bond and belong. We are social creatures. We crave that human connection. We are motivated to ensure that those relationships with our team and managers stay positive.

As leaders, we engage this drive by building a strong team culture and creating psychological safety for people to connect as humans, not just coworkers. The third drive is our desire to be challenged and learn. We are driven by challenges. We don't want to be bored. This is the drive that is tapped into when we set good goals and provide new opportunities for employees to explore, learn and try new things. The final drive focuses on our need to defend the group and have meaning at work. We are communal creatures, and we defend our group from outside threats. We also have to define who we are and our purpose, and make sure that our definition aligns with the organization. Once we're aligned with the mission and vision, we will go to great lengths to defend the team.

Finally, to be an effective leader, you need to ensure that your actions are in alignment with your beliefs. It's hard to motivate others if you are not fully committed to the course of action you are taking. Employees are keenly aware when there is a disconnect between what is being said and what they are being asked to do. You can often sense when you are out of alignment when you experience a sense of angst, some sort of feeling of discomfort within. Oftentimes, we can't name it. We may say, "Something is off." But we can't necessarily define that something. This is what psychologists call cognitive dissonance. Since we do not like this feeling, our brains sometimes overcome it—not by addressing it—but by rationalizing it away and dismissing it. As a leader, be aware of those moments when you're feeling that discomfort or angst.

Organizations can also experience a sense of cognitive dissonance, where employees feel that their beliefs don't align with where the company is going. When this happens, employees can check out and become disengaged. When looking at organizational alignment, one of the best things a leader can do is ask people within the organization how they are feeling. As leaders, we often don't ask those questions, because we are afraid of the answers. We need to make sure we ask those questions in a way that people feel safe to give truthful answers. Employees need to understand that they can voice their opinion without negative consequences. If people don't feel safe to speak up, they won't. Many times, we're wondering why a certain project didn't work or an initiative failed. It just may be because people feel disengaged.

Effective leaders understand that their job is more than just working on the business side. They are the key conduit in which their team is inspired and motivated. By understanding the underlying forces behind why and how their employees are engaged, leaders will be more effective. Behavioral science offers leaders a way to glean some of those insights and improve their performance.

CHAPTER 21

YOUR GIFTS WILL MAKE ROOM FOR YOU

By **LANISE BLOCK**

I have been an educator for over 21 years. I believed that my calling would be to teach students until I was 89 years old and passed out teaching at the chalkboard in my high school alma mater in North Minneapolis. I deeply loved teaching, the students and my colleagues at that school. I realized I needed to be the change I wanted in the Minneapolis education system. I needed to be innovative, beyond my teaching comfort zone, and show up in spaces that needed me to strategically make an impact so students could have better opportunities in the future.

I discovered my purpose as an educator the summer before my undergraduate senior year, working with at-risk youth at my granny's youth program. I was there to escape the impending feeling of becoming an adult and knowing how I would make a living after graduation.

My grandmother was a loving, formidable force and insightful; we adored each other. She spent her life fostering youth, educating them beyond the schools, and spreading hope and a sense of worthiness—helping them to understand they are more and will become more than their circumstances. She watched me interacting with, teaching and creating activities for the kids. One day, somewhat out of the blue, Granny said, "You're good with kids; you should be a teacher." She would overhear them talking about the lessons I had taught and how they felt I treated them with respect. I felt it was my mission to provide them with the best possible education I could each day.

I have since graduated with multiple degrees, taught at the same high school I graduated from, held leadership positions with the school district, and started Sankore Consulting to consult across industries in strategically creating impactful Diversity, Equity and Inclusion (DEI), and using Innovative practices to solve problems in the education, business and social justice areas.

1. Your Gifts Will Make Room

In 2015, my department was reorganized, and I was among those who were laid off. I had no idea what I would do and did absolutely nothing to prepare. I didn't fill out job applications or interviews. I was stuck with "what's next" paralysis and right back at that moment my summer before senior year in college, lacking direction for what was next.

I was laid off on Friday, June 30th with no job lined up. I continued to do the only thing I had done since finding out I would be terminated: pray. I was out of a job for almost 48 hours when I received a call from the district's superintendent's secretary. The superintendent wanted to meet with me. *Really, why?* After that meeting, he offered me a job starting that next week. I was anxious to consider the job, because his reputation preceded him, and not in a good way. Plus, we had never interacted, but he knew of some projects I had worked on and wanted to hire me as the Strategic Process Administrator, directly reporting to him.

This man, known for having high standards and being difficult to work for, became my mentor and someone I respect and admire. This role exposed me to the operations and business side of the district. I managed a budget exceeding $16 million, while leading and creating an innovation projects incubator throughout the district. I developed my skill set, executing Equity Leadership Professional Development and leading a team in creating an equity framework coupled with an Equity Diversity Impact Assessment for the district that is still used today.

This role enabled me to gain insight into strategic planning to help organizations become better DEI advocates and practitioners. I can't know the alternate reality, but I believe having an open mindset and not listening to negativity allowed my *"gifts to make room for me."* (Proverbs 18:16.)

Mindset is at the core of everything. Every space, everybody has a culture and perceived understanding of how they view the world. Have you ever considered if you identify the biases you bring into the spaces you occupy and how you address those biases?

2. An Informed Mindset is Mandatory

I first noticed the correlation between mindset and people's treatment of others in leadership environments. Then again, when I taught at a college level. Because of these observations, I now help individuals and organizations shift their mindsets in the DEI space.

In 2019, the Twin Cities was ranked as one of the worst cities for low achievement gaps, and in almost all other disparities across the board: health, housing, economic wealth, etc.

Much of my work and passion involves addressing inequitable barriers to create a better socio political environment for black, indigenous and people of color (BIPOC). For example, in my recent equity work at a local Minnesota suburban high school that has become less white over time, while the teachers are predominantly white—approximately only 30-percent of students are white, and the rest are BIPOC students—I was hired to do an equity walk and observe classrooms to help leadership ascertain areas the instructional staff could be supported and encouraged. I observed about 20-percent of students disengaged from the teachers' lessons. Student disinterest at the high school level isn't inherently bad, but the lack of effort from teachers trying to redirect student's behavior was bad.

In my feedback to the principal, I asked two key questions: 1) What do the teachers believe about educating all children? 2) Do these teachers believe all children have a right to be educated, and that it is their responsibility that students learn?

Similarly, organizational leaders can take these two basic questions and formulate them around your clients, constituents, partners and other stakeholders: What do you believe about DEI, and what is your responsibility regarding that belief?

Leadership indicated that the teachers expressed low sentiments regarding their BIPOC students' willingness to learn, because they were poor, couldn't do any better than they already were and their parents didn't think they could learn. As a solution to these assumptions, teachers actively choose to ignore students who demonstrate a lack of interest. The teachers interacted with students based on what they thought of them. Similar mindsets and assumptions, along with deeply rooted, insidious racism throughout the state, are to blame for the large disparity between the high achievement of white students, compared to the low achievement of BIPOC students.

Teachers are crucial in the development of young people. What and how we treat students carry significant weight in their future development. Rather than doing nothing, a better action would be to redirect the behaviors, have a one-on-one conversation with the students to understand their needs, or use culturally responsive teaching strategies that engage students. If we have low expectations of people, our actions will reflect poor treatment and lack of concern. These ill informed, unregulated mental models from those who hold power, make it dangerous for BIPOC people to exist and thrive in society.

For businesses, corporations, nonprofits and government entities, you must go beyond performative, one-off activities such as DEI seminars with a keynote speaker who gives you catchy quotes, and cultural potluck lunches. To get to the root of the issue— which is mindsets. Your strategies, words and activities won't matter if you don't first address your mindset.

Don't take my word for it; mental models, beliefs and biases are well documented by brilliant scientists. Take the cognitive bias and cultural inventories tests to begin addressing your individual beliefs.

3. To Achieve Different Results, You Must Be Willing to Be Innovative

Writing the inequitable wrongs in society involves taking immense risks and courage. Innovation must be included in your change process to achieve different results. Being innovative is risk-taking, and taking risks is risky. But have you ever considered that with each decision you make, you are taking some measure of risk, and hoping it will be the right one to pay off? I risked unemployment by not acting when I was told I was being laid off; similarly, I risked being miserable by working for someone perceived as a tough boss. Both risks paid off.

A secret no one tells you about innovation is that the byproduct is always a drop in production. Our pessimistic minds will always jump to the negative, "I knew we shouldn't have done this," but effective change requires time to adjust. You must ride the wave and give yourself permission to see it through, before reverting to the same behaviors.

Six years ago, I took a big risk by starting my business. My social studies undergraduate major did not train me in business. With ongoing encouragement from my husband to start my own business, I went to the secretary of state one Thursday, completed my paperwork and emerged with a business certificate. There have been times in my business when I didn't know where my next client would come from, and I had to take a risk and make certain investments that I hoped would pay off. That drop in production was necessary, because I was starting something new and learning along the way.

I didn't feel ready or confident, and it took quite some time for me to decide to step out on faith and become my own boss. The innovation of creating a space for me to make a greater equity impact by using my gifts to balance the scales, mitigate centuries old injustices and address systematic shortfalls was risky. But the change I am creating is worth it.

4. *I Don't do One-Off Speeches and Potlucks*

Companies focus on DEI through communications, making statements and putting up emotionally charged imagery that depicts a false narrative of the diverse workforce representation with hopes of attracting people of color. These performative actions may attract talent, but the organization's policies, practices and culture won't retain them.

When an organization, company or group calls me in to help address DEI issues their culture is facing, I quickly level set and tell them I don't do one time engagements, but rather a series of engagements that result in structures or protocols for impact.

To Get to the Root of Fixing DEI Issues, We Must Address the Policies, Practices and Procedures Put in Place

Oppression was institutionalized—policies, procedures and laws prohibited liberation and promoted oppression. The only meaningful way to counteract such measures is not by giving speeches and potlucks, but with new laws, policies and procedures, because that's where institutional oppression lives and where it must die. Inequitable practices show up in your business practices and pursuits. If you are only interested in DEI social events and not taking meaningful action to make a stance, your actions are performative and meaningless.

While I will not work with organizations who only want to do surface level work, I will help create their equity framework, conduct an equity audit and provide cultural inventories that include one-on-one coaching sessions and group debriefs.

How Can Individuals Create Equitable Change?

"The world is changed by unreasonable people," is a quote written in my high school yearbook by my drafting teacher. This quote reminds us that we should be unreasonable in our pursuit to create a more equitable world. You will either choose to remove yourself or work to change it. The point is that every single person has the ability to create change in some way—big or small—that will compound over time.

As BIPOC people, our duty is to be unreasonable and demand change. In practice, it can be as simple, and bold as showing up as your authentic self at work. Wearing our hair in its natural state and style is, unfortunately, a risk, but it is also educational and a stance that we will no longer assimilate to a culture given to us, instead celebrating the beauty that is within us.

As an ally, raising issues and challenging the status quo to raise awareness of inequitable practices will make people uncomfortable. It's a risk, but someone must do it. Each of us can do something at every level—whether in a small position creating smaller change or big position creating big change. Change what you can change. Fight not only for your future, but use your fight to help others create a more inclusive future for all.

While completing my dissertation, one piece of feedback my committee gave me that has remained with me is, "you are the instrument," meaning, "the means of getting something done." Start with examining yourself and doing your work. Then seek ways you can make changes in the spaces that you occupy. You are the agent of change! Godspeed.

CHAPTER 21

ROOTED PERSPECTIVE

By **LEE ANN SCHWOPE**

Picture a tree. It is the most beautiful tree you have ever seen, with lush leaves and fragrant flowers blooming, as well as seed pods hanging just right, waiting for the perfect moment to release into nature to create more beautiful trees just like this one. The branches lift to the bright shining sun that beats down on the tree, showing off just how enchanting the tree is—it is welcoming you to sit at its base and ponder life's lovely nature. Picture the trunk and how healthy and stable it is, like it has been there for centuries, waiting for you to come sit and relax.

This tree is the product of years of just the right mix of sunshine and water—nature's symbiotic relationship, which provides a mutually beneficial interaction between weather and the trees that provide so many resources for the planet. As we look at this beautiful tree, we might think that it was perfectly made or that it didn't have any trouble becoming rich, healthy and productive. But actually, what has given the tree its vitality is hidden in the rich soil. Did you know that a tree's root system is as big or bigger than the actual tree, spread deep and wide underground? This magnificent tree has spent years perfecting its roots system, in order to create the beauty we see.

As you stand next to this perfect gift nature has provided, you notice a smaller and less healthy tree, growing just out of reach of the sun's rays. This tree has not received the sunlight and water it needs. It is weathered and worn, unable to prosper. The leaves are a little wilted and there are no flowers or seed pods. While some branches are lifting to the sky, there are also some that are dry with no leaves, hopelessly faltering in the wind like they could fall off or crumble right before your eyes. The trunk has bark that is crumbling off, exposing its vulnerable insides. And as you look to the ground beneath the tree, you can see that it is dry with little color or nutrients. It is clear that this tree has not had the resources or nurturing that the other tree has received throughout its life.

These trees represent two very different lives and can be compared to the health, value, and nurturing that people either receive or create in their personal and professional lives—or fail to receive or create. It is important, when creating an authentic life with the right boundaries, to find the right place to grow your roots and ground yourself. Below, I will explore each of the areas that require nurturing in our lives—flowers and seeds, leaves and branches, trunk and roots—and include the good and bad outcomes that can emerge due to the ability or inability to provide quality care, understanding, love, knowledge, proper perspectives and authenticity. It is also important to remember that our roots, where we hold our most inner self, need to be the strongest part of our personal tree, in order to create a stable environment for the rest of our tree of life to grow and flourish.

Flowers and Seed Pods

Acquaintances are the most fleeting and possibly distracting relationships in our lives. Acquaintances are the flowers and seed pods on the trees. We can be distracted by their beauty, but they are temporary in our lives. Flowers and seed pods are grown for the purpose of giving nutrients to various creatures in nature, such as bees and butterflies. The seed pods are purely to create more trees.

If we look at these relationships like flowers and seed pods, they are seasonal friends. These are the friendships that can teach us lessons, show us new and exciting things, allow us to explore different things, such as cultures and places, but in the end, they do not stay close to us. I encourage you to accept them, for the simple purpose of learning and growing your personal perspectives on life and the world around you. You can learn what you like and don't like by experiencing new and different things. These seasonal relationships can also help us cultivate a strong root system by grounding us more in the simple pleasures, and create a more authentic connection to the world around us.

These relationships can also be harmful, if you think of the tree above that couldn't grow them. Sometimes, seed pods and flowers don't grow on a tree due to the tree's health and vitality. This causes the tree to wither more, because it is not visited by insects and creatures. And by not having those experiences, the tree becomes even more unhealthy.

When we look at this from a personal perspective, by not allowing experiences and pleasures into our lives, even if they are temporary, we cannot gather the needed foundation to create a fulfilling life filled with beauty and enjoyable moments. Think of the ripples in a pond after a stone drops. These ripples provide more experiences for the world around us.

We can never know what these moments can do for someone else. Some of these experiences include:

- Paying for someone else's coffee when you're in the drive-thru
- A smile toward a stranger in the grocery store
- Saying hello to someone as you walk down the street
- Complimenting a stranger while shopping
- Listening to an elder's story while waiting for a doctor's appointment
- Asking questions at a dinner party to people you don't know very well
- Helping a neighbor shovel their driveway

When we block these moments from our lives, we lose the possibility of spreading our authentic, purposeful selves and legacy throughout the world.

Leaves

When looking at the tree's leaves, we learn that they are very helpful for the world, insects, creatures, humans, and the tree itself. They provide the plant the nutrients it needs, and also produce oxygen that helps animals and people breathe.

When we look at the leaves as coworker relationships, we can see that they are educational and can be fulfilling in many ways. We can have mentors who teach us more about our careers and allow us to move forward in jobs. We can also have enjoyable conversations and learn more about the world around us by taking the time to cultivate relationships with coworkers. The average person spends around 90,000 hours of their life working. When you think of it this way, this is a lot of time to spend with the leaves of your life, which can be abundant, but not always meaningful.

Branches

The branches are vital to a tree, spreading the tree's leaves, flowers and seed pods. They also circulate nutrients down to the trunk and roots. When we look at the branches as friend relationships, we can see how important they are to personal and authentic perspectives, growth, entertainment, and satisfaction. Most Americans have about nine close friends. These important relationships are with the people we learn from, grow with, and help create fond memories throughout our lives. They are also people we can count on to accept us for our authentic selves.

When friendships are not healthy, they can disturb the rest of our lives. When we think of them as the branches of the tree, we can see that if the branches are not healthy, they can make it harder to grow leaves, flowers and seed pods. This means that friendships can hinder our personal and professional lives. Therefore, when choosing our friends, we need to choose wisely and only create lasting bonds with those we can truly count on for the long term.

Trunk

The trunk of a tree is the most important above-ground part of the tree. Without a trunk, we do not have the rest of the tree. The trunk contains the family relationships, which include parents, siblings, spouses, children, chosen family, etc. These relationships are the closest to our hearts, with the people we hold dearest to us. But often, we spend the least amount of our lives with these people.

The average person spends about 230,000 hours, or about one-third of their life, sleeping. When we think about how many hours the average person spends working and add in the hours they spend sleeping, we realize that we need to cherish the time we have with these people that much more. They provide us with our core memories, the ones that last our whole lives. They also are unconditional love relationships, the people we love no matter what. They are the people who know our authentic selves. Without these people, we cannot create a beautiful tree. And when these relationships are toxic, they can harm the rest of your life, including your authentic self.

Roots and Legacy

The roots of a tree are just as big or bigger than the actual tree. This system creates the rest of the tree. When we use this analogy in relation to our authentic self, who we are at our core—our values, beliefs, hopes, dreams, and legacy—we want to make sure that the roots are given the right nutrients and care.

In order to be true to your authentic self, and create a life that is true to your roots, it is important to keep a checklist either written down or in your head that helps you stay focused on what really matters. Below is a checklist I have created that I utilize daily to ensure I keep myself on the right track. Feel free to use it for your authentic self awareness. For more information about authenticity, please feel free to pick up a copy of my book, *Perspectives: Authenticity in the Workplace*, available on amazon.com.

1. **Did I behave the way I wanted to today?**
2. **Did I act with courage today?**
    a. Emotionally honest
    b. Set boundaries
    c. Be vulnerable
3. **Did I show compassion today?**
    a. Connections
    b. Create an environment of belonging
4. **Was I wholehearted today?**
    a. Sincere
    b. Commitment
5. **Did I take care of myself today?**
    a. Kind
    b. Self-care
    c. Exercise
    d. Emotional care
6. **Did I practice gratitude today?**
    a. Grace
    b. Joy
    c. Thank you
7. **Did I feel confident in my actions today?**
    a. Calm
    b. At peace
    c. Learning
8. **Am I happy?**
    a. Low stress
    b. Smile
    c. Feedback

If we do not nurture ourselves by chasing our dreams, meditating, creating boundaries, valuing our personal authentic perspectives and growth, we cannot provide the best life we desire or grow a thriving tree that we and others can enjoy. However, when we create a robust root system that is grounded in the simple things and surrounded by the richest and healthiest relationships, we are able to create a lasting legacy that ensures. People want to build something that leaves an impact on others that lasts long after they are gone.

Some great ways to focus on ourselves include:

- Reading self-help books focused on our personal growth needs
- Volunteering our time at nonprofits that speak to our inner selves
- Fostering pets who are in need of homes
- Joining running, reading or hiking groups
- Spending time outdoors
- Helping an elderly neighbor
- Listening to music and dancing in your kitchen
- Traveling to places with different cultures
- Loving yourself on a daily basis, even on the tough days

The next time you are alone meditating or thinking about your life, make sure you consider how you can nurture all the parts of it, so you can create a world you would be proud to live in, one you can share with everyone around you. You might create the most perfect life that you can be proud of, enjoy for yourself, and leave a legacy for the next generation.

CHAPTER 23

DRIVING EXCELLENCE AND TRANSCENDING MINDSETS IN CEO LEADERSHIP AND THE C-SUITE

By **LEIGH PRIEBE KEARNEY**

People who excel in their fields seldom fit the normal population. Effective leaders may, therefore, rarely connect with others who can productively match and challenge their talents. In the business world, CEOs are entrusted with bringing companies profit, performance and positive global impact. Their strategic vision, expansive industry knowledge, stewardship of evolving team members and commitment to measurable success are exceptional assets. With these unique abilities, however, come ever-intensifying demands. To meet and exceed company expectations, CEOs benefit from sharing professional intimacy and partnership, alongside an expert coach.

Intimacy should, in fact, be an acceptable word in the workplace. Professionally intimate relationships emerge through cultivating intentional, immediate and sustained trust. In my more than three decades of executive C-Suite coaching, I have witnessed firsthand their transformative promise. In this chapter, I will illuminate critical components of professional trust and intimacy. Such insights will equip rising coach psychologists to precisely understand and empower the next generation of globally impactful CEOs. To further illustrate my expertise, I will also integrate salient testimonials from world-renowned previous clients.

Critical Components of Professional Trust and Intimacy with CEOs

Immediate Resonance
Testimonial 1:

"Leigh built instant trust with me during our first call. We were discussing my company's situation ... when she asked me a deeply personal question about how I thought my team might be viewing me and my expertise. The subsequent brief conversation led me to believe that my team had developed an unhealthy attachment to me. In that first call, Leigh won my trust by demonstrating a deep understanding of me. I believed that she would be on my side throughout the process of developing my team."

Testimonial 2:

"Leigh makes a strong 1st impression. Her considered choice of language and the directness of her questions gave me an immediate sense of confidence in her ability to deal with executives that made me comfortable."

Out of all of my clients, the best CEOs have endured some sort of crisis, trauma or major developmental event. These experiences have led them to a groundedness and a "true north" of guiding beliefs. This recognition, along with reflections on my own journey, magnify the importance of being grounded and resilient. When we understand that everyone has their own path, we are less likely to try to control or dominate their life. Even if we don't always agree with someone, we can extend grace and tolerance. As a coach, cultivating immediate trust provides the path toward the discovery of a CEO's values, motivations and what drives them to succeed.

Daringness
Testimonial 1:

"Leigh's direct and honest advice is so greatly appreciated. She is able to hit you with what no one else dares to tell you. Then, she'll stick with you and see you through the challenges."

Testimonial 2:

"Maybe most importantly, we have learned a vocabulary to discuss the difficult complexities that arise in group dynamics. Some of these meetings were fun; some were painfully—but necessarily—hard. You pulled no punches, but always had empathy. Collective trust amongst my team grew (it needed to) and continues to grow. I always felt (and I think others did, too) that you fundamentally had my back, even in the most emotionally charged discussions."

A coach or any consultant must leave their own heads. When you are truly 100-percent focused on the other person or team, you can then practice directness, formulate interventions and facilitate dialogue. Daringness helps coaches move to a deeper and more authentic understanding of what a client says, and most importantly, does not say. When I work with clients, I aim to determine their deep-rooted core values.

Courage and composure are crucial elements for coaching with daringness. Before advising, coaches must be eager to listen and embody full presence. This entails granting clients with permission to transparently process their leadership circumstances. Their reflections will reveal underlying core values, which the coach can discern and validate.

Absolute Trustworthiness

Testimonial 1:

"Leigh gained my trust with how quickly she figured out who I was, how I thought and what drove me."

Testimonial 2:

"Leigh was always open about the process, her understanding, her experience, when and how to use the information, which built absolute trust with me."

"We also cemented our trust in disagreements. We would have rich conversations and make sure we explored all opposing views."

Testimonial 3:

"Leigh is incredibly discreet. She is able to discuss real issues, while protecting the client and their confidentiality."

Absolute trustworthiness between the CEO and coach is essential. Established trust allows for the CEO to be a person without their title, think out loud, and get feedback with no agenda other than sharing input. Such dialogue often resolves or solidifies thought-processing for the CEO.

Conversations are saturated with sensitive content. If information prematurely leaks, the consequences could be detrimental for team growth. Along with protecting leaders' decision-making, trustworthiness begets a safe place to be real, confess mistakes and embody vulnerability. This process allows the client to evaluate their own thinking without consequence, leading to a more robust decision.

Chapter 23: **Leigh Priebe Kearney**

Deep Literacy in Leadership and the Human Condition
Testimonial 1:

"Leigh clearly listens deeply and asks follow-up questions that probe areas I needed to explore or hadn't considered."

"Leigh has a unique gift of reading what her clients need—even if they are not aware until she raises it."

"Leigh has a deep background in leadership theory, coaching, development and teams that support me as an executive."

Testimonial 2:

"Leigh listens … not just to the words, but to the motivations and needs behind the words. She tailors or adjusts next steps accordingly. Objectives are well thought out and agreed to. She has a fluidity in execution, which allows for what is needed at the moment."

Ongoing awareness is a prerequisite to understanding the human condition. Regarding the complex lives of CEOs, good coaches dedicate years to courageously exploring the depths and heights of life. They also commit to strengthening their field knowledge, such as how historic philosophers and psychologists theorized personality.

Coaches understand that CEOs are individuals entrusted with leading other people. Supporting clients with a humanizing ethos requires humility. A coach must be humble enough to honor the magnitude of CEOs' responsibilities, while holding judgment on senior team members' actions. Coaches help CEOs and teams compartmentalize ego and critically pursue goals. Lastly, they openly approach each assignment to discern new insights and commonalities across clients.

Agentic Advising
Testimonial 1:

"Leigh always gave me a very distinct sense that we were equals. We had a shared seriousness of purpose."

Testimonial 2:

"Leigh has never told me what to do … Leigh helps me arrive at what I already often know and does it in a way that is never brutal, but always undeniable. (How blessed I am to know and work with Leigh)."

Testimonial 3:

"Leigh was instrumental in partnering with me to bring these talented individuals into a focused team. Many individuals requested time with her to enhance their own abilities and perform more effectively."

Testimonial 4:

"Leigh embraces the individuality of the person—and does not look to change it."

Everybody bows to the CEO. This is a tension. I treat them like a person, not like someone who wields power over me. Early in my life, I learned that others' opinions and judgments of me were unfounded and, in some cases, destructive. Those early personal lessons support my respect of personal choices as worthy of support, rather than being judged as good/bad. I still work to accept a person as they are, while working to equip what they believe is the best path forward.

It is extremely difficult to be objective about oneself, especially difficult for bright, creative individuals who can explain, rationalize, analyze and think critically about information. A good coach can offer clarity and remind their client of historic conversations, important perspectives, core values and human dynamics that might be important/relevant to consider.

Refusal of Generic "Prescriptions"
Testimonial:

"Leigh is able to get into the headspace of the client-specific nuances."

"Leigh has a solid strategy for execution and understanding."

"Leigh doesn't use any generic models—she is way more refined and focused with help and guidance concerning my specific client realities. There is no textbook vanilla to Leigh."

"Leigh tailored her coaching and consulting to our specific circumstances and needs to grow our three combined businesses into one cohesive group of executives who needed to function as a real team."

"Our relationship was strategic and valuable."

CEOs are aware that they are different. Being different can be a lonely existence. Beyond their spouses, many only have a few genuine friends. Not only do they stand out from the general population, but they also are individually distinctive. There is no universal "model CEO." I approach each CEO with respect for their singularities. Each person has their own history, drives, values, strengths, weaknesses, teams of people and business/economic circumstances. One commonality, however, is that CEOs usually aim to do something meaningful. They desire to "matter" in the world. My job entails uncovering their value-driven intended impact and channeling it as a motivator. This framing compels the CEO to commit to progress, even if they must adopt new perspectives or behaviors.

Storying Psychometrics into Actionable Success
Testimonial 1:

"Leigh's facility with psychometric tools and instruments to provide researched data on what it takes to succeed—and how to apply that to my position and business circumstances to nuance positive impact is invaluable."

Testimonial 2:

"Leigh 'blew me away' translating data and listening and learning the nuance of my team and the business."

Testimonial 3:

"I experienced the foundation as an extensive, probing and fun (the fun was/is important) interview. This was paired with my taking a battery of online psycho-metric evaluations."

"The next step was the critical trust launching pad: the 'conversation'—an analytical evaluation of me leveraging the discussion and using the psycho-metrics to explore strengths and weaknesses as well as obvious and hidden qualities."

"In retrospect, you approached the 'conversation' with great care—an amazing balance of empathy and insight, blending the narrative with the metrics. You highlighted strengths (and why); weaknesses (and why); blind-spots (and why); likely reactions of others to me (and why); likely ways I work in groups (and why) leadership *traits and opportunities (and why). You didn't pull any punches, but approached the more sensitive (to me) feedback in ways that were easy for me to digest and ultimately accept. You provided actionable advice and new behaviors to try in specific situations. I believed your analysis—including the challenging parts—which accelerated the trust.*

"An added emphasis: comparison on behavioral metrics to leaders broadly. This brought context to me—and helped the 'conversation' move from the abstract to the actionable."

"I felt that your analysis started with me as a person, and then picked up the work element. I appreciated the sequencing."

I investigate as many angles to the truth as possible. Each individual has a story; thus, personalized inquiry is imperative. Key questions emerge while assessing psychometrics, which are instruments that help us understand the unique human condition. For example, does the CEO's perspective match instrument-collected data? If not, why, and what gaps can I help the executive to recognize? How can I bring clarity to the conversation and evaluative process? What hypotheses can I validate by asking generative questions that will resonate with my coachee? How might I quickly arrive at their truth and begin the real work of supporting growth for the CEO and organization? Also, importantly, which strengths of the company leader are being overplayed, and how? We all have a tendency of utilizing certain strengths as often as possible to feel competent and valuable.

Conclusion

Being a CEO requires courage and competency. Leaders must clearly see through the complexity of any organization. Their understanding of people, economics and competing issues is paramount.

Imagine if more coach psychologists learned to support CEOs within intimate and trusting relationships. Increased successful decisions and, therefore, growth-oriented people and organizations can result and benefit our world.

CHAPTER 24

LIFE LESSONS LEARNED FROM THE MAN IN THE MIRROR

By **MANSOUR KHATIB**

I am fighting endless emptiness and sadness, standing in front of the mirror, looking at the redness in my eyes, feeling nothing but darkness and pain, thinking of what brought me to this point in my life.

I watched my mother die in my arms 11 months earlier. After that, I lived like a robot, emotionless and numb, still not understanding what happened. But there, in front of that mirror, the emotional dam broke, and tears flowed like a torrent.

You see, I grew up in a middle-class family in Germany, had a very close relationship with my mother and lived a happy, carefree life with few troubles—certainly, none of the scope in which I found myself now.

As a 20-year-old, I had not experienced the death of someone close to me, so my mother's passing shook me to the core. Friends and family members said, "You will get over it. Things will get better. You will see your mom again." While I appreciated their kind sentiment, I felt empty inside, like nothing mattered. It was an extremely dark time, but something good came from it.

That tragic event was the catalyst that started me on a search for truth and purpose, and I developed a set of principles based on what I discovered.

My months' long search led me to three important life lessons that I want to share with you, in hopes you will benefit. They are simple lessons to grasp, but profound at the same time.

The three lessons are:

- Change is the only constant; you must learn to embrace it.
- Respect all life and make the most of every opportunity.
- Set clear goals and follow your principles.

Change is the Only Constant—Embrace It

The only constant in life is change. If we want to be happy, we must learn to embrace change regardless of our emotions.

That day, as I looked in the mirror, I took an oath and swore to the man staring back at me, "You will always embrace change. Whatever is thrown at you, you will deal with it. This is how you're going to live your life."

Now, when things get tough, I repeat that oath to myself. Whatever the future brings, I will not complain. I will deal with everything in the best way possible, understanding that there are things you can control and things you can't.

Chapter 24: **Mansour Khatib**

Life is about change and about looking forward. We learn from our history. We learn from the future. My motto is to enjoy the day and make plans for the next 200 years—because looking into the future keeps us young.

Perhaps the best way to illustrate this principle is through two personal experiences, one soon after my mom's passing and another after I became a tech company CEO years later.

Leaving Germany to Work in the United States

I was given the opportunity to leave Germany and go to work in New York in the travel industry. It was only supposed to be a three-month summer job. Up to that point, I had been a university student studying engineering and economics and was supposed to return to school at the end of the three-month stint.

When I met with the manager who hired me, things happened quickly. Thinking I was leaving in a couple of months, the manager came back holding a ticket in her hand and said, "Herr Mansour, you are flying in two days." At that moment, I thought about myself standing in front of the mirror. And sure enough, two days later, I was on a plane to New York. When I arrived, a friend picked me up and took me to the hotel. Like any good tourist, I immediately went to Times Square—it was 11:00 p.m., and the place was filled with people and excitement.

My friend had given me a Sony Walkman (this was 1988) and I strolled through Times Square listening to a CD by the British pop group Swing Out Sister. Their hit song "Breakout" was playing. The words of the chorus struck me:

*"The time has come to make or break,
Move on, don't hesitate,
Breakout"*

Listening to the song and looking at all the lights, excitement and people, I decided right there that I would not return to Germany, but instead would remain in New York, at least for a while. I was embracing change with my arms and eyes wide open.

Pivoting My Tech Company

I am the CEO of the technology company, GBT Technologies. When I joined the company, not as CEO, but in a marketing role, I worked on various projects. Our CEO and several board members left during the height of the COVID pandemic, and I was called on to assume the leadership role. Again, fully embracing change.

I sat down with our chief technology officer to review what we had done over the years. What came out was that we had a huge list of great technical approaches and ideas but had never brought them to market as finished products.

So, we decided to pivot and turn GBT into an intellectual property company. I got the idea from the biotech sector, and we started developing patents for microchip design and manufacturing where there was a growth opportunity. Less than two years later, we have now developed ten patents that are approved and around twenty-six pending, with the goal of thirty by the end of 2023. The inventions cover different areas, including artificial intelligence, 3-D microchip technology and a tracking system that works without GPS. One has the potential to completely disrupt microchip design by drastically reducing the time and resources needed, using the current protocols.

Respect Life and Make the Most of Every Opportunity

A second lesson I learned from the man in the mirror is that life is not limitless. It is fragile and can end so easily. It is deserving of respect and to be cherished. I determined that all my big decisions would be based on that principle.

Something else I came to realize is that life is the sum of our experiences. My mom always told me, "You can't take anything to your grave but the sum of your life experiences." The lesson she was trying to teach is to take advantage of as many of life's experiences as we can, good or bad.

That's one of the reasons I decided to leave Germany. If life is precious, I should make the most of every opportunity given to me. Over the seven years that I worked for the travel company, I was sent all over the world, to thirty different countries. I worked my way up the corporate ladder to the director level bringing more than a half-million people to the United States yearly. It was an exciting time. I loved traveling, dealing with people and helping them have great life experiences.

However, what meant the most was that it afforded me with the opportunity to learn about the various cultures and religions of the people I met everywhere I went. It opened my mind to understanding there are different ways of looking at life. That's the beauty of travel: It brings people together. It enables one culture to understand another culture, and that can't be a bad thing.

Don't Let Experience Define You

Our experiences are what make us who we are today. However, we don't have to be defined by them. We can look back at our history, learn from what happened and determine to change. I was different five years ago (and even two months ago) than I am today based on my experiences and how I have responded to them.

I call it a reversal of fortune. You can be in a bad situation, but you can also just open up and be in a totally different situation if you're willing to take that step forward. There's always risk in everything we do. But if you look at life as the sum of your experiences, you can even turn your failures to your advantage.

See Failure as an Opportunity to Learn

Now, I don't want you to jump out of an airplane without a parachute. But if you want to skydive, then go for it. Don't be defined by fear. Not everything will work out as you may want, but in the end, even failure is a learning opportunity.

I have experienced many failures in my life, personally and professionally. I lost jobs, lost a company after 9/11, lost a great deal of money and even lost a marriage through divorce. I've experienced plenty of successes, too. Today, I'm the CEO of a small publicly-traded company where we're working on patents that could change the world. Even through divorce, my ex-wife and I were still able to create a family for my twenty-three-year-old son who became a climate scientist and competitive athlete, and with whom I have a close relationship.

Chapter 24: **Mansour Khatib**

In the end, we want to leave those experiences and life lessons to the next generation—if it's good experiences and good advice. We should do that, because we want to improve life, all life to have less suffering and create equality.

Set Clear Goals and Live by Your Principles

Many people influence us as we grow—family, friends, educators, employers, politicians, religious leaders and others. Most (though not all) have good intentions, mean well and want to help. They also want to win us over to their way of thinking.

Technology has added another layer of influence. We have the internet and social media. The huge volume of information available at our fingertips is overwhelming, making it difficult to make decisions. In the end, it's all white noise. If you have not set clear goals and values or follow your principles, you will be like a dog chasing one bone after another. First, you go this way, then that way, lacking any clear sense of direction.

As my son was growing up, I taught him to be assertive, stand up for himself and not be afraid of confrontation. "Don't shy away from talking to someone, just because it could make you look bad," I said.

One of the biggest issues young people must deal with now is to start learning to evaluate, decide for themselves and not be influenced by all those other matters that I call white noise. It's like peeling an onion.

"If there's an important decision for you to take in life, then peel the onion of influences all the way down," I told him. "If you're lucky, you can peel it down to what really matters to you."

The most underrated thing you must learn and say to people who want to influence you is "no." It's a lost art. Say YES to life and NO to people who want to influence you in a direction other than the one you choose to go. Otherwise, you live life trying to please everyone else.

Confrontation is another of those secrets. Confrontation and "no" don't have to be negative. It doesn't mean fighting. It just means you have decided to live life on your own terms based on your goals and principles.

Conclusion

Many people gauge success in life based on money. I have nothing against money, but that's not the only measure. Success in life is also about our experiences, enjoying life, understanding that life matters and living by established goals and principles.

Because we are the sum of our experiences, we should not be afraid of challenges but embrace them, good or bad. Neither should we fear change. That, too, should be embraced. Our experiences, change and how we respond are what define us and make us better people.

Each day, as I look in the mirror, I reaffirm my commitment to these three lessons and vow to always embrace change, respect life, focus on my goals and follow my principles. Sometimes, I fall short—I'm only human—but I aspire to take full advantage of everything those lessons teach.

In the end, it seems that I am living my mom's life lessons. If mom was alive today, I think she would be pleased.

CHAPTER 25

REVOLUTIONARY 4-D BRAND ALIGNMENT: PUTTING THE "HUMAN" BACK IN HUMAN RESOURCES

By **MARK A. MEARS**

"If you could get all the people in the organization rowing in the same direction, you could dominate any industry, in any market, against any competition, at any time."
—Patrick Lencioni

Based upon many lingering impacts of the global pandemic, we are seeing a new world of work emerge, a change that will be felt for years to come. People are leaving unsatisfying jobs or toxic work environments that no longer suit them. We are witnessing the creation of a more flexible, autonomous gig economy. This has resulted in labor shortages across many industries, causing management to revolutionize their approach to optimize human resource practices in a new era of work.

I believe this is the start of a more humanistic, purposeful way of life and work that can be more fulfilling for individuals as well as more profitable for the organizations we work for. I call this movement.

The Purposeful Growth Revolution

Let's take a closer look at what revolution means. These definitions are timely and relevant in addressing this still-unfolding, multi-dimensional phenomena impacting our life and work:

Revolution (noun)

1. An uprising of the people:

History shows that when people feel oppressed or lack growth opportunities, they revolt against authority. In fact, an uprising of the people spawned revolutions that led to the formation of new forms of government, policies, ideologies and movements (for example, the American Revolution, French Revolution, Arab Spring, #MeToo, Black Lives Matter).

According to some, we are in the midst of "the Great Resignation," as people are leaving the workforce en masse for a variety of reasons. Some have been touched by the pandemic directly—getting sick themselves or losing family or friends to COVID-19—while many others have been affected indirectly by long periods of isolation or the loss of connection with those they love, the things they enjoy doing, or the need to put life plans on hold.

All these factors are certainly cause for self-reflection. But I believe one reason has risen above the others—we are all asking, "Is this all there is to life?" And, given that adults spend approximately a third of their lives working, many people may wonder if it's possible to find purpose and meaning in both our life and work.

Chapter 25: **Mark A. Mears**

On January 11, 2022, MIT Sloan Management Review published an article by Donald Sull, Charles Sull and Ben Zweig about a massive research study in which 34 million people from a wide variety of industries were interviewed. While the results varied by industry and even among companies within the same industry, one important piece of data stands out. In 2021, "toxic culture" was cited ten times more frequently than the second-most cited reason for resigning. And compensation was way down at number 16 on the list!

I don't care for the term "the Great Resignation," because it suggests that we have decided to give up and resign from the workforce, quitting altogether. Or possibly worse, it suggests that we have resigned ourselves to an unsatisfying status quo and decided to quit … and stay. This has spawned a new term, "quiet quitting." I think we can agree neither of those outcomes are great.

I prefer to view this era as "the Great Repurposing," which helps shift the work paradigm to a more humanistic balance that benefits the *who* we collectively serve. I believe it all starts with purpose. When we lose our way or face change on life's journey, it is time to "repurpose" ourselves in preparation for our next great adventure. What may seem difficult is actually a golden opportunity to reevaluate what (and who) is most important in our lives, as we seek to fulfill our unique purpose in both life and work.

To that point, instead of starting with *why*, I believe we should actually start with *who*—more specifically who we serve among four different, but integrated categories, all revolving around *purposeful growth*:

- **Spiritual:** God, religious deity, spiritual belief system
- **Relational:** Family, spouse/significant other, friends, neighbors, communities
- **Personal:** Mind, body, spirit, soul
- **Professional:** Organization, team members, clients/customers, networks

When we lock into our mind a mental image of the faces of *who* we "serve," it leads us to our *why*, and then naturally, to our *how* and *what*.

The reason I have chosen to focus on the word serve is because I believe it captures a deeper level of meaning and related engagement, caring and commitment. Servant leaders are considered the very best type of leaders as they inspire love, trust, respect and loyalty—the core fundamentals of any successful, mutually rewarding relationship.

2. *A dramatic change in the status quo:*

The second definition of "revolution" is a reference to the spirit of innovation in changing the world and how we progressively live, work and play (including innovations like electricity, telephone, trains, cars, planes, computers, smart phones, drones, artificial intelligence and augmented reality).

Throughout history, major growth opportunities traditionally occur as a result of some type of catalytic event, like war, weather, famine or a discovery.

Chapter 25: **Mark A. Mears**

I think it is safe to say the scourge of COVID-19 (and its variants) is a catalytic event that has touched us all, probably most in our ability to connect with one another. Let's rewind back to the spring of 2020, when we were all ordered to "shelter in place," forcing us to use digital communication devices such as Zoom to keep our businesses going, as well as our interpersonal relationships.

There were a few words or phrases we learned then:

- **The Official Word of 2020:** Pivot
- **The Official Meme of 2020:** "Um, you're on mute!"
- **The Official Question of 2020:** "Can I share my screen?"

While COVID-19 remains with us in some capacity, companies are deciding whether to return to 100-percent on-site employment, 100-percent remote employment, or some combination of a "hybrid" work environment.

A recent study by Nicholas Bloom, a Stanford University economics professor, suggests that, as a result of COVID-19, "working from home is here to stay, with hybrid arrangements fast becoming the dominant strain." Bloom concludes that companies may see approximately half of their employees return to work, while 10-percent of employees will continue to work remotely and 40-percent will have a hybrid schedule with some days remote and some days in the office. The genie is simply not going back into the lamp, so we must pivot accordingly.

How do you create a sense of place and build cooperative interpersonal relationships when not everyone is in daily face-to-face contact?

Given the confluence of technology (hi-tech) with humanity (hi-touch), here are just a few ideas to help cultivate a fertile and productive place for remote or hybrid collaboration:

- **Personal Life Sharing:** Getting to know people on a more human level—within their home environment—provides a deeper level of empathy that can help the team grow stronger together.

- **Team-Building Exercises:** These exercises can also be used for crowdsourcing solutions—unlocking the collective wisdom of the team—to help overcome key challenges that directly or indirectly affect the broader organization.

- **Continuous Learning Opportunities:** Create a forum to learn and share information, best practices, and new tools/resources. According to a recent survey conducted by LinkedIn of 2,000 of its members, people who learn are 24-percent more likely to feel happy at work."

- **Reward/Recognition:** Instead of the dreaded annual performance appraisal, what if the team member and manager co-crafted a purposeful growth plan that integrates the personal and professional growth goals for the team member within their department or organization? The plan could be reviewed together on a more frequent basis.

Remember, *diversity* just gets us in the door, *inclusion* gets us a seat at the table, *equity* gets us an equal voice, but without *belonging*, we may not feel comfortable being truly vulnerable to give our very best for fear of potential rejection.

Whether in person, remote or hybrid, it is vitally important for leaders to cultivate a sense of belonging that will allow all team members to feel part of a safe, mutually respectful environment that helps them fulfill their purpose in alignment with shared team and organizational goals.

3. A circular orbit around an object:

While the first two definitions of revolution focus on the importance of change, the third, "a circular orbit around an object," struck me as foundational in helping us unlock the four interwoven, purposeful growth processes.

- The earth *revolving* around the sun = **life/existence**
- The wheel *revolving* around an axle = **movement/productivity**
- The compass hand *revolving* around points = **direction/guidance**
- The clock's hands *revolving* around hours in a day = **time/rhythm**

The universe has a natural and undeniable rhythm that revolves around most living things—people, animals and plants.

Our unique purpose is the epicenter of our universe—everything we do must revolve around it for us to fulfill our growth potential.

My decision to add the word *revolution* to *purposeful growth* is much more than hyperbole or word craft. When you examine the word r-***evol***-ution a bit closer, you can see it contains the word love, written backwards!

Since the dawn of human consciousness, most of us have wrestled with the question, "What is the meaning of life?" But for me, that question is a bit too passive and generalized. I believe in repurposing this question to be more active and personalized: "What does life mean to you?"

> *"The meaning of life is to find your gift.*
> *The purpose of life is to give it away."*
> **–Pablo Picasso**

The concept of purpose has been gaining a lot of traction recently. From spiritual teaching to scholarly research, there is solid evidence that connecting individuals to their higher purpose helps increase job satisfaction, productivity, longevity, loyalty and outer directedness that benefits others.

Researchers Aaron Hurst, Brandon Peele, Tim Kelley, Zach Mercurio and their team at The Science of Purpose have assembled statistics supporting the power of purpose in our lives.

Individuals with a connection to their purpose experience:

- 63-percent increase in income, wealth and leadership effectiveness
- 64-percent increase in fulfillment
- Learn twice as much
- Are 4 times more engaged
- Are 175-percent more productive

Companies with a connection to their purpose experience:

- Higher margins as purpose-driven firms are 30-percent more innovative
- 73-percent of customers will switch to higher-purpose brands
- 55-percent of customers will pay more for higher-purpose brands
- 47-percent higher Net Promoter scores and related length of tenure
- 54-percent more fulfilling work relationships

Now, let's establish the power of aligning purpose as a broader, multi-dimensional concept that impacts all brands.

4-D Brand Alignment

Like all relationships, a brand is nothing more than a promise, or series of related promises, that impacts stakeholders in ways that build trust.

While many people see brands as one-dimensional, there are four different, yet interrelated brand dimensions that must be aligned and integrated—all revolving around purposeful growth. There is one's *personal brand*, the *internal brand*, the *external brand* and the *employer brand*.

Each of these integrated 4 brand dimensions must closely align behind 4 related components:

- **Aspirational**, or aligned with long-term vision
- **Inspirational**, or aligned with a daily mission
- **Institutional**, or aligned with shared values
- **Operational**, or aligned with strategic and tactical plans

The word "aligned" represents the connective tissue that binds together any successful team or organization. Think of a rowing team who must follow the rhythmic cadence of the Coxswain to ensure all oars are in the water and rowing together. Called "swing," this coordinated approach powers the boat across the water as smoothly, efficiently and productively as possible to attain ultimate victory.

Let's apply this important principle to maximize our potential for purposeful growth.

1. **Personal Brand:** Every member of a team has their own personal brand that represents the alignment and integration of four key areas of service: spiritual, relational, professional and personal. We are all whole people, not simply workers or nameless employee identification numbers. It's called "human" resources for a reason. Every organization contains people with a diverse array of backgrounds, experiences and perspectives. We must feel safe to be who we are in the workplace by bringing our "whole" self to our jobs, while keeping the promises we make to ourselves and holding true to our values.

2. **Internal Brand:** Our internal brand consists of all stakeholders connected to establishing, leading and following our purposeful vision, mission, values and strategic and tactical plans (for example, the executive leadership team, team members, board of directors, shareholders and investors). This represents the promises we make to each other. Our culture must create a nurturing environment to align and integrate the uniqueness and diversity reflected in the personal brands of our team members into one belief system, as we work together to accomplish our common goal.

3. **External Brand:** Our external brand consists of our target audience—customers and clients—who represent the beneficiaries of our differentiated value proposition, along with its related media and messaging, as we engage to help enrich the communities we serve. This audience must see and feel that our actions are aligned with the advertised product and service messages and related benefits we promise.

4. **Employer Brand:** Our employer brand represents the heart of the organization that we put forth, both to attract new team members and also to retain and grow our existing team members. Here we must actively live-out the promises we advertise in ways that create a deep sense of belonging, which helps to align and integrate the organization behind our shared purpose and business goals.

The following are examples of great 4-D Brands who "walk the talk" by living out their shared values across all four brand dimensions.

Patagonia

While numerous organizations tout sustainability as part of their purposeful approach to doing business, few actually put their money where their mouth is. One such company is Patagonia, whose stated purpose is inspirational and aspirational, even as it says nothing about any type of product superiority, market share or profit goals.

We're in Business to Save Our Home Planet

Wow, very powerful indeed! Patagonia is a great example of a 4-D brand that lives out its purpose every day in multiple ways that provide its stakeholders with a deep level of engagement. The Patagonia purpose can be experienced in several ways.

- **Supportable:** Patagonia donates *1-percent of sales* to help support grassroots organizations all over the world.

- **Measurable:** Patagonia *Action Works* helps to connect individuals with a passion to get involved with grassroots organizations in ways that truly make a difference on a local and regional level.

- **Sustainable:** Patagonia *Provisions* supports sustainable food growing and supply chain techniques that are environmentally safe.

- **Recyclable:** Patagonia *Worn Wear* is an initiative that helps repair damaged products and accepts trade-ins for store credit, instead of having customers discard them in a landfill.

In fall 2022, Yvon Chouinard, the founder of Patagonia, announced the creation of a trust fund that essentially gives back all of the company's profits to projects that fulfill the Patagonia purpose.

Chapter 25: **Mark A. Mears**

Canva

Another great example of a 4-D Brand that lives out its purpose is Canva, a firm based in Sydney, Australia, that developed a globally accessible graphic design platform used to create social media graphics, presentations, posters, documents and other visual content.

Empowering the World to Design

Canva has developed a very simple, yet powerful and purposeful two-step plan.

- **Step 1.** Build one of the world's most valuable companies.
- **Step 2.** Do the most good we can do.

Instead of setting out to accomplish those goals in that order, Canva has committed itself to doing both since its inception in 2013. Here are some examples:

- Canva is now valued at $40 billion with 65 million people from 190 countries designing in Canva every month, in total creating more than 7 billion designs.
- Canva committed to a 1-percent pledge. The company has committed 1-percent of its profits, 1-percent of its product, 1-percent of its team's time and 1-percent of its equity to be a force for good in the world, based on company values.
- Canva has more than 130,000 nonprofits in its nonprofit program. Those organizations can use Canva Pro for free.

- Canva's One Print, One Tree initiative plants a tree for every print order. So far, the company has committed to planting more than 2 million trees.

Talk about a 4-D Brand that lives its purpose in a profitable manner benefiting all stakeholders.

KPMG

I read a *Harvard Business Review* article highlighting an approach that Big Four accounting firm KPMG used to define its purpose. Instead of devising it within the C-Suite and trickling it down to its associates from on high, KPMG took a different tack.

Higher Purpose Initiative

Through its higher purpose initiative, executives at KPMG reached out to its associates to help the firm define its purpose by telling stories of how their work helped make a positive difference in the world. Then, the company shared those stories throughout the organization to place the proper emphasis behind its unique purpose.

By employing a bubble-up approach that involved its associates in the process, KPMG created a much deeper emotional engagement than they would have built through a more traditional top-down approach. This helped inspire KPMG's associates to pay more attention to the value they continue to bring to their clients every day.

You see, purpose must be truly authentic, 100-percent believable, extremely relevant and consistently applied throughout the organization. If those elements are firmly in place, the business results will certainly follow, drawn forward like a magnet.

Chapter 25: **Mark A. Mears**

While I am sure these and many other organizations are making progress, I believe we have just scratched the surface on how to integrate and align the personal brand of every team member within the other brand dimensions–the internal brand, external brand and employer brand.

Labor cost is traditionally the biggest line item of a company's profit and loss sheet, including not just salaries and benefits, but also the cost of recruiting, hiring, training, recognition and rewards. Given that, alignment behind one's purpose can optimize productivity and lengthen an individual's tenure. This leads directly to improved profitability–the goal of any business enterprise–while providing an opportunity for the brand to make a positive, lasting impact on the communities it serves.

> *"Always remember, your focus determines your reality."*
> **–George Lucas**

To succeed within "the Great Repurposing," the old, outdated "command and control" style of management must give way to a more humanistic, loving and nurturing style of servant leadership that aligns all brand dimensions within a unified 4-D Brand that stands behind the power of purposeful growth. This is the blueprint for success in the new world of work, where there can and should be a symbiotic relationship between purpose and profit to serve all stakeholders–team members, clients and customers, business partners and communities.

Let's put the "Human" back in Human Resources!

To find out how you and your organization are aligned on the importance of purposeful growth, you can take a free purposeful growth self-assessment at https://www.MarkAMears.com and download a report customized with your results and related Seeds 4 Growth to inspire you along your personal and professional growth journey.

The Purposeful Growth Revolution is on! Are you in?

CHAPTER 26

CREATING THE MOST VALUABLE RETIREMENT ASSET: ONESELF

By **MARK ANDREW THIEDE**

"Serendipity. Look for something, find something else, and realize that what you've found is more suited to your needs than what you thought you were looking for."
– Lawrence Block

The home of Two Wrasslin' Cats Coffee House was built in 1784, four years before U.S. Constitution ratification. Two hundred and 28 years later, I purchased this cute antique Cape as home for my coffee house adventure. Aside from a fountain, gazebo and meandering brook, the property was unassuming like many properties in East Haddam. Yet in 2020, Mark Clymer, a regular customer and amateur archeologist spotted a fascinating stone protruding from the ground near a new electrical conduit. Mark concluded that the stone, a piece of Hudson Valley flint with an ergonomic handle and sharpened edge, was likely made by people long ago.

To gather proof, Mark dug nine test pits, in which he uncovered a collection of artifacts that would pique the interest of Dr Sarah Sportman, the Connecticut State Archaeologist. In only nine days of excavation, the archaeological team uncovered over 800 artifacts to date, which led Dr. Sportman to conclude that the Two Wrasslin' Cats Site likely represents an encampment of Paleoindians 10-12,000 years ago! The findings, first presented at the 2021 annual meeting of the Eastern States Archaeological Federation, have since been published in the 2023 Fall edition of the *Uconn Magazine*.

Like this beautiful discovery, I describe my 67 years of life as a series of serendipitous occurrences. Together, these events have led me to where I am meant to be, helping those I am meant to help and making discoveries that benefit others. As a PhD in Molecular Biology and Biochemistry (U of Connecticut, 1986) I had a fascinating three-decade journey performing and leading discovery research in the pharma-biotechnology industry. While that work focused on the discovery of new treatments for connective tissue and inflammatory diseases, and enhanced survival of cancer patients undergoing marrow transplant, I always had a strong yearning to exploit my creative potential and most of all, eliminate the personal compromise that comes with working for others.

So in 2012, serendipity struck again in the impression left by frequent business travels to Seattle's coffee culture; my daughter gifting two "wrasslin' kittens," Bruno and Larry, named after wrestlers Bruno Sammartino and Larry Zbyszko; and a last batch of homemade beer fictitiously made by "Two Wrasslin' Cats Brewery." This became the launch of my "work in progress" idea of a retirement project; a leap into the business of owning a cat-themed coffee shop, and it's enabling me to find a "retirement" path in a community that I love and am very proud to be a part of.

Chapter 26: **Mark Andrew Thiede**

Two Wrasslin Cats Coffee House

I could clone a gene, etc., but had no experience creating and running a small business. My first action was to order a copy of the FabJob Guide, Become a Coffee House Owner, off the internet. I decided to bring the business to East Haddam, Conn., and identified a couple of potential properties. I then attended the American Barista & Coffee School and the American Specialty Coffee Conference in Portland, Ore., in April 2012. I had to source equipment, furniture, coffee and create (yes create on the fly) a desirable menu and comfortable space. It didn't start off as a "cat-centric" coffee house, as my business learning curve was steep.

My coffee shop is as original as its moniker. A whimsical cat-themed coffee shop with a vivid blue and green facade, and two five-foot carved felines that greet you above the door. The antique portion of the house was minimally modified, while the two car garage and modern bedroom space were transformed into a service area and kitchen. The beverages, food and even the artwork on the walls are sourced locally. The community collective of cat figurines and pictures fill the walls and shelves and act as a testament to my loyal cat loving clientele. Many first time customers visit TWC, because they've seen our social media ratings, have heard about it from friends and most of all, need to experience it for themselves. To be honest, I didn't know what it would become in time, as success was my goal.

Two Wrasslin' Cats Coffee House opened its doors to its first customer at noon on May 31, 2013. The first menu that customers ordered from was hand-written on a piece of foam board. A baker and assistant made delicious fresh baked goods in the morning, while breakfast sandwiches and an evolving list of lunch sandwiches were served until closing. After two months, I discovered that I had over-hired and that the bakery was lagging behind the desire for breakfast or lunch sandwiches. So changes and hard decisions needed to be made before long. By the end of that summer, I had gotten my hands around the critical expenses that were needed to operate this new unique business, and a printed menu soon followed. And Two Wrasslin Cats lived another day!

Catification of the coffee shop would soon follow. A considerable amount of TWC's success lies in the cute and catchy names for its products. We offer lots more than just your regular espresso and coffee drinks, or breakfast and lunch sandwiches. We offer the Catnapiccino signature blended espresso drink in three flavors. For breakfast, you have the Littermate or Kitten Classic sandwiches. For lunch, there's the Catprese, Calico Chicken or Furry Curry chicken salads and the Kitten Club or Krazy Katt sandwiches, to name a few. Some are named after family cats, like Janet's BLT or Trudi's Catch of the Day. TWC's unique interior is a testament to a shared love for the feline species and the joy that cats bring to my family, neighbors and guests.

In February 2020, the original Two Wrasslin' Cats, Bruno and Larry, left for the big wrasslin' ring in the sky. In September of that year, I adopted two beautiful sister cats, HerQuleez and Anneteus, named after two gods who wrassled in Greek mythology. They became the New Wrasslin' Cats, and in the winter of 2022, I sealed off the front two rooms of the 1784 building, internal and external entrances, and created a separate business entity called the New Wrasslin' Cats' Lounge, LLC. It is currently the home of five beautiful and sweet and socially adapted one-year-old sibling cats. This adjunct business was

Chapter 26: **Mark Andrew Thiede**

created as space for periodic visitation and relaxation with cats, as well as offering these cats' hearts and purrs for animal therapy for the disabled, seniors, patients with cognitive deficits, substance recovery and other populations in need.

Our shop is located in East Haddam, Conn., a small community of approximately eight thousand people. This bucolic town offers many year-round and seasonal attractions and amenities, including Staehly Farm Winery, Goodspeed Opera Theater, Fox Hopyard Golf Course and Gillettes Castle State Park, as well as beautiful hiking trails. The Two Wrasslin Cats has been listed on this distinctive list of local attractions.

"To be yourself in a world that is constantly trying to make you something else is the greatest accomplishment."
–Ralph Waldo Emerson

Personal Values

I learned my values from my parents. Not by being overbearing or lecturing, but by being amazing and consistent role models. I've always strived to be a positive role model as well, not just for my children, but for everyone I meet. I had the pleasure of employing each of my three children before they moved onto their own paths. The foundation of TWC is that everyone should feel safe, welcome and equal. It's not just simply that "the customer is always right." It's that the customer is a fellow human who deserves shared respect and kindness.

My parents brought me up in a church setting, and with the passing of time, we all became distant from religion, but kept our values.

My mom would acknowledge our shared doubts about religion. But I always felt that those years taught valuable lessons about how we as a family treat others. This has always been a very important piece of who I am. As I enter my tenth year as the owner of Two Wrasslin Cats, I look back and it is clear to me that my values have been essential to not only my business success, but also my commitment to being a community asset. These essential values that have been a pillar of my business and life are:

- **Integrity**—the quality of being honest and having strong moral principles; moral uprightness
- **Kindness**—the quality of being friendly, generous and considerate
- **Empathy**—the ability to understand and share the feelings of another
- **Equality**—the state of being equal, especially in status, rights and opportunities
- **Charity**—the voluntary giving of help

Practicing these values in the day-to-day operation of every aspect of my business makes each day special and value-filled. My interactions with my customers always demonstrate kindness and openness. The atmosphere of my coffee shop is that of a family where, "I welcome everyone who welcomes everyone." No one is excluded, unless they exclude themselves or others. I am known throughout our community for being a safe place and for knowing everyone's names, even if I have not seen them for years. I have built a business that is able to support other organizations through donations, through the use of space and through being an engaged community citizen. It is our unique value-driven culture that keeps people coming back.

Chapter 26: **Mark Andrew Thiede**

Keys to Sustainability Without Experience

When starting my business, family and friends alike were in disbelief. They could not understand why a PhD scientist, earning great money, would leave his field of expertise, his career, to open a coffee shop. One of the few individuals who saw my vision from the start was my mother. She felt like I could do this effectively, because of my capacity to manufacture solid authentic communication. She believed in my ability to build strong interactions and significant connections with others. She probably thought I was nuts, too, but she knew I sometimes just wouldn't listen.

Before opening, and during the early days of business, I had many people telling me what I should do and how I should do it. This was a very confusing season for me. Once I began tuning out unnecessary noise from outside well-meaning people, I was able to concentrate more on day-to-day operations efficiently. I quickly learned to adapt, by embracing and initiating necessary changes. I started with nine staff members, and by the end of my first summer, I was down to four staff members. Downsizing staff was a difficult, but necessary decision that improved my business. I realized that I didn't need more staff. I needed to be lean and efficient. And I needed to read the tea leaves (or is it coffee grounds?).

Since my success was not based on strong business experience or background, I had to develop skills in every area, from operations to marketing, as well as staff management and everything in between. I am still learning, because it is a never-ending process. My scientific training has kept me in a position of learning. I learn something new every day. I have the unique ability to drop things that are not working and move forward with things that work. I have learned how to make this business work for me.

As I got older, I realized that having shorter work days was very important to me, so I changed our hours. I have had to change our menu, and even our layout, to be something that I am proud of and something that I find enjoyable. If I didn't like something, I made an intentional decision not to do it.

Activism

The one thing I learned from being in business is that you can succeed or fail on the way you manage your customer base. One advantage I possessed going into this adventure, besides perusing the FabJob Guide, *Become a Coffee House Owner,* I never read a business book or took a business course. I never read how one shouldn't voice your feelings behind your service counter, or for that matter, in the space that surrounds your place of business. If I had, I wouldn't be writing this chapter.

I have used my business platform to take a stand for activism and social issues that are close to my heart, such as women's rights, anti-racism, pro-transgender rights and anti-hate. My business displays banners and flags prominently hanging outside the shop showing our support for these causes. For years following the 2016 presidential election, TWC proudly displayed a sign that paraphrases New York Daily News columnist Shaun King, which states: "Dear Muslims, immigrants, women, disabled, LGBTQ folks & all people of color, we love you – boldly & proudly. We will endure."

In 2016, it became clear that many members of our community were hurt by the election results. In January 2017, we held a vigil for the women's march at our location—one of three marches held in Connecticut—and 500 people attended. I was proud that Two

Chapter 26: **Mark Andrew Thiede**

Wrasslin Cats could be part of something so positive during such difficult times. In the midst of the chaos in the world, my mom was actually dying at the time, but she passed away just five days after the march. It meant something really special to me, knowing she had seen her children standing up for what we believed in before she passed away. I had discovered that my mom protested and that she marched against the Vietnam War, back in our home town of Torrington, Conn.

I started this business with a desire to make money, but it has evolved into so much more. I have been lucky enough to create a business that now serves as a community center. It is a hub for important work and the good people meeting the needs of underserved communities.

I evolved over the last nearly 10 years and I listened to my customers. They clearly wanted a place to connect with others and find support. My staff and I have become an essential staple in the community by bringing people together. We have hosted and worked with autism youth programs, youth and family activities, Narcotics Anonymous and Alcoholics Anonymous (AA) meetings, the art league, prevention council, local politicians and the local school district. We will soon be partnering to host pet therapy for children and those suffering from addiction.

"When in doubt, do something."
–Harry Chapin

I have developed a new and unique business model, which would be highly beneficial for those entering retirement, or who are already retired. It makes no difference if they are wealthy or living on a fixed income—this model can work for anyone. It is now my desire to share this knowledge with others, and inspire them to take similar steps toward achieving their own goals in retirement. I want retirees to know that there is still something they can do in their later years. They can create a profitable community driven business, which is enjoyable for them, but also brings value to their surrounding communities.

Too often, people in retirement become fixated on money matters, since it becomes such a critical concern at that stage of life. When I started my own business, I was initially motivated by the desire to earn, but somewhere along the way, I found so much more than just financial gain. My focus shifted from being about the money, to instead being about the impact I could make through doing something enjoyably meaningful. And now, sharing this newly gained knowledge with others and encouraging them to take action, is equally as important.

CHAPTER 27

DON'T TAKE NO FOR AN ANSWER

By **MARK R. WARREN**

After creating two high-tech companies, I stepped into the wine category, with no experience, and took that company from zero to sale in seven years. The alcohol industry—dominated by huge players and layers of almost impenetrable barriers—made for an interesting and challenging journey.

It all started at a tech startup, where I took a sales job that I thought would give me more nights and weekends with my kids. That's where I met my current business partner, Tom Beaton. Instead of being a solution, sitting in a cubicle from 9-5 made me feel like a caged animal at the zoo. So, I started looking around for other opportunities. Tom and I created a tech services company that served as a value-added bridge between the startup we were working for and their clients. Eight months later, Tom and I left the startup and launched our company, Velocha, in the middle of the 2008 financial crisis.

Velocha was a white glove services company that did national rollouts of kiosks and digital signage. At the time, Blockbuster was trying to chase down Redbox, so they licensed their name to NCR, which put out Blockbuster DVD units to compete with Redbox. We had access to 15,000 technicians across the country who began installing these. But managing all those people was not fun. After we sold that company, we definitely wanted to go into products versus services.

Tom and I were both into wine and started to think about what our unique approach to wine could be. I had been into CrossFit for years, and my wife competed in triathlon events. Whenever we went to a marathon or Ironman competition, there were all these people trying to be uber healthy. But, outside of the top tier athletes, everyone there still wanted to drink. Most of the events only offered beer, and occasionally spirits. That sparked the idea: What if we could make wine that fit the lifestyle of athletes?

We started with athletes, but in the end, we landed on the Yoga Mom as our ideal customer who drove the brand. Yoga Moms are what I call the mid 30s to late 40s moms, who either work or run a house full of kids and still want to have a couple of drinks on a Tuesday night and not get up and have a headache. We created a low sugar, clean tasting wine that tasted great and still had full alcohol. We called it FitVine Wine.

Gorilla marketing played a big role in our early years. In 2015 and 2016, we were literally pouring wine inside of CrossFit gyms and yoga studios. We went to marathons and mud runs, and learned everything we could about our customer and the category. Applying all that information helped us grow our business.

The alcohol industry is extremely challenging for newcomers, with its legacy three tier system. Basically, after Prohibition ended,

Chapter 27: **Mark R. Warren**

everyone who was bootlegging booze was allowed to become a distributor. Then, they set up laws. Suppliers cannot sell directly to stores.

Alcohol is different from every other consumer product that can go sell directly to Walmart. In the United States, all alcohol is sold through state distributors. So, my direct customer is not Whole Foods, it's the distributor for Massachusetts: Martinetti's. Martinetti's has the legal right to sell to stores, restaurants and bars. No one entity can be any two of these things. We are considered the supplier who makes the wine. I cannot own any equity in a distributor or a retailer.

The only place where a winemaker can sell their own product is in the state where they make it. Someone could come to our winery in California and buy direct from us or we could sell to stores direct in California. For every other state, we can only legally sell through a distributor. That means, there is a built-in middleman who is protected by law. Even worse, in over a dozen states, you have the franchise laws that were put into effect by Henry Ford. If these distributors are horrible, you can't fire them.

A big part of our brand was delivering a transparent message to the consumer that they could believe in. Like food, wine can be overproduced. The government allows a lot of crap to be added to everything we eat and drink. In wine, you can have 76 different flavor additives. A lot of people are like my wife who can go out to dinner and consume an unfamiliar wine and within 15 minutes, her hands are swollen, and she can't get her ring off. People get flushing and headaches and other symptoms, because of these additives in the wine.

It's tricky being transparent and delivering that message to the consumer. You can't go pointing fingers at other winemakers. Seventy-four-percent of the wine sold in the United States is sold by three companies. Pointing a finger at one of the 800-pound gorillas creates a David and Goliath fight. It was a huge challenge to balance delivering our message, without picking a fight with the entire category.

To give you one example, Cameron Diaz launched a wine competitive to ours. They copied a lot of our messaging, but they went up to the next price point, so it really didn't hurt us. She made the mistake of saying, "Our wine is organic and clean." Several huge groups, like Gallo, The Wine Group and Constellation, went after her. "So, you're saying everybody else has dirty wine?" Together, they own every single publication, and they started tearing her apart. They even lobbied to the federal ATF and TTB agencies to get them to write language making the use of the word "clean" illegal.

In the alcohol industry, you cannot have any language that references health. Even though the media can run stories about how red wine can be good for your health, we as manufacturers can't even re-post an article like that. There was an article written in Food and Wine Magazine about the potential benefits of red wine. We re-posted that on our blog, without making any claims ourselves, and we got a warning from the feds. We had to take that article down.

We've learned from our retailers to never demonize anyone else in the industry. Such severe restrictions on how we can deliver our message makes it very challenging to compete and stand out in an industry where so few own so much. People asked us all the time: "How did we ever get FitVine Wine approved by the feds?" "Fit" for us stood for how wine fits into your lifestyle. Our message focused

Chapter 27: **Mark R. Warren**

on being transparent. We created a wine with the lowest sugar we can. We use no flavor additives. We never use the word clean. We might say, "Our wine is clean tasting, high quality and still full alcohol. How does that fit into your lifestyle?" We danced around health and wellness as much as we could, even though we started by launching inside of CrossFit gyms and yoga studios. It was tricky.

Once we got to the level of stores wanting to carry us, distributors were standing in our way. They gave us every excuse. We don't like your label. We don't like your name. We don't believe in the product. When we started the brand, we were selling online only, and we could ship to 40-plus states. That's what we did the first two years, using social media, and pouring wherever we could to drive the brand. But customers had to go to the website, order it, and have it shipped to their house.

Once we were selling a fair amount of wine online, we wondered if we could get these consumers to become our salespeople. We started running ads saying, "You guys love our wine and you're always asking, where you can get it. Can you start asking stores to carry it?" Within a couple of months, Whole Foods called us and said, "We can't believe how many people are coming in every day saying, "This is a perfect Whole Foods brand. Why don't you sell this?" Our customers helped us get our first distributors and really drive velocity.

We started in retail in 2017 in six states. By the end of the year, we were in 42 states. A few months later, we were in all 50 states. Next, we had to make the shift from mom-and-pop distributors to go after the big, blue-chip distributors that can handle the larger volumes. It took about 18 months to consolidate to the top tier distributors around the country.

As we went bigger, we became a smaller piece of the pie, because the big guys handle the Gallo's of the world. Now, we have to figure out how to get the attention of these big guys so they will actually do their job for us. Every time we grew, whatever it took to get to the next stage ended up creating new hurdles.

As we built out our sales team, we had to make sure we were hiring people who had experience and relationships in the alcohol industry, with both the distributors and the retail stores. People who have been in the industry for a decade in their region can walk into a retail liquor store and know the manager. With solid relationships, they can say, "Hey, here's the new brand I'm selling. Can I get a stack on the floor?" At the distributors, they have to know who all the key players are. Who's writing the purchase orders? Who's managing the street team? Who's managing merchandisers?

My job in operations involved phone calls, emails and meetings. I was doing 200 flights a year in 2018 and 2019. Distributors would bring their wholesales team together in house monthly for a general sales meeting. They would have a full day of suppliers pitching products for 15 minutes each. Sometimes there could be 30 back-to-back meetings in a row. It was a serious challenge to get people excited about selling our brand.

When COVID-19 shut everything down, we still paid raises and bonuses, and we didn't lay off any of our sales team. When things opened up, we told our people to take whatever security measures that they were comfortable doing. The big brands had to put strict regimes in place. But because we were a small company, we could do what we wanted.

Chapter 27: **Mark R. Warren**

Retailers were really struggling. They had a hard time even getting employees. Managers were working 20-hour days just to stay open. We told our people not to go in and pitch them anything. Go in and bring them coffee, bring them lunch and help them stock their shelves. We did that for months and when we got on the other side of things and people were back to selling, that paid massive rewards. When our salespeople walked in, managers asked, "What do you guys need? We'll give you whatever you want." We asked for a 60-case stack on the floor as an end cap and they said, "It's yours." Done.

What we were allowed to do in Texas and Florida was months ahead of what our teams in California were able to do. They were not allowed to go into stores. So, we had them do Zoom meetings with salespeople from distributors. Normally, they would buy everyone lunch, but everyone was working from home. So, they called GrubHub and had lunches sent to people's houses.

We relied heavily on our teams to come up with workarounds that would work in their state. It was hard to keep people motivated during COVID-19, but this gave them a new excitement level, due to the reactions from the stores and distributors. And it allowed us to leapfrog everyone else and compete like a Gallo, Bacardi or Patron. This was personal, because everyone was scared. They were worried about how they would pay bills or keep their store open. What we did went a long way. If you can find ways to bring a positive to a negative situation that you can't control, it can have a huge impact on your business. What our salespeople did during COVID-19 had a profound impact on our business for the next 18 months.

At the end of 2018, we did a capital raise and brought in a family office. Unfortunately, we were never aligned. They wanted EBTDA and we wanted market share. Four years later, they had the ability to force a sale. It wasn't a sale we were looking for at the time. We felt there was still a lot of growth and we wanted to continue building the brand, but we sold the company in the fall of 2022. We immediately began working on our new brand, 2 Bears Wine.

When we started in the wine business, everyone wanted to remind us that we were stepping into a category where we didn't know what we were doing. I believe that not coming from the alcohol industry actually served us. Yes, we made plenty of mistakes, but we didn't know enough to fall into the trap of, "This is how it should be done."

Alcohol is a copycat business. If someone comes out with a successful peanut butter whisky, there will immediately be seven more just like it. With a few exceptions, big brands don't innovate. They buy innovation. Coming from the outside, we rattled the cages of the industry. If you truly believe in what you're doing, put 100-percent effort into it, and don't let anyone tell you no.

CHAPTER 28

A HEALTH AWAKENING AWOKE THE ENTREPRENEUR IN ME

By **MATTHEW J. MCCARL, SR.**

One of my favorite people to quote is Darren Hardy: "Don't fake it till you make it. Be real, be transparent, be authentic and be yourself." My story of success stems from two significant injuries leading to surgeries that sent me on a path to finding better healing alternatives.

1. Helpless to Helpful on Purpose

I was going to bed one Friday night, and as I threw the covers back on my bed I couldn't stand up. Have you ever noticed how the worst things seem to happen on a Friday?

I decided to tough it out and planned to go to the chiropractor on Monday. That plan failed. I ended up spending Sunday in the ER due to excruciating pain. The ER performed their typical 2007 protocol—a series of tests, a follow-up referral suggestion to my doctor and a prescription for pain medication.

I followed up with my chiropractor a couple of times, but still felt odd every time I got off the table. He ran some tests and suggested an MRI. Turns out, I had completely ruptured my L4-L5 disc in my lower back and needed major surgery. The recovery time kept me out of work for six months. When I returned to my position as a RV technician in 2008, I was told the RV company had been sold and that I needed to find new employment.

Growing up on our family-owned 80-acre farm, I watched my dad go through cycles where he worked in Plywood mills, got laid off, then rehired and laid off again. I worked for an RV company for 20 years until being laid off, similar to what I had seen with my father growing up. Watching Dad on the farm, I intuitively knew there had to be a way to live and afford the things I needed, without relying on working for a company.

The house my wife and I began our family in was located about three blocks from the fire station. I would wake up at night hearing sirens rushing out of the station. One night, I dreamed about the time I felt the most helpless growing up. In the dream, I watched EMTs work on my grandmother while she was experiencing a medical emergency one night in our home. I was around middle school age. At this time, my elderly grandmother lived with us. It was the most helpless I have ever felt to that point in my life. I couldn't do anything but stand back, observing the paramedics hurling questions, connecting machines and checking her vitals. That feeling of helplessness stuck with me. I believe that was one pivotal moment that sparked my desire to help others.

I became a volunteer firefighter in 1992. I was shifting from the RV industry, as a new hospital was starting and was seeking people with emergency service experience to work in the emergency room. My skill set was a natural fit, and working in the ER allowed me to help

Chapter 28: **Matthew J. McCarl, Sr.**

more people. I got certified as an emergency medical technician (EMT). Today 80 to 85-percent of all fire department emergencies are now medical.

For over 30 years, my mission has been to help people. Helping others is my life's purpose. It drives me. It piqued my curiosity to become a volunteer firefighter, then later an EMT and now the founder of a wellness clinic.

Before you set out to action on something you desire, evaluate your purpose for being and your values. Question if that thing aligns with who you are, who you want to be and how you want to be remembered. None of us get out of this thing alive, so we must live on purpose.

1. Treat Your Body Better Than Your Vehicle

"If you want a new outcome, you will have to break the habit of being yourself, and reinvent a new self."
–Joe Dispenza

I was working in the medical field in my new position at the ER and was very out of shape, because of my previous lifestyle. I was 39 years old and 260 pounds, out of shape and probably not the best role model for the patients. I realized I needed to be in better shape and treat my body better than my vehicle.

I was setting small goals to shift my lifestyle, when out of the blue, I started experiencing chest pains. After a stress test, the doctor prescribed an aspirin regimen. I was much too young, in my mind, to be on heart attack and stroke prevention treatment. Due to what was happening, the aspirin regimen was the best medical course of action. Since I was only 39, I felt that was not what I wanted to do being that young.

We only get one body in this lifetime. Yet, most of us will treat our vehicle better than we treat our bodies—the vehicle for our souls in this lifetime. We can modify our bodies, but we can't trade them in or upgrade them for the latest and greatest model.

Consider how we buy luxury vehicles that require premium gas. You wouldn't one day decide to put regular or mid-grade gas in your car from that point on. It would ruin your car. We tend to want to maintain our vehicles—buy new tires, get tune-ups, oil changes and more. Our bodies are ours until we depart this life. We deserve the same effort of maintenance that we give our cars or better.

Your health and wellness is up to you. It's more than going to the doctor and allowing them to care for you. You must actively choose to watch your diet and work out to have your best life ever. Treat yourself well now so you won't have to take many medications later.

I started actively making long-term wellness investments that would compound over time. I researched and implemented healthier food habits, started shifting my mindset around food and shopped outside aisles in the grocery store—fresher foods, less processed and boxed foods. I invested in P90X to help achieve my health goals and created a small side hustle. I ate better, worked out and lost about 90 pounds between 2010 and 2012.

Healthier living and consistency had paid off. I knew more about using food for fuel while still enjoying the foods I wanted. I was stronger physically and mentally. I was treating my body better.

Chapter 28: **Matthew J. McCarl, Sr.**

It was arm day in July 2012. I was in my workout room doing curls when I tried to do a curl with a 20-pound weight on my right arm, and it would not curl. My doctor referred me to a physical therapist for a few weeks, but I needed another surgery—neck surgery. I had a pinched nerve in my neck for my right bicep. One of the side effects of my surgery was that the neurologists bumped the nerves in my left hand that caused tingling and numbness in my ring and pinky fingers.

I was on my second road to recovery. I decided to attend a wellness conference in Tacoma, Wash. I checked out vendor after vendor, until I discovered one of the vendors demonstrating how our bodies can heal themselves from many ailments simply through oxygen therapy under pressure.

After the conference, hyperbarics became my new target of curiosity and research. It was my new mission to help heal the tingling and numbness in my fingers. I dove into research on hyperbarics and connected with the NLHW owners. The owners were seeking investors to create multiple locations. They agreed to allow me to be a 15-percent investor and help me set up the Eugene, Ore., clinic.

2. A Business Model is a Recipe

"Seek out positive people who have achieved the success you want to create in your own life. Remember the adage: 'Never ask advice of someone with whom you wouldn't want to trade places.'"
–Darren Hardy

One in five businesses fail in the first year of opening. One reason new businesses fail is that they lack a realistic business plan. Business models are like the recipe for creating a successful business. Your brand needs to align with the parent company's standard when franchising. You don't deviate from the brand.

Think of investing in the Mcdonald's franchise and owning a location. You know what to expect from McDonald's, because the McDonald's brand and marketing are strong. McDonald's has mastered the art of training employees to uphold their brand and recreate their recipes so we all know what to expect. We expect consistency; no matter what McDonald's we visit, the fries and the Big Mac should taste like McDonald's. Should a location deviate from that brand, it changes the customer experience by creating a product that is no longer of the McDonald's brand. Similarly, the same is true when franchising in any other business.

In 2013, roughly one month after meeting the NLHW owners at the conference, I called them seeking advice and guidance on bringing a clinic to Eugene. The business model at the time required investors, so I went to work finding ways to acquire the needed funding to open my location. One day a few months later, the owner called me with an update that they had decided to shift to a franchise model, with me to become their first franchisee. The decision was easy; I went from 15-percent investor to 100-percent owner of my own NLHW franchise location in Eugene.

A year after my clinic was open, two other individuals were seeking to franchise their own locations, but were unwilling to follow the business model step-by-step. Ultimately, not following the recipe led to business failure.

Being consistent and constantly seeking guidance from the experts allowed me to defy failure in my first year as a new business.

Chapter 28: **Matthew J. McCarl, Sr.**

As part of starting the franchise, I bought an in-home hyperbarics chamber for research and in an attempt to relieve the tingling and numbness from my two fingers still present eight months post surgery. Ibuprofen had become a part of my daily routine, and one hour of treatment was like taking 40 ibuprofen. After the second treatment, I felt the difference. The numbness and tingling in my fingers was relieved, and I had regained full motion after six months of consistent treatments three times a week. My wife experienced results for a cancerous brain tumor. With consistent in-home treatments over a couple years, she went into full remission. Now, we were part of the success stories of the very business I had opened.

3. Don't Let the Big, Scary Things in Life Stop You

In 2015, we were finally able to open New Leaf Eugene. The only location of the original parent company. I understood the success I desired would stem from the advice I implemented from the parent company. Persistence, patience and following the model paid off. What was a tough obstacle to overcome for the original owners created a better business opportunity for me.

I always side-hustled for those multilevel investments, but never created a business that gave me complete control or replaced my full-time income. After giving to an industry that one day let me go and told me to have a good life, I was fearful of spending so much time building something that would just go away. But the investment paid off.

Use the big, scary things to fuel you to innovate and find opportunities to better your business.

COVID-19 temporarily closed NLHW, like many businesses, but it also created a great opportunity for some small businesses to thrive in new ways. This was a scary time that was bad for many folks, but it also fueled business innovation. COVID-19 helped to highlight our necessity for clients and to create better cleaning practices.

Purpose kept me curious to continue to seek better ways of living, which led me to discover what eventually became a profitable business. I certainly didn't know that I would be the only New Leaf Hyperbarics Wellness in Eugene. I just kept pushing forward.

CHAPTER 29

MAKE IT MATTER

By **MEGHAN MACKAY**

A sudden flash and loud crack shook my knees and made me dizzy. "You just lit up," said a man standing fifty feet in front of me, his eyes wide with wonder. At 16 years old, I had been struck by lightning in the vast and unforgiving Nevada desert.

Five years later, I found myself in a very different kind of desert, teaching at a failing school, bereft of any kind of flourishing—the kind of school where nobody believed "these kids" could read or write, let alone dream of becoming doctors, poets and scientists. Every day, I told myself there had to be a better way than the desolation of misery and failure that everyone accepted. While my students lined up for recess, another teacher's angry, thunderous roar—aimed at the children—shook me to the core. At that moment, it struck me that schools, intended to be the great social equalizers, were not created equal, and I knew I would find a solution to that barren landscape surrounded by concertina wire.

I joined a small group of revolutionaries to draft a plan for a new kind of school that would champion belonging, freedom and stronger outcomes for its students. I was in charge of the standards of excellence and collected a few examples so we could debate whether our standards aligned with our beliefs about the students' capabilities and with our vision for a school—and a future—full of possibilities. Ever since I felt that jolt of freedom and independence when starting a school with members of the community, I have contributed to the design and founding of many more schools. I love working on teams with others to seek equity in education, and I am willing to fight for every child and all school communities to have access to high-quality K-12 educational experiences. To make good on this promise, I believe we need a coalition of leaders nationwide who have creative solutions, alternative perspectives, flexibility and the autonomy to achieve extraordinary results.

Too often, change is not achievable, because leadership turnover leads to a more fragmented community. In a 2022 survey from the National Association of Secondary School Principals, nearly 40-percent said that they planned to quit in the next three years; 14-percent of those respondents claimed they planned to leave within the next year (NASSP, 2022). To combat this problem, five years ago I started a nonprofit invested in the success and sustainability of education leaders called the LeveragED Foundation. My team and I cultivate networks of diverse leaders and connect them to each other through ongoing experiences for enrichment and professional growth, offering access to compelling opportunities, curated resources and thought partnership.

Tackling Educational Challenges

The slow limp out of the pandemic has exposed the failure of education to offer experiences and produce outcomes for (and trusted by) under-resourced communities. As a result, education leaders and their teams are now tackling one of the nation's most intractable problems: ensuring a high-quality education for all children.

Chapter 29: **Meghan Mackay**

If the United States does not have highly qualified leaders who sustain their leadership and put children first, the dismal results of the nation's schools will only plunge further below where they need to be. In 2019, pre-pandemic results revealed an average of only 40-percent of fourth graders, 33-percent of eighth graders, and 25-percent of 12th graders showing proficiency in math, and reading proficiency rates of about 34-percent among all students (National Center for Education Statistics, 2019). In 2022, only 36-percent of fourth graders, 26-percent of eighth graders, and 24-percent of 12th graders showed proficiency in math, and reading proficiency rates of about 31-percent among all students (National Center for Education Statistics, 2022). Couple these declining rates of proficiency with the exodus of teachers and leaders post-pandemic, and we have a massive crisis on our hands. According to a recent RAND study, teacher turnover was 12-14-percent in high-poverty, urban districts serving primarily students of color (Diliberti & Schwartz, 2023).

To research further how to best support the ongoing professional growth and sustainability of educational leaders, specifically those who choose to work in historically under-resourced and under-represented communities, I am pursuing a doctorate at NYU's Steinhardt School of Culture, Education, and Human Development in Leadership and Innovation, where I am collaborating with a cohort of peer leaders determined to make transformational change within their organizations.

Through my work at LeveragED and my research at NYU, I support projects in which educational leaders can realize their maximum career capabilities and accelerate transformation both on school campuses and off campuses, in communities themselves.

Know Who You Are as a Leader

Over the years, I have learned that better understanding how I show up, communicate, overcome challenges, and develop my people allows me to be a more effective leader. I am a big-picture person, love a challenge, and am confident we can figure things out as a team, even when the answers are unclear. I enjoy sitting in a place of uncertainty, asking questions rather than responding with answers. Because I have an outsized tolerance for change and adventure, I can rally people around turning a vision into action and tend to take the lead, even when there are still details to work out.

I am most fulfilled when I am creating with a group of people, addressing organizational problems while tending to the human elements of change. Though my natural working style is strategic and action-oriented, I think a lot about how I show up on a team, how I might adapt the way I communicate and operate, and how I can leverage the strengths of others. Because I know my blind spots, I intentionally build diverse teams with complementary strengths to execute my vision. By sharing this information about myself, I think it helps others navigate how they might best work with me.

In my leadership journey, I have been humbled by several experiences when I had not considered my positionality as thoughtfully as I should have. One experience sticks with me: A teacher in one of my schools was tapped to become a leader before she felt she was ready, and she wanted to stay in the classroom for at least one more year. It was apparent to me that she would make a great leader, but I also respected her position, and told her that she should ask for what she wanted. "That's easy for YOU to say, Ms. Superintendent. I'm afraid I don't really have a choice. I'm just a teacher, and I bet there will be consequences if I say no."

My intentions were good, but I had not thought about how much pressure she was under, nor how vulnerable and powerless she might have felt to say no. I offered to advocate for her, but what if she hadn't pushed me to think about what her consequences might have been? What if my advice had led to her being asked to leave? Though she ultimately became a leader and has been successful, I continue to reflect on situations like that and ask myself what could go wrong if I were to ignore positional power. When I recognize my biases, I become a better listener and more curious about others' perspectives. As a leader, monitoring and moderating some of my initial instincts is critical for intentional, strategic and empathetic communication.

Teamwork

At LeveragED, my team members and I have created "self manuals" to communicate our natural working styles to one another as colleagues. These helpful guides include what energizes us and what drains us, our values and motivations, our preferred pace of work, and our natural roles. Teamwork can be stressful when conflicts arise, the outcome is uncertain, or when members come with a deficit mindset. Having an awareness of each other's strengths means we can maximize our time together. An asset-based approach matches our strengths to challenges, engenders professional trust, and speeds our success.

When my team and I work with education leaders, we do this same "self manual" exercise with their teams to foster increased communication, acceptance, intentionality and strategy in the ways they interact with each other and their school communities.

Inevitably, we have conflict, or issues that are tricky to navigate. As a leader, I encourage team members to assume the best of each other and to approach the problem with curiosity. I also try to be as transparent as I can about what part I play in contributing to the issue. Our team has made it central to our mission to make our thinking more visible, so as to reduce any obstacles to success. This helps build our collective strengths.

High Expectations and Connection to Others

I expect a lot from people. When I am committed to something, I do not stop until I achieve the goal. If I want others to follow, I know I need to support them in doing their best work. Ongoing professional development that builds skills and cultivates a growth mindset that leads to excellence is key to earning the autonomy we seek in our lives. I hire people whose values and work ethic align with this vision of excellence, and I continually seek out education leaders who are hungry for challenge, support, and connection to others.

Chip Conley's *Wisdom @ Work* has inspired me in this later phase of my career. The relationships we have at work are often separate from our personal relationships, but I tend to blur the lines and try to integrate my relationships. As an educator, I need a group of people in my corner who play different roles in my life—mentors who model and hold up mirrors, so I understand myself more clearly; advisors who provide specific expertise; coaches who offer tactical approaches; systems gurus who can help me develop process; mentees who learn from me; and editors who can get inside my mind and help me prioritize and simplify. I consider everyone with whom I work to be a contributing sculptor who sees something special in me and chisels away to help me access it.

Chapter 29: **Meghan Mackay**

Education leaders are constantly building social capital through professional relationships to ensure we do right by children. None of us can do this work alone. Through connection and support, we can help each other clarify where we are and where we want to go, note the obstacles, and set a path to becoming accountable to finding sustenance for our collective success.

Amplifying and Extending Brilliant Ideas

I am committed to elevating the voices, ideas, unique experiences and collective knowledge of leaders. To ensure children have access to high-quality schools, I like to imagine the notion of alchemy (without all the ancient mystery and secrecy). With some golden ideas (even just veins in an untapped mine), I believe I can help unearth brilliance, working with my team members to spread ideas and implementations beyond a starting place in one corner of the Earth.

Some people call this codification. My teammates and I like to think of the process as thoughtful translation, because we listen carefully; ask questions to expand those ideas; pay close attention to one's language, tone and accent; and try to understand the intended audience.

We recognize that the knowledge, contributions, and experiences of historically marginalized leaders and historically under-resourced communities have been neglected, disregarded and disrespected in far too many circumstances. We believe these are the very ideas communities need to thrive. I hope that together, we can extend these ideas to overcome current inequities and gaps.

Will Lightning Strike Thrice?

Let's hope! I would like to avoid yet another zap in a desert, and instead make an electrifying impact through the LeveragED Foundation, which I believe can be a catalyst to connect educators, celebrate what's working in education, and use our collective strengths and experiences to commit to a more effective, equitable and exceptional future. Together, we can energize each other to continue to sustain careers in education and make every school day matter.

Resources:
- *https://www.urban.org/research/publication/students-alternative-schools-serve*

CHAPTER 30

THE POWER OF DELAYED GRATIFICATION

By **MHER M. VARTANIAN**

Entrepreneurship and life go hand in hand. When you start your own business, you eat, sleep and breathe it. It consumes your life. Everyone who is serious about their business understands that their business is a part of them. At least for a time, it defines you. It's your mark on the world. Some say entrepreneurs are born, while others say entrepreneurs are self-made. I think it's a little of both.

I grew up in an entrepreneurial family. As the son of immigrants, I am a first generation American. My mom fled war-torn Lebanon and my dad fled war-torn Syria, both in the 1970s. While they arrived from different locations, they met here and set out to live the American Dream. Today, they own their own small business and they own real estate. They have assets. They carry zero debt and they were able to send two kids to premier, Ivy League universities.

I had a stay-at-home mom. I didn't even know what that meant, until I was in high school and heard, "Let's go over to Billy's house. His parents aren't home." We never went to my house, because there was usually someone at home. It was a real eye-opener to realize that my friends' parents were both college educated and they both had to have full time jobs to afford their lifestyle. My dad didn't graduate middle school in a third world country and my mom didn't have to work. Our house was bigger than my friends' houses and we had nicer things. I started having these realizations at a very young age.

My dad owned a dry-cleaning business. It wasn't fancy. When I was a kid, I was even embarrassed to think, my dad cleans clothes for a living. My friends' dads were engineers, architects and accountants. Apparently, I thought those jobs were cooler.

I started working at the dry cleaners when I was eight years old. One Saturday morning, my dad asked me, "What are you doing today?" I said, "Nothing." He said, "Come with me." It wasn't too intense, just things like sweeping the floor. That was important for me, because I learned about responsibility. When I learned to drive as a teenager, it gave me greater opportunities to work and earn my own money.

During the summers, I opened the shop and closed the shop, freeing my dad to run errands and do whatever he needed to do. He always said, "I would rather hire you and pay you than hire someone outside the family." I didn't fully understand what that meant, until one Saturday night. I closed the business, emptied the register and brought the cash home to my dad. There was something visceral about putting cash on the table. Over dinner with my parents, I realized, I helped contribute to our lives. My work impacted my family. I think a lot of people live their entire life without feeling that what they do matters. I experienced that from a very early age, and it made a huge impression on me.

My dad also taught me to have a good relationship with money. He always insisted I keep money on me. Even at eight years old, I

Chapter 30: **Mher M. Vartanian**

always had $60 in my pocket. Throughout middle school and high school, I remember going to our local convenience store, Wawa, with my friends. While my friends were pulling quarters out of their pockets, I could say, Arizona Iced Teas are on me. I had cash. I was enjoying the money I had made. It was a little thing, but when you're a kid, it's a big deal. I could go to the toy store and buy myself toys. I enjoyed them more, because I bought them myself with the money I made.

As I got a little older, I began to think about other ways to make money. From the age of 10, I started to create side hustles. I sold snacks at school out of my backpack. At 12, I started selling things on eBay. My mom had to drive me to the post office so I could mail packages. It's interesting how a little dose of entrepreneurship can change your life. It's not actually about money. It's about freedom. As a kid, I was able to do things without having to ask my parents for money and wait for that verdict. When my parents did give me money, they wouldn't let me buy anything stupid. And because I was earning my own money, I naturally felt less likely to spend it on something stupid. Entrepreneurship and freedom go hand in hand. But freedom also forces you to learn responsibility.

Even when you feel married to your work, at the end of the day, you still have as much freedom as you want to take. You have a piggy bank full of freedom. You can take as much as you want out, and you can save as much as you want. There are consequences to actions, but ultimately, you are in control of your destiny, and no one is telling you what you can and cannot do.

People arrive at the entrepreneurial mindset in different ways. In my current role, I work with entrepreneurs, business owners and high net-worth individuals. I've noticed that the successful ones all have a similar core belief and value system. Obviously, there is a correlation between money and freedom. The more money you have, the more freedom you can buy yourself. I truly believe this, because everything has its cost. Everyone's time has value. Even if you're working 9-5, the person who hired you is thinking that your time is valuable to them. That's why they hired you.

Entrepreneurship basically comes down to understanding that delayed gratification exists. Entrepreneurs want to build something and grow it over a long period of time. You have to find that spark that drives you to keep going, until you finally see the fruits of your labor and receive that delayed gratification, and the huge dopamine spike that goes with it. Entrepreneurs understand that inner drive. I think we all have it, but some people have more of it and they chase it. Once you've had a taste of success, it can become like a drug. The trick to success is to keep moving the goalposts and advancing your goals.

When I started out in commercial real estate, my first goal was to get a listing. I did that my first week on the job and soon after, I had several more listings. My next goal was to sell one of these properties so I could get a paycheck doing this. That took nine months, but I finally sold a Taco Bell, off Interstate 95, in Maryland. More followed. My next goal was to buy real estate.

Then, I started training junior agents and building a team around me. I partnered with my current business partner, who has become one of my best friends and is like a brother to me. I started buying investment properties on an annual basis, which made it possible for me to buy a house. Now, I'm working on a development project.

That's the new delayed gratification I'm chasing. This project will be four years in the making, once it's fully stabilized. That's a huge undertaking that is only possible, because I kept hitting my previous goals, and I know I can hit those again consistently. Once you achieve one goal, you can start to build systems around yourself to achieve your goals over and over.

Closing a deal out now is not as exciting as it used to be. The first time a six-figure check hit my bank account was insane. The second time, it was great. The third time, I thought it was great, because I needed that money to execute the next thing I wanted to accomplish.

As an entrepreneur, I want to buy more, build more and create another business. My wife and I also want to start a family soon. You can't quantify that in the same way you can a business goal, but it still comes down to goal setting and planning. What do you want to do? What do you want to have? And what do you need to do to achieve those things? That involves a constant, systematic approach to self-evaluation and course correction. The "delay" part of delayed gratification is not about sitting around waiting for something to happen. It's something you actively participate in and direct.

When you're just starting out, it's hard to be systematic. When I'm training new agents, they tend to just have their heads down, plowing forward, until they make their first few bucks. When new agents ask me, "How can I make money as fast as possible?" I tell them, just throw everything you have at it until you start making money. Once you alleviate the anxiety of not having enough money in your pocket, you begin to think about your business in a systematic way. At that point, you have enough data to analyze what you're doing. You can make as many business plans as you want at the start of your new venture. But in the end, you don't know what you need to be doing, until you actually do it. In the beginning, you must constantly tweak your plans. You start by tweaking them weekly, then monthly, then quarterly. Eventually, you review and make changes annually. From there, you can start setting new goals.

When I make projections, I take a conservative position and assume I am going to make half of what I anticipate. That encourages me to live within my means and not overextend myself. Then, I start planning out one, two, five and 10 years into the future. I use those numbers personally, because that's how treasuries are priced. Then, there are 20 and 30-year numbers, which we also target, as best we can.

I don't recommend doing anything too lofty in the beginning. I always tell my junior agents to start by paying off all student debt. Then, start investing heavily in your 401k before you're 30 years old, because that's how you reap the most benefits in terms of contributions into a 401k, Roth IRA, or whatever you have.

Goal setting is more than just income targets and investment planning. It includes building a life. As entrepreneurs, we don't have a 9-5 job with guarantees of cash income. I tell my junior agents every single day, I'm not your boss. I don't control your life. You control your life. I'm here to help you, and we are going to work together to get things done. We are partners in this work. Feel free to take my approach and model my success, but at the end of the day, this business is a meritocracy.

I'm big on the idea that what gets measured gets improved. Consistency is key. You must put your goals on paper. Write your goals down at the beginning of every week. What are you going to do? What numbers do you want to hit? How many phone calls and client meetings do you want to have? Every week, set achievable goals and be consistent in your execution of those goals. We tell our agents to aim for 300 calls per week. But if you know you are going to be out on the road for a day or two, and 300 calls doesn't make sense, don't set yourself up for failure. Adjust your goal to an achievable number.

Every Saturday, as you think about your week ahead, everything seems possible. But as the week progresses, a million unexpected things pop up. If you know you're not going to be able to hit your goal, don't beat yourself up. Do what you can to accommodate the unexpected. Hire support staff, refer less important tasks out, wake up earlier or go to bed later to get things done. Do what you have to do to stay consistent with your main tasks. The main purpose of planning is to think about what systems are needed to support and amplify our goals.

Delayed gratification can be a tough sell in our instant gratification and short attention span world. People think of it as painful, boring or something their grandparents would encourage them to do. For me, delayed gratification is about your vision. You're not waiting for anything. You are creating your life. You are in charge. Plan it. Execute your plans. And you will create a life you want to live.

CHAPTER 31

MENTAL HEALTH IS THE DRIVING FORCE BEHIND THE SUCCESS OF YOUR BUSINESS OR PRODUCT

By **MYNTILLAE NASH**

At the intersection of work and life, lies a valuable lesson. Our jobs and lives are intertwined in ways we may not even realize. When we are feeling balanced and energized, ready to take on the world, our performance at work thrives, as do our personal relationships. When we get bogged down with stress from either side, it can feel like an endless cycle of diminishing returns.

Being mindful of the relationship between your job and life is essential for your success as business owners. It is worth taking the time to invest in yourself so you can be mentally prepared for any situation, while still maintaining a healthy balance between work and other areas of your life. Being consistent with this will allow you to grow, both personally and professionally, without sacrificing one for the other.

That begs the question, how do we create better overall mental and physical wellness as business owners? The answer is that you have to make it a priority and put in the work to heal. Unfortunately, many of us have become accustomed to ignoring our own needs in favor of achieving our goals. Subsequently, we end up neglecting our own wellbeing.

For years, I have struggled to understand how my mental and physical health are inextricably linked. Between the physical symptoms and mental exhaustion I was experiencing, I felt completely out of control of my own life. I felt compelled to push myself further. I was working as much and as hard as possible, because that's what I could control.

I have been drawn to creative activities since I was a child. This passion has served me well in my career. I started off in the field of graphic design, and then transitioned my skills into web design and user experience (UX) design. Working in this industry requires exceptional attention to detail, which allowed me to combine my creativity with my work. My passion for the work I do resulted in me not setting limits or boundaries for myself or for my clients. I was not fully showing up for myself in business or in my personal life.

Then something happened that was so disruptive, it jarred me out of the cycle I was in. It forced me to take a step back and realize that there were some big changes I needed to make in my life, in order to heal and thrive.

I was in a severe car accident that left me significantly injured. For the first time since I could remember, I had to ask for help to be mobile and do small things. Being injured obviously affected my work as well. The parts of my life that I had control over were suddenly not in my control anymore. This event forced me to reflect on the trauma cycle that brought me to a place where I was overworking and under-caring for myself. Something was about to change, and I began to see clearly what needed to happen.

Chapter 31: **Myntillae Nash**

I knew that if I wanted to find long-term success within myself, and as a business owner, I needed to take an introspective look at what was going on beneath the surface. How is this affecting my work? How is this affecting my body and life as a whole? When I became aware that my abuse in childhood and my abusive romantic relationships were causing me to recreate a push and pull in all areas of my life, my healing began to grow from there.

I decided it was time to start investing into understanding myself so I could move forward toward advancing in every aspect.

I realized I was not only burning out, but using every available source within me for fuel, and collecting more to burn the next day. I left no room for me. It came at a high cost. I would not feel empowered to invoice when I should have. I would do more than I was being paid to do. I would exist in a toxic work environment, all in an effort to provide value and be valued. I had not yet learned that my intrinsic value began with me.

This mindset led to diminished creativity and motivation on my part, as well as exhaustion. I was spending all of my energy on my business. I realized that if I did the hard work to heal, I could work smarter instead of harder, as they say.

I became determined to deal with the trauma that led me to making decisions that were not in my favor. I was giving my all in multiple areas of my life, and reaping incomparable benefits. My business, my relationship and my physical body all reflected my previous, subconscious, undervaluing of my contribution. I methodically built my own foundation of prioritizing myself while valuing my own contribution to the world around me.

It's not something to be taken lightly, and while I've built on my strategies for growth over the years, it is an ongoing process. My growth will always be and should be just that, a process.

First, I had to remove the obviously toxic elements in my life. I ended my abusive relationships and ended toxic business relationships. I set boundaries and limits for myself, in order to ensure that I can maintain control of the resources I have. Those elements weren't easy, but then came the harder part. I had to do the work of healing the inner wounds and learned behavior that compelled me to accept those things into my life in the first place. I also implemented new habits and processes that have allowed me to continue to grow.

Here are my top tips and strategies that help me continue to grow.

Taking Breaks

Taking time to do things I enjoy has a positive impact on everything in my life, including my work. Making sure I have time off energizes me both physically and mentally. That helps me be more productive and focused when tackling big challenges. I find myself better able to think clearly and make decisions more quickly and accurately.

Before I began this journey, I would not have felt like it was a good business decision to take a week-long vacation, or an impromptu mental health day, simply because I needed it. Now, I understand that taking these breaks is actually a fantastic business decision. Stepping away from what I am focusing on in my business, and throwing myself headlong into a new adventure, offers me a fresh set of eyes on my life and work once I return to it. But that isn't the only reason to claim your own enjoyment of real life and absorb new experiences. Doing these things helps us evolve into better versions of ourselves.

Work-Life Balance

As business owners, it's important to make sure we aren't overworking ourselves. I'm sure you're no stranger to feeling the drive to work 24/7. How often do we take over a project we've assigned to someone else, because doing it ourselves is faster than the explanation would be? Creating this balance can be difficult, because many of us suffer from perfectionism. That perfectionism has been a huge contributing factor in us being where we are today. It's hard to let go of the reins sometimes. However, overworking can eventually lead to lower productivity and diminished quality of life at work and at home.

This can look like taking regular breaks throughout the day, and delegating the tasks and projects that you can. Set yourself working hours, and stick to them. Doing these things will ensure you can develop and maintain a fulfilling life outside of work. Instead of just crashing at the end of the day, you'll have the energy for your favorite activities and even find new hobbies to enjoy. You will have more time and energy for your family and friends. I am able to be more productive now that I have made this a priority.

Exercise

Taking time for yourself to exercise is essential to maintaining your health and mental wellbeing. As our society and technology advance, we have to move less and less. Many people use grocery delivery, instead of walking around the grocery store and ordering various other purchases to the front door. We've come a long way from having to plant and harvest our own food. While this is amazing, we now have to put mindful effort into being physically active, in order to be and remain healthy.

Exercise is an investment in your future. As a visual and UX designer, so much of my work is done on the computer. If I spend all of this time sitting while working, my business is advancing, but my body is not. The return we can get from investing in our bodies is invaluable, not just in old age, but almost immediately. When your body is able to move and improve, your opportunities for enjoyment in life increase. A hike can turn from a chore to a joy. Yoga can become an uplifting, calming and rejuvenating experience. Running with your pet becomes just as much fun for you as it is for them. Exercise is an investment in yourself. Set aside time to do whatever type of physical movement you like to do. Find activities you enjoy, and try different things until you find what works just for you.

Mindfulness

Meditating and practicing yoga have enabled me to become a better person for myself, my loved ones and my business. When I take the time to listen to my body, tune into how it moves, and recognize its needs, I'm able to have a more authoritative approach to challenges in life and business. Understanding how stress affects my body and my mind allows me to take care of myself where it counts.

Mindfulness isn't only found in meditation; it's an exercise in empathetic analysis of ourselves and the world around us. It is an appreciation of the circumstances that brought each situation into being. Mindfulness and empathy play a large role in my business, because I have become better equipped to understand users and better serve my clients.

My personal journey has fostered a deep level of empathy and compassion for others. This attribute is essential in my role as a UX/UI designer and web developer. A key element of my job is to understand the problems users face and create solutions. Empathy toward the user is an incredibly important skill, but some designers may not have this foundation naturally. Everyone's skill set is different. It's important to lean into what makes us unique, in order to flourish where the strengths are.

My life experiences that I have overcome helped me develop a deeper level of empathy that greatly drives my ability to understand the user of any product I design. I strongly believe that understanding how people think, feel and interact with a product is the key to creating intuitive tools for my clients. This hard-won skill of relating to others gives me a unique advantage in knowing how to effectively collaborate in teams, as well as understand what my clients need.

Working together with stakeholders and developers to identify unique solutions for successful products is something I'm passionate about. Whether it's software, an app or a website, finding ways to improve the user experience is what drives me. It starts with understanding who our users are and what they need. That's the value I enjoy providing to my clients.

Every day I am grateful for the decision I made to focus on my mental health and learn to heal from my past trauma. The results have been remarkable. In the years since I started this journey, I have achieved more success in life and business than I ever could have imagined.

I hope by sharing this story, others will be encouraged to make their mental health a priority and reach new heights. We are capable of amazing things when we take care of ourselves first—something that should never be taken for granted.

CHAPTER 32

THINK LIKE A VENTURE CAPITALIST

By **OKSANA MALYSHEVA**

You may not think about Venture Capital (VC) on a daily basis, however, even without you knowing, it has changed your life. How many times have you tapped Twitter, ordered on Amazon, or flipped through Google (within even the last hour)?

Let's face it, we're all daily devotees to innovation funded by VCs. How does our industry elevate the obscure into unicorns? Success saddlebacks on grit. You and I know that, so we'll take it as a given. I'm here to explain why venture capital rockets grit even further. The answer comes from a string of magical moments: pushing your toes to the threshold, taking a deep breath and leaning into the unknown. It's making a habit to take charge with curiosity, rather than fear.

Radical ideas are, by definition, against common reason. In the everyday drawl, "safe" becomes a routine as much as it becomes a cage. In our daily life and our daily work, we are conditioned to focus on the incremental, to manage risks, to balance equally what can go right with what can go wrong. But radical ideas only change your life when someone stops for a minute to think: What if everything went right? As I will explain later, as a VC, it is my job to focus on what can go right before and above everything else.

You are hearing from a VC who never even heard about this profession growing up, and who absolutely never envisioned it as her own. I look back and realize that ignoring the boundaries the world built for me, as well as trusting the moment and the leaning into experiences I walked through, were my first personal lessons in thinking like a VC. In many ways, I now think I was meant to do this, even when I did not know this world existed. I am also convinced that if I was not lucky enough to find this field, thinking this way would have pushed me forward and brought more joy and growth into my life. Being an Accidental VC comes with humility and introspection, and because of this, I can see and want to share how thinking like a VC can improve your life, just like I think it has improved mine.

I was born in Kiev, Ukraine, back when it was part of the Soviet Union. Being a VC was not on my to do list (must less something I even imagined could exist). Although my life story may come across as very determined and confident, that certainly was not how I felt going through it. I started my career as a physics geek, feeling awkward in a string of classes where I was once told, "Girls can't do physics." However, I finished my PhD. During my lunch breaks, I was exposed to snippets from business journals. That began my illicit love affair with business.

Later on, I started working at McKinsey. Then I became a marketing strategist at Motorola, where I was part of the team that launched RAZR. For the past 15 years, my passion has been growing, coaching and investing in serendipitous startups. I use every single part of my seemingly unrelated careers to nurture each one of them.

Chapter 32: **Oksana Malysheva**

Risk Doesn't Always Feel Good

Looking back, I realize venture capital touched every aspect of my life, even before I had heard of it. Risk doesn't feel good while you're walking in it. Yet, VCs must be able to walk in that uncomfortable precipice for years. I had no idea that all those doubt-filled nights throughout my career, were training me to grasp this concept.

Breakout ideas do not feel the way you expect them to. Mine were filled with doubt. For VCs, you must be able to live in that uncomfortable space. Otherwise, you fail. It takes a certain mindset to step into a breakout idea. From there, you also need to maintain the endurance to stay. This takes an optimistic eye for potential and making a habit of dreaming. Visualize what could go right, rather than ruminate on what feels wrong.

How Does Venture Capital Work?

As a newcomer to the United States, I see entrepreneurship as what makes America unique in the world. It's a culture of serendipity. And within that, venture capital plays a significant role. As an observer, I curiously admire this economic system, which was not natural to me at first and, as a result, never ceases to inspire me.

America is extremely entrepreneurial compared to almost any other place in the world. It's fairly easy to form a company here. It takes less than an hour. Even the language is entrepreneurial. Brand names become verbs—like Uber. What enables the entrepreneurial spirit in America is that if someone has a fantastic idea, but not necessarily the capital, they can approach investors and, for a stake in the company, they can get capital. While raising capital is never easy, people in the U.S. are willing to bet on crazy things. They can envision the future and they are willing to fund it and take the risk.

As the managing partner of a VC fund called Sputnik ATX, I jokingly describe my job as running a kindergarten for gifted and talented startups. The birth of a company happens when two people sit down together and draw something on a napkin. For my fund, the minimum requirements to apply are having a product and a customer you've convinced to buy that product. We teach companies how to evolve the product and grow and scale their company with our capital. It's extremely rewarding as a VC to support startups and watch them grow. If everything goes right, they could potentially become a unicorn. That's what we're looking for as VCs. When the company goes to IPO, that's when we know our culture of serendipity has paid off.

No one loves to fail, but in the U.S., compared to other cultures, if you start a company and it closes down, unless you've done something unsavory, it's actually a positive experience. If you fail, you get another chance. No shunning. No stigma. That is extremely unique. This type of resilience exists in degrees in other countries, but in the U.S., it's particularly strong. It drives our economy forward, and it drives innovation forward.

To me, capitalism and entrepreneurship are magic. If you look at the top 10 companies by market cap: Tesla, Facebook, Google, Twitter—all the value, all the jobs, all the impact, good and bad. All of these companies were venture-backed and didn't exist just 25 years ago. When they first appeared, their ideas seemed crazy. Yet together, with a venture partner, they rode serendipity all the way to the Forbes' 100.

Chapter 32: **Oksana Malysheva**

The VC way of Thinking

The job of a VC like me is to find companies poised for breakthroughs. They are the drivers of innovation, the future billion-dollar valuation, the unicorns.

When we do this, sometimes we will look insane to the outside world. Let me show you why. Imagine this: Go back in time 15 years. Two design majors come up to you and say, "We've started a new business to make rent. We lease air mattresses in our apartment to strangers." Would you be as excited for them as they seem to be?

Now imagine you make a bet. It's not just your own money on the line, but money entrusted to you on that crazy concept as well. Would you back out? Odds are, most of us would probably have to see the world differently to make that bet. What if I were to tell you though that those two design majors were the future founders of Airbnb? Looking back, the right choice is obvious. We all know their story. They took on all the biggest and most established hotel chains and are now worth $30 billion. Yet, the best of the best in my industry couldn't see the potential. Those who did, were called insane early on, and genius in the rear view mirror.

The primary job of a VC is to focus on how an idea could go right and build a bridge to get there, no matter how crazy it seems. It has been very well studied that the human brain evolved to weigh every negative interaction five to seven times larger than their positive interactions. It is not necessarily surprising that the humans who thought the rustle in the grass was just the wind were bitten by the poisonous snake and died, while the more paranoid humans survived to pass that paranoia onto future generations. The push to serendipity often goes against our genetic programming.

Established businesses see opportunity and tend to assess chances of failure first. A risky move might be good for a company, but it also carries significant threat. That can mean anything from lay-offs, to also the possible threat of destroying the business entirely. Most people don't make bold moves and they aren't necessarily wrong for thinking that way. Failure is punishing. But radical moves that have a high chance of failure, also have a disproportionate payoff when they succeed.

As a VC, my biggest mistakes are mistakes of omission, not commission. An easy way to distinguish an experienced early-stage VC from someone who is just entering the game is that the new investor, or angel investor, talks ad nauseam about what could go wrong, the risk profile and five-year financial projections. None of this is relevant. Good investors are going to push entrepreneurs to envision the future. Let's think together about how this could go big. How can it go right? What is the scenario? Where is the unicorn?

This is a very different way of thinking from traditional business training, and it took me years to learn. It's easy to read about, but not so easy to internalize. If you think about the Airbnb example, 90-percent of business executives would have laughed them out of the room. And frankly, a lot of VCs did as well, yet here we are.

Huge companies like Amazon, Google, Facebook, Twitter, Apple and Netflix, all started as an impossible idea. An impossible idea may make you look like a maniac, but without those crazy ideas, none of these companies would exist. You could argue that these companies are fundamental to our quality of life today. However, they were all once crazy ideas.

Chapter 32: **Oksana Malysheva**

Due to the massive risk from startup companies, we actually invest in baskets of companies, knowing that some of them will fail. Others will return a flat amount of money, not in proportion to the amount of risk we've taken. And, there will be a few that deliver disproportionate returns and essentially pay for this whole big basket of average performers. We invest in a lot of crazy ideas, knowing that at least one of them is the right crazy idea. Failure isn't a sign of doing something wrong. It's a part of the process.

The key to surviving this stage is patience. Going from serendipity to stable success usually takes a new business a whopping eight to 10 years. My fund currently has about 50 investments across many different industries. However, since Sputnik ATX has only been in existence for about five years, we are still somewhere in between the start and finish of the unicorn lifecycle.

Allow yourself to Dream and Envision what is Possible

How can VC thinking be applied to your everyday life? Whether you are an entrepreneur, an executive, or just a growth-oriented person, you can apply the traits of a VC mindset to improve your own life. It can be your job, your growth, your relationships—literally anything.

For a normal businessperson, you should be thinking in a more traditional way most of the time. You have a job that pays rent, childcare and college tuition. I'm not inviting anyone to disregard any of that. But I am inviting you to carve out time on your calendar when you are un-hassled, and hopefully well slept, when you can give yourself the luxury to envision… what if everything goes right? What is my disproportionate risk? No dream ever becomes externalized without being envisioned first. If you don't dream of creating a unicorn, you won't ever see one.

When you envision where you want to go, it may seem too far to reach. Try to envision a bridge. If you think of the Bay Bridge from San Francisco to Oakland, it flows over the water between supports. Instead of thinking about the entire bridge, what supports can you create? A support can be a plan you undertake, a side hustle you're going to try, becoming a consultant, or networking your way to a person who has already done what you want to achieve. Success isn't built on one serendipitous moment. It's the first step. What is your plan from there?

I invite you to look at the world from a different vantage point. Scheduling time to think like a VC can be similar to meditation, such as practicing envisioning, It is a useful tool for anyone who wants to move their career forward.

When you spend time asking yourself what can happen if everything goes right, your options expand. You'll have more ideas and you'll be better equipped to bet on the choices and opportunities that come from them.

The final key for VCs in regards to breakout thinking, is to surround yourself with the right people. Envision potential, not limits. Elevate your self-belief and extinguish your self-doubt. But don't worry if you don't always feel that way. Like many women leaders, there are days where I have supreme confidence and days where I have extreme self-doubt. I'm always fighting to keep them in balance. This is normal, but there's no need to invite more doubt than

Chapter 32: **Oksana Malysheva**

necessary. Who do you need to be to make your dreams come true? What do you need to learn? Who do you need to network with?

Give yourself grace when you take on something difficult. Implementing your breakout idea will not feel the same as standing in front of the finished project. Your doubts make you human; they don't determine the worth of your ideas. Dream big. What makes you human is what makes you powerful.

CHAPTER 33

THE SECRET TO LEADERSHIP SUCCESS

By **PETRIA MCKELVEY**

While many people measure success in dollars and cents, accolades and awards, I am intentional about measuring it by the level of impact, care and concern for people. With over 34 years in the medical billing industry, I have managed to successfully run my own company, Precision Medical Billing (PMB), for more than 28 years. As an advocate and a champion for healthcare providers of all calibers, I work diligently to make sure they receive every dime they deserve.

Insurance companies have mastered how not to pay healthcare providers. The insurance companies get richer and richer, because they collect premiums from consumers, but deny claims from our healthcare providers. I've come across so many doctors and nurses, among other healthcare providers, who are such nurturers that they don't care as much about getting paid as they do about the wellbeing of their patients. They simply want to make sure their patients are okay. This is why my passion is advocating for independent providers so they can keep their doors open and remain profitable, which in turn helps consumers by keeping healthcare pricing down.

As one who has loved working with money and numbers, I just knew I was going to work in investment banking or financial services.

But after tapping into the medical billing industry at the young age of 20, what started out as a job simply to pay the bills, soon became a passion and a full-time career for me.

Growing up, and the same is true today, I will faint at the sight of blood, so I never thought about healthcare. However, I never knew about the operational side of healthcare. Once I was exposed to it, I realized that I'm still dealing with numbers and money, and this is where I've been for the past 34 years, and I still love it!

But, let's be clear. It's not just about the money. It's really about the healthcare providers and the heartfelt care they have for their patients. Healthcare providers take an oath, and they are really serious about that oath. For most healthcare providers, their passion is the wellbeing of their patient. My passion is the wellbeing of healthcare providers. It is that attention to care and concern that sets my company apart from the rest.

One of the core leadership principles I stand on is care and concern. We genuinely care, and it shows in our work. Because of that, we don't take on everyone as a client. We only take on the clients we know we can genuinely help. If I feel like I can't help them, I don't take them on as a client.

However, it's not just important to show care and concern for clients. It's just as pivotal to show the same care and concern—if not more—for my employees. I'm not oblivious to the fact that my company has grown leaps and bounds, because of the strength of my team members. When I started almost 30 years ago, I was a solopreneur. Today, I have over 40 employees.

Chapter 33: **Petria McKelvey**

I feel like I work for my employees. I'm the visionary of the company. PMB is a giant, and I can't do it all myself. So, I have to make sure my employees practice self-care, too.

That leads us to the second leadership principle that I attribute to my success: company culture.

We have seven particular core values, which we hire based on them and use them to retain people. We have a wonderful team and a great culture. I don't make my people conform to who I am. I understand that one employee may need to be managed one way, while another employee may need something totally different. Some people need verbal accolades. Others are motivated by awards and bonuses. Every employee is unique, which helps create a strong culture.

It's also important for employees to take "brain breaks" regularly. I encourage my employees to work hard, but also play hard. I encourage them to take regular vacations and block out time to simply clear their heads, as needed.

True self-care is so important. I tell my employees all the time, "If something happens to you, and you're gone tomorrow, I'm going to put out an ad for your position." Don't let any job kill you. We are people, not robots. I want my employees operating at 110-percent, not 30-percent.

As a firm, but fair leader, I encourage my employees to remember that there is always tomorrow. The work will be here tomorrow. They don't have to work 24 hours to complete everything in one day. For many companies, that's not effective, nor efficient. That's why, when many companies or potential clients think they are interviewing my company, we are actually in turn interviewing them as well to determine if they are a good fit with PMB's culture, core values, and the care and concern PMB holds as a brand.

Although PMB has clients throughout the U.S., Alaska, Guam and Hawaii, I'm not afraid to fire clients and employees alike if they seem to be out of alignment with the company's vision, mission and goals. I encourage leaders of all backgrounds to hire slowly, and fire quickly. It's absolutely true that one bad apple can spoil the whole bunch. Protect your team and protect the company culture.

Whether you're a leader in the healthcare industry, or in a leadership role in general, below are three keys to help you become an effective leader in any marketplace.

You Must Spend Money to Make Money

When I first started PMB this was a hard lesson to learn. However, you must spend money to make money. You shouldn't be afraid to spend money. You should look at it as an investment, not a cost. In order to gain a greater level of expertise in retaining talent for your company, you're going to have to invest in hiring skilled staff within your industry. It will save you in the long run.

While I believe in saving, I urge leaders to save from a point of responsibility, not out of fear. Fear will truly paralyze you and hinder you from making more money than you already are. You have got to trust the process. Your time is actually more valuable than money. This leads us to our next pivotal key.

Chapter 33: **Petria McKelvey**

Fear Kills More Dreams than Failure Ever Will

Fearful leadership is not effective leadership. More than likely, you're in a leadership role, because someone saw something in you that you didn't necessarily see in yourself. As a leader, the company isn't just depending on you; your people are, too. If you operate in fear, so will your team. Mistakes are inevitable as you grow into your role as a leader. Too many leaders ponder, "What if I fail?" instead of, "What if I succeed?"

This mindset causes you to stall or freeze altogether. But the truth is, nothing changes if nothing changes. In order to get results you've never achieved in your company, on your team, or during your tenure as a leader, you have to take risks. You have to take chances. You have to move forward in some instances when you can't see the whole plan.

As leaders, we have high hopes for our teams and the impact they can, and will, have on the company at-large. But, over time, lack of confidence, constant correction without accolades, and costly mistakes can cause them to lose hope and *play it safe*. Contrary to popular belief, failure is not the worst thing that can happen. Many people who seemingly fail end up "failing" their way to greater success. Fear is designed to protect you from the false evidence that appears real.

Even when you seemingly fail, you will still learn. Even when a project or assignment doesn't work out the way you thought it would, you gain new skill-sets. As a leader, you're out front, leading the pack. You set the example for those who follow you today, and those who will come down the line years after you.

Some of the world's greatest inventions are here today, because a leader dared to dream, pushed past fear and refused to quit until they achieved the desired outcome. Leaders lead. You have a responsibility to lead people into the deep, even when you don't know the totality of what lies beneath the surface. I often tell my employees that the real failure is in quitting. Therefore, quitting is not an option.

Hire Slowly and Fire Quickly

In every company, leaders have to be able to navigate diverse types of people and personalities. To that point, it's critical that leaders choose employees who are going to fit in well with the culture of the company. It's not enough to have education and job skill-sets. One bad apple can indeed spoil the whole bunch. I've been through a lot of employees in the past 28 years. Today, people compliment me on how strong my team is, but they have no idea what I've gone through to get this level of team and great culture at PMB.

Always Think Ahead

Long before COVID-19 and the concept of "hybrid" workspace was a thing, I was working from home. Luckily for me, when I gave birth to my son in 1994, I didn't have to choose between putting my son into daycare and/or latchkey, or taking an extended maternity leave. My leader at the time understood the importance of work/life balance and didn't want to lose me as an employee. She allowed me to work from home two or three days a week and come into the office two or three days a week.

It was that same leader who told me to go spend $8 and get a DBA to start my own business. As a young mother, staying home and working remotely was transformational. It also gave me the courage to step into my purpose and passion in the midst of starting a great career journey. Today, I extend that same grace to my employees.

I have always allowed my employees to work a couple of days from home, based on how long they've been with the company and based on their performance. COVID-19 wasn't a shakeup for us, because we were already set up to work from home.

Bonus: Always Be a Visionary

You cannot only think about today. You will fail if you just think about today. You must think years ahead and always with technology in mind, the state of your industry and how it's changing, as well as the workforce as a whole, so you're not caught off guard. Don't be afraid of trying new things and continuously thinking outside of the box. And trust those smart people you have hired. Some of the best ideas at PMB come from my staff, not me.

Today, like many companies, we are hiring a lot now. With the significant growth of the company, I'm also hiring for positions I didn't have before. Based on the changing needs of the clients, as well as the employees, I may not have a job description for a particular role. But, I'm not afraid to do the research to create it! To date, my longest standing employee has been with the company for more than 15 years, a feat that not many companies can boast about.

CHAPTER 34

MY ROAD TO HUMANITY

By **PHILIP AYLES**

Grace and patience go together.

I grew up in Dayton, Ohio. I joined the Army National Guard at 17. The military has offered me a life experience that has had peaks and valleys, but has ultimately led me to find resilience, self-acceptance and love.

My career has also included working as military police; a civilian police officer; a member of the reserves to train the Iraqi Police in Baghdad; and then I deployed with the reserve unit. We did great things over there. I got to see what it was like to see a post war environment and how our service helped others. I have had over two decades of service in humanitarian crisis operations, and a lifetime of lessons I hope can humbly spark a call to action within yourself, which will inspire strength and the value of being kind to yourself during times of challenge.

Before the military, I had undiagnosed Attention Deficit/Hyperactivity Disorder (ADHD). What do you do when everything interests you and you can't focus on one? Perhaps not understanding this part of who I was is what led me into the vast world of the armed services.

The military, for me, was a necessity. It was my last resort. Working for the military gave me a breadth of experiences. They were tough mentally, physically and tested me on every level. The military gave me the opportunity to see the world and how we assist other countries. I realized I have been desensitized to a lot of things. I initially lost that sense of humanity, because we had missions to do in very dangerous places.

Coming out of the military was really a shock to my system and mental health. All of the connections I had when I came home were gone. I already felt incredibly isolated from being in Iraq. I felt alone, like being in a prison. The only difference from being in prison was that the guns face out. That experience turned this extrovert into an introvert.

The way of the military can be very competitive. But, when I got out, I was almost more intimidated. I started to look around for work. I must have applied for 300 jobs. But employers went for other candidates. I was overqualified and too expensive. Going into a "normal," non-military job, I don't think that they understand my previous work experience and skill-sets. It took eight years post military for me to find my footing.

I had another challenge in my life when I got back. My wife and I separated. She went out of the state where we both resided, and I had all three of my girls by myself. I didn't realize the dynamics of the house while I was gone. They challenged me. But, I prioritized … I focused on my daughters. God put me here for a reason. I realized one night that they needed me there so they could have a future with more purpose, direction and motivation.

Chapter 34: **Philip Ayles**

I didn't know them, because I was gone so much. By all rights, I was living in their house and I had some learning to do. But for the most part, I was blessed to be a part of their lives. I focused when they needed it. Today, I am a proud father. I taught them how to fish. They are my best accomplishment in life. The other job titles I have carried are just that—titles. The title of father has sincerely humbled me and has provided me with the sense of prioritizing my responsibility in their development.

My daughters helped me to understand my emotions. I used to take aggression with aggression. I had to learn patience. It takes time. I realized I failed with controlling my righteous ideology earlier in my career and perhaps personally. However, as I began my own journey of what I didn't realize at the time was my own healing, I didn't have time to look backwards. Only time to look forward. While time was of the essence for me to find ways to be positive and productive, it became more apparent that I needed time to reflect on the areas I desperately needed to see change.

Through my challenges, I have realized it is important to stop and see where you are at and re-evaluate where you want to go. As a leader, I realized that I have to be the inspiration for others. I saw this with my children. I realized the world and people are interacting differently with each other than when I was not in a war situation. Being a father demanded I live in the moment. I made the connection between the leaders I admired, and recognized that they, too, change direction based on what is happening in the world. Their passion trickles down. I saw this in my daughters. I recalibrated my mind. I truly believe in leading by example. My daughters helped me to see the power in that with their own accomplishments.

My experiences in the military allowed me to live history. Combined with my other personal history, I decided I wanted to forge ahead by creating a new chapter for myself.

In the service, we start over every new place we go and we get accustomed to that. I had to look at my new life post-military in the same light. Part of me thought I knew everything. But, I realized I needed to network with people who do know. I needed to make connections along my journey where everybody benefits. I decided I wanted to take this knowledge and share with others, and help them with getting through life's challenges with more determination, and most of all, support.

Becoming The Mindful Leader

I don't judge anybody anymore!

I realized I was self-righteous. I had to let go of ego and pride, because those two things will cause you to make the worst decisions in your life, and prevent you from being the best person you can. To the ones I called out, I was the worst person, because I scared them. In the military, when I was in other countries, I had so much humanity. But here, I found it different. It was such an individual culture, versus the collectivity I had experienced. However, deep down, I knew that sense of community could be found. I looked at myself like breaking the shell of a military dog that goes from nothing and alone to do search and rescue. This analogy really helped me to relate to people again.

One of the most significant life changing moments is when I almost lost my daughters emotionally. This is how I became more

Chapter 34: **Philip Ayles**

mindful. I was aggressive with them to get their attention. Absolutely not abusive, but in my tone and sternness. Even though they lived with me for a time, they went back to live with their mom.

And then, I realized I had really lost everything, including my car and my house. I bought an RV and I told myself to, "slow down, you don't know what you are doing," and I headed toward the east coast. I had a conversation with one of my daughters, who was always honest and understanding, and she explained that what I was doing, "was wrong, and you need to get a hold of yourself." That was the most emotional turning point in my whole life. And I realized what I was doing was not considerate of others. I had to make a choice.

Not too much longer after that, I met my current wife. God smacked me on the back of the head. This woman changed my life. I admit I was quite rustic. I needed some refining. My wife loves horses. She took me on like I was a wild horse out in the field. She told me she thought to herself, "He's got good in him. But, he needs to learn to control himself." She only knew me for eight months and traveled the country with me. Looking back, that was pretty amazing. And most notably, she recognized that I had Post Traumatic Stress Syndrome (PTSD).

We later bought a townhome in Jacksonville, Fla. I went on a PTSD study and it unlocked all of the walls I had put up my entire life. I discovered things about myself in a way I had never thought about. Once I threw that ego out, I realized I'm the cause of everything in my life, good or bad. And the pain I suffered was the pain I created. I loved everybody else more than I loved myself. And I got tired of sacrificing myself and acting as though I didn't care. I didn't want to die alone. I didn't want to see my daughters disconnect from me.

Life constantly throws curveballs at you, and I had to gain control over my triggers. It took this significant emotional event to pay attention to what's going on at that moment. My wife also helped me to realize that if I was a piano I would have lots of keys to get played, and I can choose to make a symphony or a screeching mess.

Once I realized my triggers, I was not the same person I was yesterday. It's about having the courage, even when you are scared, to become resilient—get out and do it. I accepted the challenge and the experience. But it took patience.

What would you do if you were told you had five hours to live? Nothing else matters. You have that every day. You have 86,400 seconds in a day. How you spend them is up to you. But you need to balance out your existence. It's how you recover from the challenges.

Realization and practicing these ways of being, led me to being more mindful. Mindfulness of what is in front of me, and not dwelling on what is behind—more people centric, holistic and authentic, by making the best out of the situation you can. Getting out of your own head and into the moment. Life is a culmination of experiences into who you are. It's about what you learned from these experiences, not what you experienced. It's also about being honest with yourself. Not making excuses, but understanding and taking the time for change.

Self-care is not being selfish. Put your mask on first before you can help someone else first. I am more religious since being in Jacksonville, because it is a sense of community. I see a purpose in everything. We learn more from our failures—it's how you get through it. Are you living the best life you know you can? Pursuit of

Chapter 34: **Philip Ayles**

happiness is in the Constitution, but why don't we use it more? Our forefathers took 10 years to write it, but pursuit of happiness was in it. If it involves violating others, then that is criminal, but if you are not hurting others, let's work on making better life choices for ourselves, which will in turn help others. We all want the same thing and to live in peace.

If my words can help anyone get out of that hole or offer inspiration to help them to just climb higher, we can help each other together! I have faith in this. Since I got baptized, I put my faith in God, and I truly want to see the good in the world.

Renewed Energy Renewed Purpose

Meeting my wife—her kindness and patience—during my refining time, made me a more palatable person. I never knew what love was, until I was with her. She is a true partner. This is what I had always imagined what marriage would be like.

I trust her. I couldn't trust anyone before.

I sat all four of the women in my life together and I told them they are the four people who I put above myself. They are the reason I do what I do. This gives me tremendous hope. I now believe I'm easy to love. I can say that with confidence, after five years into our relationship. I can get my family's input and support at any time. That is why I wake up every day. It motivates me another day to see what I can get accomplished. They give me a reason to keep going, and they make me want to be a better man than when I was younger.

Finding this love and support has helped me to realize my own passion to help veterans and first responders to recover from their own traumas. If I can help in any way to prevent someone from committing suicide or other harmful behavior, I want to be of service.

Let's get you to the present. This is one reason why veterans isolate themselves. Life didn't work out the way they wanted and that can be a hard reality. I want to help in breaking through the trauma for a happier life. I, too, had to be willing to take the steps and be brutally honest with myself. I learned to have patience, if things didn't go the way I wanted them to. I want to help others realize that. You survived and your situation made you more resilient. We can respond to and recover from all of life's trauma. Who you bring into the mix can make a difference. I can attest to that.

My family has been my rock. But, I was always spiritual; I had a Jesuit education. Today, we are so interconnected, more than any other time in human history. The differences are what makes us great, because there is not just one way to do things. The sense of community and lifting up others is rewarding for intrinsic reasons. We are all in this world together. We have to love and trust each other for who we are.

Dr. Martin Luther King said love breaks through hate. Patience and mindfulness can lead us to creating success and fulfilling lives together!

CHAPTER 35

BUILDING A STRONGER AND MORE SUSTAINABLE BOTTOM LINE

By **SALLY HANDLON**

Introduction

Businesses, like humans, are individual entities. And, like humans who rely on core essentials, businesses of all kinds, from nonprofit to for-profit, also rely on core values to sustain and thrive.

For individuals, those core components, which lead to a healthy life, can include: drinking water, purposeful movement, eating nutritious foods and sleeping seven to eight hours routinely.

Our choices in these four areas will positively or negatively impact our health and wellness. Over time, poor choices in these areas can contribute to chronic illnesses and impact our longevity.

Businesses are no different. There are four areas, which contribute to sustainability and success. These areas and their scope include people (from the board room to custodians, as well as investors and clients); planet and environmental sustainability; place, or the surrounding community; and profit and prosperity, the financial bottom line.

The four core values and the decisions made around them guide the successful implementation of a business' objectives and goals.

As you are well aware, the business landscape has dramatically been altered the past few years. You can no longer predict the future using past history. As many management experts will advise, today's business leaders need to function with agility, flexibility and transparency, while continuing to incorporate ongoing key management skills related to communication and technological advances.

How does an individual or group incorporate all these continually changing directions?

First and foremost is by having good health! Good health is a necessity for good business. The pandemic revealed that lesson. Good health also supports the ability to make changes in direction with more clarity and less stress, for the leader and organization.

Let's look at the four key areas for individuals: Drink, Move, Eat, and Sleep.

Drink

Our bodies are approximately 60-percent water, although organs and body systems may take more or less. Everything under our skin works in water. Twenty-percent of water sources can include the food we eat, but the remaining should be filled with good old water. When we age, our bodies are less able to signal our need for water. Either we think we are hungry or we become somewhat dehydrated. Dehydration can lead to mood swings, decreased cognitive function and fatigue, to name a few. Consider the poor decisions that could be made if you or your team members are not hydrated.

Move

Technology has brought about many changes within a workplace. For many, sitting at a desk has made their days less active. Some experts consider sitting to be the new smoking. It is recommended that individuals get a minimum of 30 minutes, five days a week of purposeful movement, intended to affect our cardio-vascular, respiratory and lymphatic systems (which relies on movement to maintain flow). Exercise, which can be as simple as walking daily, has a positive impact through stress relief, mental acuity and strengthening internal systems, including digestion. A lack of exercise can lead to a greater risk of developing high blood pressure and decreased blood and oxygen circulation. To make good decisions, our brains require a consistent flow of blood and oxygen.

Eat

Over an average lifetime, it is estimated a person will eat 25 tons of food. Are you okay with accumulating non-food ingredients in your body with each bite—pesticides, hormones and GMOs? Our bodies are amazing machines, but they need the right fuel to function well. Our bodies want to trust us—if we eat something the body doesn't recognize as a nutritious food source, it will store it in fat cells until (and if) the liver can process it. This can cause weight gain and create an internal environment that may slowly build toward an autoimmune disease. In the short term, unhealthy eating can impact body stress, fatigue and work capacity.

Sleep

We spend about a third of our life sleeping. Quality and quantity of sleep is as important to us as food and water. Without sleep, you can't form or maintain the pathways in your brain that let you learn and create new memories. Lack of sleep makes it harder to concentrate and respond quickly. In order for the body to do its maintenance, it needs at least seven to eight hours of sleep, on a consistent basis, and preferably at a consistent time of night, seven nights a week. Lack of sleep can lead to poor decision making, loss of brain function and emotional instability.

Individual Summary

To begin this section, I'll paraphrase Dr. Art Bronstein, an author and primary and preventive care physician: Our body is the greatest high-performance machine on earth. It is rated to last up to a hundred years or more. It is adaptable to climates, environments and life situations. It is able to endure and survive conditions of extreme hardship and deprivation. The body's engineering is a masterpiece of nature, more complex, durable, sophisticated and intelligent than anything crafted by man.

Businesses are made up of individuals, but they are also considered to be "corporate citizens." In 1946, famed management professor Peter Drucker wrote in the *Concept of the Corporation* that every business leader has two responsibilities: for the performance of their institution, and for the community as a whole. He equated the variety of business institutions in a community to an orchestra, as various instruments work together to make music.

Chapter 35: **Sally Handlon**

Forty-eight years later, John Elkington, an author, serial entrepreneur and authority on corporate responsibility and sustainable development, wrote for the *Harvard Business Review* about the concept of the triple bottom line: people, planet, profit. "The triple bottom line wasn't designed to be just an accounting tool," he said later. "It was supposed to provoke deeper thinking about capitalism and its future."

Before getting into the four core values, there is one more business expert to acknowledge: Judy Wicks, who founded the White Dog Café in Philadelphia, in 1983, and wrote a book about her experience. She was one of the first businesses to fully promote the triple bottom line. She later went on to add another "P" to the concept: Place. Considering these Four P's—People, Planet, Profit, Place—are suggested for leadership guidance as we continue to navigate the unchartered waters of this century. It can be overwhelming to try to anticipate what direction you, your company and the world are headed in. And there is a lot of varied advice on how to navigate these changing times. This is where employing the four core concepts come into play.

People

In the digital age, we find ourselves in an "always on" world. The work/life balance seesaw isn't balancing. The only way to truly leave your work behind, regardless of your position, is to unplug all your devices. For many, due to the needs of family or habit, it isn't easy to do that. It is important to provide a healthy environment for stakeholders where they feel empowered to do so. Supporting the four core components will benefit both stakeholders and the business.

Based on information gleaned from the "great resignation," health has become a number one priority for employees. It is also a consideration of boards and stockholders for key leadership positions. By keeping in touch with all stakeholders, you become more agile and flexible; their feedback, insight and actions will provide guidance.

A recent Gallup survey found that "taking care of your employees' health in the workplace is not only beneficial to them; it also creates an effective and efficient working environment that benefits the business. Employee health and productivity go hand in hand: A mentally and physically healthy individual is more optimistic, creative and motivated."

Planet

What is the impact of your business on the planet? What are the impacts of its products, services, employees and operations? Our environment is being impacted by our past selfish needs and desires. Today's workers and investors are interested in employers that are socially conscious. Unfortunately, since the 1950s, businesses have been more focused on short-term earnings. Being considerate of our planet requires longer-term thinking and expectations. This can be addressed through small steps. Some examples of ways businesses are showing their concern about the planet include:

- Donating a portion of earnings to environmental efforts or environmental organizations
- Reducing carbon emissions; educating employees on their carbon footprint

- Recycling of office and operations trash; create a zero-waste plan
- Using energy efficient products
- Finding sustainable materials or recycled products for use in your operation
- Finding local sources for your business and manufacturing needs

Profit

Profit has been the primary driver of most businesses. Whether it is for-profit or nonprofit, a business can't stay open without earning money. However, profit doesn't need to be the only bottom-line goal. Some of the leading businesses from the 1950s disappeared, because they focused solely on financial profit, often measuring the wrong things and being driven by greed. This list includes Kodak, Xerox, Polaroid, Blockbuster, MySpace and many more. For many businesses on this list, the innovativeness of employees was not valued, and shareholder vision was focused short-term.

Place

This is where business operations are conducted, in your immediate community, whether it is one location or multiple. The operation is utilizing local resources, such as talent and community infrastructure. Yes, the company is providing work opportunities, but what else could the company do to ensure a healthy and economically sustainable community?

Place is becoming more important as employees work virtually or in hybrid environments. Frank Feather, an author and futurist, shared a concept that *the more global we get in our business life, the more important our local community.* Our local community allows us to connect and recharge, a concern that the recent pandemic elevated. *The Great Good Place*, by Ray Oldenburg, also underscores the importance of place for local gathering and sharing, which helps support an economically sustainable community. One of the ways that Judy Wicks' business supported her community was by providing competitors with her sourcing contacts, a reminder that the Miracle on 34th Street doesn't have to be a fictional approach to business.

There are many ways to support "place" in your business operation. Employees can volunteer locally or the company can donate a percentage of profits. You as a leader can provide expertise on boards or community projects, or offer leadership to the business community.

Summary

Lifestyle impacts the choices we make as individuals or companies. If we take the time to understand the choices that we have, both personally and professionally, as well as the long-term effects of those choices, we will make better decisions today.

In the case of business, you can create a culture that emphasizes the business purpose, including its vision and mission. The Four Ps can help you navigate rolling waters by providing guidelines for leaders as well as employees making daily decisions. This sense of purpose provides investors and clients with the assurance that the

Chapter 35: **Sally Handlon**

business is here for the long-term, both on this planet and in this community.

Resources:
- *www.ded.gov/physicalactivity/walking.index.htm*
- *https://www.ninds.nih.gov/Disorders/Patient-Caregiver-Education/Understanding-Sleep*
- *https://popsci.com/your-schedule-could-be-killing-you*
- *https://blog.hubspot.com/the-hustle/corporate-citizenship*
- *https://sustain.wisconsin.edu/sustainability/triple-bottom-line*
- *https://hbr.org/2018/06/25*
- *https://bthechange.com/best-for-the-world-event-why-white-dog-caf%C3%A9-founder-judy-wicks-believes-in-the-power-of-a-local-226235097ea4*
- *https://www.gallup.com/workplace/404105/importance-of-employee-wellbeing.aspz.aspx*
- *https://www.e-careers.com/connected/10-businesses-that-failed-to-adapt*

CHAPTER 36

ENGINEER FROM THE OUTSIDE-IN

By **SCOTT E. LEBEAU**

When operating a small business, financial constraints, staffing needs and operational difficulties are challenging factors; however, competition is your biggest challenge. More than 12 million small businesses in the U.S. don't have a website and can't afford to use social media campaigns. The need to advertise and get your products in front of your customers to drive sales is by far the number one challenge small businesses face. Most small businesses don't have backend departments with marketing support to deliver on the requirements and demand of social media, or posting frequently and often, while keeping new posts relevant. With only 40 hours in the work week, many small business owners report finding themselves working 80 to 90 or more hours, just to get the essential business things done.

I've worked in the banking industry for 30-plus years, helping community banks create products that will help their customers. Gone are the days when your best marketing asset was face-to-face marketing. Before the internet, a commercial loan officer shared a marketing strategy with me that I will never forget. He told me that if or when I was reading any type of public content, such as a newspaper, magazine or trade publication, and I saw an article that would be of interest to a current customer or a prospect, to cut it out, and photocopy a good number of copies. He advised me to take that article out on calls and to make a point to drop the article off with a note saying something like, "Came across this and thought you might be interested." I'd drop it in the mail if I knew it would be some time before I saw that customer again. This technique has allowed me to continually add value to my customers, and it is that same value that I hope to bring in new ways.

My best asset is my ability to network and connect with people. My kids have repeatedly asked me if I know everyone, and if I don't, do I have to talk with everyone? Because of this, we have been known to stay at functions longer than they would like. In fact, when I mentioned to the kids I was quoting them for this book, they both smiled and laughed.

1. The world does shrink when you talk to people.

I was at a bank seminar in Atlanta, and on one of our last evenings, several of us decided to go out after dinner and have a few drinks in Buckhead. We found a bar a block off the beaten path. After a few minutes, one of the guys in our group started talking with a girl who had walked in with us. Several minutes passed before some of us decided to go over and "save" her, as we could clearly see she wasn't interested. It didn't take long after joining the conversation for us to realize we knew some of the same people. See, she was best friends with two of my cousins who lived in Knoxville. Better yet, we had actually spoken on the phone as she was trying to get me and a couple of friends to go to a New Year's Eve party several years prior.

I don't think there is anything special about how I network; it's just the willingness to engage in conversations and learn more about them. Most small business owners are willing to talk about their businesses—after all, it is their passion. If you listen and ask a few questions, it's truly amazing what you can discover. I believe this allows me to effectively help customers and small businesses solve their challenges. The magic in networking is getting to know your customer, understanding their needs and seeing if you are able to help them. If you can't help, you point them in the direction of someone who can.

The entrepreneurial spirit has always been with me. My objective is to help the customer as best I can, even if that means suggesting they go somewhere else.

2. "Like a tiny blade of grass in a great big field." — Bob Seger

More than one million small businesses were started during COVID-19, making an already competitive market even more competitive. This has made breaking into the search engine algorithm key to making your business stand out. Your small business is like Bob Seger's quote, "A tiny blade of grass in a great big field." With so much information feedback within search results topics, it's easy to understand why 75-percent of internet users never scroll past the first page of search results. A small business will invest a great deal of time and money in expert website optimization and daily targeted social media posting, and that's just the start.

A recent Fundera study reported that while 75-percent of small business owners feel that internet marketing is the most effective way to attract new customers, 61-percent say their biggest challenges are generating traffic and leads. Even if your small business has a website, to engage and convert leads into customers from internet searches, your business must make it to that first page of results. It's now become fairly common knowledge that content marketing is one of the best ways to increase brand exposure; with 81-percent of shoppers researching online before purchasing, your why and the solution you offer must be clear to effectively position yourself online to drive results. However, the best content in the world still won't help your small business generate leads, unless the public can discover it in the first place. This is why understanding search engine optimization (SEO) and pay-per-click digital advertising is a must. Even with the technologies that automate small business marketing, the top two channels for customer research are online reviews at 55-percent, and company websites at 47-percent.

When small businesses turn to search engines to market their business, the qualifications require small businesses to be established for a minimum period of time, before getting a seat at the table. Just because you're starting on your own, doesn't mean that you should have to start at the bottom. Your staff and customers are looking at your knowledge and experience, while you look for someone to give you a chance.

Consider an accountant who worked at a firm for 20 years and then decides to go out on their own. When they walk out the door, they don't leave their knowledge or experience. Unfortunately, when the accountant creates their website, the search engine algorithm may rank their website poorly, because they are a "new" business. In this situation, the search engine gives no credit to 20 years of experience.

There are many reasons that small businesses fail, and for the most part, it's not because the owners are not putting in the effort;

though I am sure it's only human nature for a person to give up when their efforts have failed to produce success. It's one of the hardest things to do, and has been part of my job in the past, to wind down a business that the owner has worked at 12 hours a day for 15 years. It's been my experience that, in so many ways, the driver is about information. It could be information about your product or service, or information helping you to understand how to manage your business. Could too much readily available information and not knowing where to begin, or how to find the information, be why so many businesses fail?

My mission now is to help small businesses strive for networking and person-to-person connections to create a loyal customer base and network.

3. Outside-in engineering

To sustain and grow your business is not as easy as just having a website to engage the visitor and then convert them into customers. A company competes within a search engine environment to engage and conserve customers, which is the place where all information online is centralized and ranked by algorithms that dictate its competitiveness. As I considered ways to help small businesses and community banks overcome this challenge to get their products in front of their customers, I wanted to build a different kind of community that not just made sense to me, but to the end user as well. To do this, we placed great emphasis on getting their feedback.

For years, I worked in an industry that created products they thought their customers needed, and then went out and found those customers, with less of an emphasis on gaining consumer feedback.

Inside-out engineering is what I have come to call traditional business product creation. Businesses tend to ask their staff about solutions to their customers' needs, as opposed to consulting with their customers. A product will roll out to its consumers for feedback after the business has decided what the solution should be, look like, feel like and how their customer experience should be. Outside-in engineering is the opposite of this model. The focus should be outside of the developing world. The solution is co-created with input and feedback from end users. In our case this was small business owners. At One Source Direct, our board members are also our consumers who we look to for insights and feedback to continue the development of the platform.

Challenge yourself to take an "Outside-In" approach and build solutions by discovering what your consumers need and not what solutions work for you. I think you will be pleasantly surprised. Use people to pilot or confirm your hypothesis. By people, I mean those outside your company. Ask your customers, potential customers and people who have never heard of your company to take a look and solicit their feedback. Get as many perspectives and opinions from as many people who are willing to give it. It's this type of feedback that will help you engineer a better product or service. This focus on the end user, and not profits, will enhance your final product and the customer's desire to buy with you. Consumers love to be a part of the process and be heard, but also to know that their input is valued.

4. Expect this to go somewhere unexpected.

When discussing the idea for One Source Direct with a friend, he told me to "expect this to go somewhere you didn't expect this to go." This possibly could have been the best advice I could have been given.

Chapter 36: **Scott E. LeBeau**

On Nov. 5, 2014, I met with a friend and colleague at a local coffee shop to discuss the idea and get his feedback. Like many conversations I had since then, I presented the concept and then waited for their feedback.

When we look to bring a new partner on board, I typically get asked my thoughts about what I want; I find it difficult to respond. For example, when I met with a potential marketing company, they wanted my suggestion for the marketing campaign look. I told them I was not a marketing person and that my idea was a blank whiteboard. I wanted to keep an open mind as marketing is not my field of expertise. I felt the same way when it came to coding. I have the business idea, but didn't have the software design and code background to create it, or know if what I envisioned was even possible. I needed to rely on others, and their area of expertise, to do what they needed to do.

Have you ever noticed how we get so caught up with purpose, trying to understand the "how" of what we are trying to do? Often doing so over-engineers the solution and creates more strife in the process. Allowing your idea to flourish and go places your initial vision didn't expect, the possibility to create something great or better than expected is ripe. Keep your mission and purpose close, but be open to the possibilities of seeing your vision thrive in ways you've never imagined.

My business is not in the same place. What started with the abstract idea that I pitched to several friends along the way has grown and evolved, and become something even greater, while keeping intact my original purpose and vision to help businesses—Connect, Create and Grow.

As a business owner, if it wasn't for my instinctive curiosity to understand and know people, I wouldn't be able to connect with them about the solutions they need. Networking is how I have been so successful. I am your partner! We are sitting beside you as we co-create, and not at the top of a dreadful tower, looking down, dictating what solutions are best for you.

CHAPTER 37

THE MARKETER'S GUIDE TO DIGITAL TRANSFORMATION

By **SHAMIR DUVERSEAU**

In his 2018 documentary, *Quincy*, Quincy Jones recalled that growing up on the south side of Chicago in the 1930s, he wanted to be a gangster until the age of 11. Why? Quincy stated, "You want to be what you see, and that's all we ever saw."

I love that quote as a reminder of the importance of youth exposure. If a young person never sees an example profession or life to strive for, how can they reasonably know what careers are possible?

African-Americans are underrepresented in the digital and technology industry, comprising of only eight-percent of employees. At this rate, companies staying relevant and increasing their audience bases may be creating a challenge and missed opportunity, by not recruiting and retaining more Black people. To close this gap, one must solve what I call the Quincy Phenomenon. While diversity isn't just about grooming, recruiting and retaining African-American workforces, it also means not overlooking other professionals of diverse races with diverse professional backgrounds and experiences.

True digital transformation requires a good foundation, proper tools and the right resourcing—from marketing to data to experimentation, automation, user experience design and coding. To have all three requires embracing the strength in diversity. Hire diverse people who are qualified and reflect your customers. The perspectives gained will lead to a competitive edge that can only come through diversifying your talent. More importantly, you need perspective and expertise to see beyond the obvious when change is necessary. Diversity is simply good business.

I started Smart Panda Labs 13 years ago to create more control in my schedule and freedom over my life. Going into business for myself was uncomfortable, but a necessary change to obtain my desired lifestyle. I've worked many years, predominantly across the travel industry, helping large Fortune 500 and 100 companies find ways to best set up their user interfaces, in order to appeal to their customers and understand their consumers' digital experience expectations. Evident in every project is the consumers' desire for a simple and easy-to-use digital experience, regardless of what it may take behind the scenes.

The goal of digital transformation is to deliver a better customer experience beyond IT systems. Usually, the delivery falls on the marketer, and enterprise marketers don't focus very well. We have a hundred balls in the air, trying all types of transformation tactics, making changes to all kinds of content, and trying all kinds of new campaigns—the list seems endless. All too often, all this is in a vain effort to "get stuff done" and "see what sticks." Marketers want the look and feel of the user interface and experience to be on brand, and the IT experts want the systems to work seamlessly and cohesively, connecting to all the tools and systems in place.

Think of the relationship between a marketer and IT professional like a consumer and contractor. If you wanted to build a new home from the ground up, you wouldn't draw a picture of the house with no dimensions or detail and give it to the contractor to build. At least, I hope you wouldn't. Contractors are much like IT; the details matter so they can deliver the request, while marketers are bigger picture and aesthetic thinkers. You need both to build a house, just like you need both expertises for digital marketing.

The Modern Marketer is a Technical Marketer

Digital marketing has many technical components that are a challenge to work with, and marketers tend to get scared by that. I was not one of those marketers. The scarier the task, the better. I wanted to be the bridge between marketers and tech specialists.

The philosophy I coined, The Marketer's Guide to Digital Transformation, has helped me drive change in numerous organizations to deliver better customer experiences. My philosophy might seem simple and easy, but sometimes the simplest strategies are overlooked.

Companies strive to stay relevant in the digital space and ahead of the competition with marketing that appeals to broader audiences. Marketers must:

1. **Establish a foundation by identifying proper resourcing and critical components to move forward**
2. **Create a framework for data insights**
3. **Experiment**

Establish your foundation by determining what resources and processes you need optimally to complete the job. As mentioned above, the more diverse your resourcing can be, the more creative the solutions. What do you need to get the job done? What skill-sets must be present? What type of technical support will you need?

Your foundation begins with basic tactics. Drive quality traffic to a solid user experience, nurture your newfound audience, convert them into customers and build a relationship with them. Now, you're actively creating digital experiences.

Once the foundation is laid, determine the critical tactics or marketing tools and data—email automations, landing pages, advertising campaigns, etc.—needed to execute from a digital standpoint. Gather data from these tools. Marketers spend a great deal of time and effort trying hard to get people what we think they want. We based this on our experience and vast expertise. What if we used data more often as a tool to listen to our customers?

As you drive digital transformation in your organization, make listening a part of the foundation by using the right tools. And I don't just mean web analytics. Gather experience analytics and the voice of customer data. Strive to get a sense of what people are doing, how they are doing it, who is doing it and why. The best way to do that is to have them tell you, explicitly and implicitly. Ensure listening is a part of your framework by consistently extracting insights from the tools to inform experiments and enhancements to your digital experiences.

Once your framework is running, observe and pull key data insights. Learn from the data. Garner insights that tell you what you should do to make this all work better. It is crucial to extract the right set of metrics to understand what the data is trying to tell you.

- How are you measuring what's happening?
- How is it performing; what is it doing?
- How are you driving insights from that data?
- How are you experimenting with what you are learning?

Too often, companies tend to choose the wrong metrics and data sets to analyze. The data sets chosen are not driving toward key OKRs; instead, they are gathering data for data's sake. Then employees generate dashboards and send them out in emails that no one is looking at. Good data should be insightful and, most importantly, actionable.

Data gathering and experimentation should be a constant cycle feeding itself, allowing for learning and strategic action. If the data provides a meaningful indication of a problem to solve or the potential to improve, move on, experiment and iterate. Use that data, your research, your experience, your gut to uncover how you can improve. Test it. Repeat. That's your framework. Now, you are in the cycle of true digital transformation. Doing all of this will be a gift to your customers.

The foundation, framework of data insights and experimentation creates a cycle where you can learn, iterate and improve. This cycle is critical to success and adapting to the people, market and competitors who are always changing. Without this cycle, how can you possibly keep up?

Experimentation is Key for Relevancy

Change is scary, and experimentation has no guarantees. It's full of the unknown and possibilities. Not every experiment will lead to success; likewise, not every experiment will fail. A few of my favorite examples of successful experimentation involve wine, television and music.

The Champenois (inhabitants of the Champagne region) were jealous of their Burgundian neighbors 200 miles south for having the finest red wine in the world. Champagne produced thin, light-bodied wines that mysteriously frothed and bubbled. Futilely for decades, they tried to rid their "poor quality" wines of this devilish device and concoct red wines that would outclass Burgundy. One day, a 17th Century monk looked at Champagne's wines differently, reasoning that "maybe the sparkle in Champagne isn't so bad after all!" This monk didn't drink wine, but he was an avid winemaker and savvy businessman. We now know his new concept of sparkling wine as Champagne. This monk was Dom Perignon.

In the late 80s and early 90s, MTV sought to generate more ad revenue for a broader audience. They flirted with the idea of broadcasting sporting events, going so far as hosting game shows like Remote Control. In the end, they settled on creating a soap opera, but that had a high expense to produce. So, they asked themselves if they could create a soap opera without actors, actresses and sets— just regular people (each paid about $1,400 total). And with that experiment came not only *The Real World*, but the birth of reality TV as we know it.

Recently, as I was listening to a live radio broadcast, Rick Springfield introduced a song by Run DMC. Rick reminisced about the first time he heard Run DMC was performing on Live Aid. In short, Rick was unimpressed by three guys with a turntable. Well, as he now admits, he was wrong, and the rest is hip-hop history.

As an even more practical example, Smart Panda Labs was once hired to help a company that had a valuable tool for experimentation that they weren't using and they no longer wanted to keep. We asked all the probing questions to understand the current state and desired future state. It seems they wanted to be purchased, so revenue and profitability were key to their valuation. In other words, they needed to generate revenue without increasing costs, and experimentation was the key to doing that.

We focused on tracking and extracting the right data points and metrics to better understand the consumer experience from their e-commerce site. From the data, we mapped the issues and saw that one key issue wasn't the amount of money the company was spending to drive traffic to the site, but that customers weren't converting, because they were losing them at key points in the process, which hurt the company's profitability. We used experimentation to improve the e-commerce experience and drive conversion. Ultimately, the company started to see a greater return on ad investments in customer conversions and improved customer acquisition costs, valuations and profitability.

What do all these examples have in common? A willingness to try something new—experiment.

The idea of experimentation is off-putting to many. The fear of losing upwards of 90-percent of tests may feel like a risk you and your career can't afford. Fear of the unknown is natural. I must caution you that you will fail before you succeed. Think of that failure as an inevitable opportunity to learn.

As an enterprise marketer, don't allow the fear of the unpleasantness of failure to deter you—analyze, experiment and iterate. You must learn by trying new ideas, methods, technologies and philosophies. Today, the internet is a medium of constant change. The world is changing. Like it, fear it, whatever. It is what it is. Something unpleasant can yield something good. The monk took something that was frowned upon and devalued, and created something that is now highly valued and enjoyed. MTV created reality TV from an experiment. Grab your turntable and change with it.

Experiments are about creating solutions to identified problems. Experimenting is not just copying what others are doing, even if you know what they are doing is working (and you usually don't know). Experimenting is about iterating for your customers and your business—both matter. Your experiments may not create a new television genre, but they can drive learning and results relevant to your business and you. You just need a framework that gets you started, and who knows what'll come next.

So, build your foundation with the right resources and tools. Ensure you have the correct framework with the fundamental metrics to gather customer data. Validate the problem by gathering and analyzing data to fuel experimentation, and then hypothesize a solution. Use the framework for ideation and experiment through omnichannel campaigns and measure their effectiveness. Do less. Measure more. Test a lot.

CHAPTER 38

MOTIVATE THE UNMOTIVATED

By **TIM KINTZ**

The big story being told right now is that you can't find good people to hire. We hear that the younger generations are lazy, entitled and they don't want to work hard. They want all the money, but they don't want to do the job. While some of that is fact in some areas, it's far from absolute. I hate hearing this, because I have seen the reverse. In 1990, when I started selling cars, there were 50-year-old sales guys who were lazy, entitled, not wanting to work hard and not driven by money.

There are some badass millennials out there. There are Navy Seals, athletes and incredible salespeople. If you allow the idea that you can't find good people to leak into your mindset, you will miss out on some great hires, you'll manage the ones you currently have ineffectively, and eventually lose them.

While this same complaint existed 35 years ago, today, we use it as an excuse. It has become a way to justify not training and developing good people. We need to pivot how we recruit, hire and retain top talent. Now more than ever, leaders need to learn how to motivate people.

Everybody is motivated differently. Some people are motivated by money, others are motivated by status, titles, time off and even charitable giving. Today, you have to be a better leader than ever and learn what makes each one of your people tick. And don't assume it's money.

How many times have you gone out to a restaurant and been motivated to buy something by an unmotivated employee? I believe employees are not motivated, because they don't have the right leadership. As leaders, we can either choose to approach this as a problem and complain, or we can attack this opportunity and rise above our competition. I prefer to see challenges as an opportunity to gain market share, while everyone else is focused on what they can't do.

Finding Good People

There are a lot of good people out there and chances are that you've hired good people in the past who didn't work out. When you look for good people, there are a few areas that need to be addressed.

1. Most good people already have jobs.

Does your recruiting target them? I'll be the first to admit that recruiting is a challenge. The number one rule is to always be recruiting, because the best time to hire a good person is when you don't need one. When I worked at a car dealership, I can't tell you how many times I'd look at someone and think, there's no way this person can sell a car. I wouldn't buy a car from this person. Then, the next thing that came out of my mouth was, when can you start? There's a mindset that we just need bodies.

I often ask managers, are you better off being wrong staffed or short staffed? They usually say they're better off short staffed, until they have so many customers that they don't have enough people to help them all. That's when they say, "We need more people on the floor," and that's when they hire the wrong people. You may never know exactly what the wrong people cost you in terms of turnover and customer experience. That's why you have to make sure you are disciplined in your hiring practices.

2. Have a solid onboarding program.

You need to be committed to your people, if you expect them to be committed to you. Once you have committed to a new hire, you have to understand that you are committing not just to them, but also to their family. You owe it to them to help them succeed by giving them everything you have.

3. Have an ongoing training and development process to keep them growing.

Ongoing training should take place multiple times per week with lots of interaction and practice. And every manager in the department should hold training classes. When you all take turns, it creates accountability and ownership. People are as good as they are going to get on their own. It's up to us to help them get better.

4. Compensation plans must recognize and reward top producers.

Your compensation plan needs to match your company's goals. That may sound obvious, but I've seen companies pay on volume and their profit suffered, while others paid on profit and their volume suffered. If you want to hire the best, your compensation plan needs to be the best.

I always make sure I'm recognizing my top producers and rewarding them better than everyone else. So often, I see that under-achievers and average people are overpaid and the top producers are underpaid. If you look at sports, the top producers are the ones making the stupid money. The bottom guys are making good money, but not nearly as much. You want to pay your top people so well that they can't afford to leave, and train your people so well that they could leave and go somewhere else anytime. Then, treat them so well that they would never want to. I call that the Golden Handcuffs.

Another big mistake I see is when leaders take their best salesperson and promote them into management. Why would they do that? It doesn't make sense. They are two totally different skills. Rarely do top salespeople make great managers. In sports, great players rarely ever become great coaches. They don't understand players who are not willing to put in the time. Why weren't you here early? Why aren't you watching game films until midnight? Great players were internally motivated to do that on their own. They don't know how to coach people who are not. There are two parts of a pay plan. I am a big believer in separating compensation from rewards.

You compensate people for doing their job and you compensate everyone equally. Then, you reward people for going above and beyond. That way, everyone is on the same pay plan, but not everyone is getting the same rewards. As they hit different levels, they get different bonuses. Your pay plan is not designed to motivate. Your pay plan is designed to compensate. A bonus plan is designed to motivate.

Internal and External Motivation

It's important to distinguish between internal and external motivation. Internal motivation is something you have to create. Internal motivation gives a person the drive to want to set goals.

Chapter 38: **Tim Kintz**

As a leader, you can help someone develop internal motivation by helping them develop their vision. Where do they want to be in three, five and ten years? If you help them develop their purpose, then every day when they come to work, they are internally motivated. They know they are doing a task today, because it will take them to their ten-year goal.

So often, there is no long-term vision. People just want to make it through their eight-hour day, go home, drink a six-pack and watch reruns of Jerry Springer. And pretty soon, they're going to be on an outrageous daytime talk show. But if you can help people identify their vision, and then help them break it down into goals, that gives purpose to their plan and to their life. There has to be something bigger than just getting a paycheck every two weeks. Giving someone a vision and a purpose creates that internal motivation.

External motivation is what you do. That's the rah rah, Knute Rockne speech, and let's run out the tunnel all fired up. As a leader, that is something you have to do on a regular basis, especially in sales. So often in sales, you fail more than you succeed. People need that coach on the sidelines patting them on the back. If you just threw a pick six interception and lost the game, you need that coach to keep motivating you, pumping you back up, and reminding you that failure is just a stepping stone to success. It's only a failure if you don't learn anything from that experience.

Money is another form of external motivation. Cash spiffs and other bonuses are important, and you want to do that periodically. But be careful that they don't become an expectation. There are two things you need to have to be good at external motivation. Number one, in the words of John Maxwell, "How do kids spell love? T-I-M-E!"

It's not the teddy bear that lets them know you love them. It's spending time with them. How do your people know you care about them? Same thing: T-I-M-E. How often as leaders do we get caught up answering emails, doing spreadsheets and focusing on the big picture without realizing that the big picture only happens when each individual does their job?

Make time to spend with your people. If you don't find the time to do it right, you'll never have the time to do it over. People don't go sideways in one day. They don't become former employees just because they woke up and said, I'm quitting. It's a little bit every single day. If you spend time with your people every single day, then you'll be able to keep them on the right track. There will always be issues, but you want to deal with them before they become major issues.

Doing your one-on-one coaching sessions with each individual player makes a great team. People don't care how much you know until they know how much you care. If you want to motivate the unmotivated, spend time with them. It has to be planned in your day. They have a time slot, you have to be there, and there are no distractions. That person has to be the most important person in the world to you when you are with them for that ten or twenty minutes.

And the only way you know if you did a good or bad job during that one-on-one is if they are better at the end of it than they were at the beginning. Maybe they are better at a specific skill or task. Maybe they are better at being organized. Or maybe they just have a better attitude. Sometimes, you have to help them take a checkup from the neck up, because people can't always do it on their own. Not everyone is self-motivated.

Chapter 38: **Tim Kintz**

Emotional Bank Accounts

Another challenge for leaders is understanding that you have to build emotional bank accounts with your people. The best way to make a positive deposit into someone's emotional bank account is by catching them doing something good. As managers, we are often good at catching people doing something bad. When something's not right, we are really good at pointing that out. But when you catch them doing something good, even if it's a little thing, do you tell them, hey, great job on that yesterday? That's a deposit into their emotional bank account.

Of course, in business and in life, we're always going to have to make a few withdrawals. There will be times when I need to ask people to do things they don't want to do. I may have to call them out, because they're not doing a good job. But if I build up those emotional bank accounts, I can make a withdrawal without being overdrawn. So often, managers don't make enough deposits and they are always overdrawn with their people. That's why they have high turnover and low motivation. And, that's why they struggle as a leader. You want to be the leader that your team needs and deserves. Stop managing your department and start managing the individuals within your department. That's how you make a difference.

The best salespeople I've seen don't chase the money. They chase being the top salesperson, because they know the money will take care of itself. All salespeople love to be recognized. It could be public recognition or private recognition. Just make sure you give it.

My company has fun tools for dealerships to use to motivate their salespeople. Every Saturday morning, you can call the people who did well up front and recognize them. They love being recognized in front of all the other salespeople.

I'm a big believer in Levels of Excellence Charts that rank salespeople based on their performance. So often, managers are afraid to have rankings and put up achievement boards, because the bottom guy might get his feelings hurt. I can't run a successful business worrying about the bottom guy's hurt feelings. I will spend time with that bottom guy to help him get better. Even Tom Brady has to take a few losses. That's just life, but everybody needs recognition. I truly believe that we need to bring fun and friendly competition into our businesses. That's how great coaches and leaders get everyone working together.

Imagine this. Twenty years from now, all the people you ever managed or led are in a room. Then, I ask them, who was the manager or leader who made a difference in your life? Who is that person who helped you become better than you ever thought you could be? The question is, will your name come out of their mouth?

As a leader, you have the opportunity to make a difference in people's lives. If you take being a leader to heart and do the right things, if you spend time with your people, if you train them, and if you care more about them getting better than they care about themselves getting better, your name will come out of their mouth.

Being the leader who can motivate the unmotivated is a choice you make every day. That choice can change the lives of the people you lead. And it will change your life, too.

CONCLUSION

By **ADAM TORRES**

Our team at Mission Matters hopes you have enjoyed reading these amazing stories of entrepreneurs, business leaders and executives. While each leader has a different story and background, one common trait is shared among them all—they are never done working on their craft.

We have created an interview series with expanded content, showcasing our authors, which can be found on our website (www.MissionMatters.com), podcasts and social media channels.

The best way to explore is to visit us here:

We hope you enjoyed this 10th volume of **Mission Matters Business Leaders** and hope that the information will help you along your journey.

To your success,

Adam Torres

P.S. Don't forget to listen to our podcasts at:
MissionMatters.com

APPENDIX

Adam Torres | Foreword | Page iii
Co-Founder Mission Matters
MissionMatters.com
Instagram: @AskAdamTorres
Twitter: @AskAdamTorres

Brad Weber | Chapter 1 | Page 1
President
hello@InspiringApps.com
hello@InspiringApps.com
InspiringApps.com
linkedin.com/company/InspiringApps/

Brooke Sousa | Chapter 2 | Page 9
Life Entrepreneur
Instagram: @brookesousa

Bryan T. Vielhauer | Chapter 3 | Page 15
President
bryan@decalimpressions.com
decalimpressions.com
linkedin.com/company/decalimpressions
facebook.com/decalimpressions
instagram.com/decalimpressions
youtube.com/@decalimpressions

Carlton Millinder | Chapter 4 | Page 23
Independent Travel Advisor / PlanNet Marketing Rep
cmillsluxtravel@gmail.com
https://carltonmillinder.inteletravel.com/booktravel.cfm
https://www.plannetmarketing.com/cmillinder84
https://www.facebook.com/carlton.millinder/
C Mil Lux Travel (Facebook Business Page)
https://www.facebook.com/profile.php?id=100088168812659
https://www.linkedin.com/in/carlton-millinder-mba-88aa1b12/

Chelsea Johnson, MD | Chapter 5 | Page 31
Founder/ Physician Executive
DrJohnson@conciergecare-pediatrics.com
Conciergecare-pediatrics.com

Collin Plume | Chapter 6 | Page 41
President and CEO
management@nobleira.com
www.NobleGoldInvestments.com
https://www.youtube.com/c/noblegoldinvestments

Curt Maier | Chapter 7 | Page 49
Vice President of Business Development
Company: IBA
curt@ibainc.com
www.ibainc.com
Facebook:https://www.facebook.com/profile.php?id=100072463374547
Linkedin:https://www.linkedin.com/in/curtmmaier/
Twitter:@maier_curt

Cynthia Gallardo | Chapter 8 | Page 57
Founder and CEO of Legacypreneur™ Academy housed in Synergy Solutions Pro, LLC & Cynthia Gallardo Law, LLC Legacy Law Boutique™
cynthia@cynthiagallardo.com / cynthia@cynthiagallardolaw.com
www.cynthiagallardo.com
Instagram: @cynthiagallerdolegacy
www.cynthiagallardo.com
www.cynthiagallardolaw.com

David Reich | Chapter 9 | Page 63
The Observationist
Entertainment, Education and Enlightenment
Senior Customer Success Manager - IBM
Chief Magic Officer - IBM
David Reich, LLC - Master Magician, Mentalist, Hypnotist, Lecturer and Course Creator.
contact@davereich.com
www.davereich.com
LinkedIn: www.linkedin.com/in/davereich
Facebook: www.facebook.com/Observationist

Dr. Diana C. Stephens | Chapter 10 | Page 73
PhD, MBA, MMus, BMus
Founder and CEO, Mindful Job Alignment
dcmstephens@gmail.com; support@mindfuljobalignment.com
https://www.linkedin.com/in/dianacstephens/
https://www.linkedin.com/company/mindfulness-job-coaching
www.mindfuljobalignment.com

Greg Johnson | Chapter 11 | Page 81
Executive Coach
greg@abovetherim.us
Web: www.abovetherim.us
Linkedin: www.linkedin.com/gregljohnson

Jason Kennedy | Chapter 12 | Page 89
Jason Kennedy
President, AutoInterests Group
jason@autointerests.com
https://autointerests.com
https://tracksidesystems.com

Jennifer A. Ingram | Chapter 13 | Page 99
Entrepreneur, Author, Executive
Jeningram85@gmail.com
www.Jeningram.me
www.CalibratedLens.com
https://www.linkedin.com/in/jen-ingram-62801a4b
https://instagram.com/jeningram.me?igshid=ZDdkNTZiNTM=

Jennifer Johns Sutton | Chapter 14 | Page 107
CEO/Founder, Bright+CO and OrangeWIP
jennifer@brightcomarketers.com
brightcomarketers.com
orangewip.com
https://www.youtube.com/@hellochaospodcast/
Listen on Apple Podcasts: https://podcasts.apple.com/us/podcast/hello-chaos/id1622445449
LinkedIn: https://www.linkedin.com/in/jenniferjsutton/
Twitter: @jjmediamaven

Jessica Z Brandenburg | Chapter 15 | Page 119
Reluctant Entrepreneur or Independent Consultant
www.linkedin.com/in/jessicabrandenburg

Jessica Nava | Chapter 16 | Page 129
Chief Growth Officer
jess@moxieexchange.com

Joseph Fannin | Chapter 17 | Page 139
Founder/ CEO
info@fanninprofessional.com
www.fanninprofessional.com

Keith Angell | Chapter 18 | Page 147
Certified Board Director, CEO, Operating Partner
angell@pythian.com
https://www.linkedin.com/in/keithangell/

Kevin M. Campbell | Chapter 19 | Page 155
CEO
https://www.linkedin.com/in/kevin-m-campbell-93b2861/

Kurt Nelson, PhD. | Chapter 20 | Page 163
Founder & Chief Behavioral Officer - The Lantern Group
Founder & President - Brain/Shift
Founder & Co-host - Behavioral Grooves Podcast
kurt@lanterngroup.com
www.lanterngroup.com
www.brainshift.shop
www.behavioralgrooves.com

Dr. Lanise Block | Chapter 21 | Page 171
CEO, Sankore Consulting
staff@sankore.consulting
https://www.sankore.consulting/
Sankore LinkedIn
Professional LinkedIn
Sankore Twitter
Sankore Facebook

Personal Facebook Page
Sankore Instagram

Lee Ann Schwope | Chapter 22 | Page 179
Partner, Amphora Consulting
las@leeannschwope.com
LinkedIn - https://www.linkedin.com/in/lee-ann-schwope/
Twitter - @Lee_Ann_Schwope
Facebook - https://www.facebook.com/LASchwope
www.leeannschwope.com
www.amphoraconsulting.com

Leigh Priebe Kearney, PhD | Chapter 23 | Page 187
Founder, LPK Consulting and Osprey Leadership Consulting
leigh@leighkearney.com and leigh.kearney@ospreyleadership.com
https://www.leighkearney.com/home

Mansour Khatib | Chapter 24 | Page 197
CEO, GBT Technologies Inc.
mansour.khatib@gbtti.com
https://www.gttbi.com
https://www.linkedin.com/in/mansour-khatib-0230282/

Mark A. Mears | Chapter 25 | Page 205
Chief Growth Officer, LEAF Growth Ventures, LLC
mark@markamears.com
https://www.markamears.com/ & https://www.linkedin.com/in/markamears/

Mark Andrew Thiede, PhD | Chapter 26 | Page 221
Owner
twowrasslincats@gmail.com

Mark R. Warren | Chapter 27 | Page 231
Co-Founder
mwarren@2bearswine.com
www.2bearswine.com
www.linkedin.com/in/mark-warren-174298108

Matthew J. McCarl, Sr. | Chapter 28 | Page 239
New Leaf Hyperbarics & Wellness
Office Address: 1200 Executive Pkwy #230, Eugene, Oregon 97401
Office Phone: (541) 636-3278
matt@newleafworld.com
Website: https://www.newleafeugene.com/
Facebook: https://www.facebook.com/newleafhyperbaric
Instagram: @NewLeafHyperbarics

Meghan Mackay | Chapter 29 | Page 247
Executive Director, LeveragED Foundation
mmackay@leveragEDfoundation.org
https://www.linkedin.com/in/meghanmackay/
https://www.leveragedfoundation.org/
https://twitter.com/MackayMeghan

Mher M. Vartanian | Chapter 30 | Page 255
mher@hyperioncapitalcre.com
@TheRealMher
https://www.linkedin.com/in/mher-m-vartanian/

Myntillae Nash | Chapter 31 | Page 263
Founder & Product Designer
myntillae@myntifreshdesigns.com
Myntifreshdesigns.com
instagram.com/MyntifreshDesigns
https://www.linkedin.com/company/myntifreshdesigns/
https://www.linkedin.com/in/myntillae-nash-72787414/

Oksana Malysheva | Chapter 32 | Page 271
Managing Partner
oksana@sputnikatx.com
www.sputnikatx.com

Petria McKelvey | Chapter 33 | Page 281
CEO
PrecisionMedicalBilling.com
MyClearVisit.com
PMBinstitute.com
linkedin.com/company/pmb-precision-medical-billing

linkedin.com/in/pmbtria
facebook.com/pmbprecisionmedicalbilling
facebook.com/groups/homecarebilling
Facebook.com/PMBinstitute

Philip Ayles | Chapter 34 | Page 289
Founder & CEO Ayles Solutions LLC
philayles@aylessolutions.com
Website: Aylessolutions.com

Sally Handlon | Chapter 35 | Page 297
Founder/President
sally@hbrllc.com
www.handlonbusinessresources.com
www.hbr.com
www.bodyconstruction.me
www.linkedin.com/sallyhandlon

Scott E. LeBeau | Chapter 36 | Page 307
scott@onesourcedirect.net
https://onesourcedirect.net/
Facebook: https://www.facebook.com/One-Source-Direct-209804284410949
LinkedIn: https://www.linkedin.com/company/onesourcedirect
Twitter: @1_source_direct

Shamir Duverseau | Chapter 37 | Page 315
Managing Director, Chief Strategist & Co-founder
https://smartpandalabs.com/
https://www.linkedin.com/in/shamirduverseau?original_referer=https%3A%2F%2Fwww.google.com%2F

Tim Kintz | Introduction, Chapter 38 | Page v, 323
Kintz Group LLC, President
Tim@KintzGroup.com
KintzGroup.com
Facebook: https://www.facebook.com/KintzGroup/
InstaGram: https://www.instagram.com/thetimkintz/
LinkedIn: https://www.linkedin.com/in/tim-kintz-89383712/
YouTube: The Kintz Group

MISSION MATTERS
PODCAST

WITH

Adam Torres

MISSION® MATTERS x ARABICA® Since 1976

WWW.ARABICA1976.COM

OTHER AVAILABLE TITLES

Purchase at **MissionMatters.com**.

In the ninth edition of *Mission Matters (Business Leaders Edition Vol 9)*, Adam Torres features 26 top professionals who share their lessons on leadership. In these pages, through inspiring stories, you'll discover:

- How to Transform an Organization
- How Simple Questions Can Lead to Amazing Innovation
- An Effective Way to Work with Global Teams
- The Simple Truth of What Motivates Us
- Optimization Best Practices for Entrepreneurs
- How to Lead with Internal Controls to Drive Revenue
- And much more!

....

In the eigth edition of *Mission Matters (Business Leaders Edition Vol 8)*, Adam Torres features 26 top professionals who share their lessons on leadership. In these pages, through inspiring stories, you'll discover:

- How to go from a good worker to a great manager
- Why roadblocks should be embraced, not avoided
- The smartest way to trust your gut
- Why becoming a "natural leader" is easier than you think
- How to solve employee retention issues through the secrets of compassion
- The power of an abundance mindset in leadership success
- And much more!

In the seventh edition of *Mission Matters (Business Leaders Edition Vol 7)*, Adam Torres features 22 top professionals who share their lessons on leadership. In these pages, through inspiring stories, you'll discover:

- Four ways leaders can mitigate human error
- The true power of having a clear life mission
- How to create amazing digital customer journeys
- How Amazon has disrupted your business (and what to do about it)
- What it means to be ALL IN in your work
- How small changes can lead to big savings
- And much more!

In the sixth edition of *Mission Matters (Business Leaders Edition Vol 6)*, Adam Torres features 20 top professionals who share their lessons on leadership. In these pages, through inspiring stories, you'll discover:

- How persistence always beats resistance...
- Why it's so important to raise entrepreneurial kids...
- How to cure cancer in 7 (mostly) easy steps...
- Why business success is a matter of stewardship...
- The unmatched opportunities of always saying yes...
- How hiring veterans is a business superpower...
- And much more!

In the fifth edition of *Mission Matters (Business Leaders Edition Vol 5)*, Adam Torres features 18 top professionals who share their lessons on leadership. In these pages, through inspiring stories, you'll discover:

- The real cost of bad customer service!
- How to truly become a mission-driven organization!
- Seven ways women can thrive in a male-dominated world!
- Why relationships, education, achievement, and love are true values in leadership!
- How imperative it is to tell your story!
- Why it is essential to teach children how to manage online purchases!
- And much more!

....

In the fourth edition of *Mission Matters (Business Leaders Edition Vol 4)*, Adam Torres features 18 top professionals who share their lessons on leadership. In these pages, through inspiring stories, you'll discover:

- How patient care and technology meet in the medical field.
- How digital transformation is imperative for companies.
- What creating your dream retirement looks like.
- How to create a result-driven culture in your company.
- How to pivot your marketing to survive crisis situations.
- Why cohesion is more important than engagement in an organization.
- And much more!

In the third edition of *Money Matters (Business Leaders Edition Vol 3)*, Adam Torres features 13 top professionals who share their lessons on leadership. In these pages, through inspiring stories, you'll discover:

- Different approaches to leadership and people management.
- Rules for success from a Green Beret.
- How to effectively manage a company full of millennial employees.
- How to transform your marketing mindset.
- Where customer success and employee success meet.
- What manifesting your success in business looks like.
- And much more.

In the second edition of *Money Matters (Business Leaders Edition Vol 2)*, Adam Torres features 18 top professionals who share their lessons on leadership. In these pages, through inspiring stories, you'll discover:

- How to harness the entrepreneurial mindset.
- Why scaling your business for sustainable growth is vital.
- How to grow your eCommerce business.
- Lessons learned from sales experts.
- How to level up your leadership.
- How to manage your energy.
- And much more.

In the original edition of *Money Matters (Business Leaders Edition)*, Adam Torres features 15 top professionals who share their lessons on leadership. In these pages, through inspiring stories, you'll discover:

- How to create a clear path for growth.
- Why every business should act like a media company.
- How to build a community to last a lifetime.
- Lessons learned from professional soccer.
- How to maintain a well-connected brain for peak performance.
- How to create harmony through union in business.
- And much more.

In this latest edition of *Mission Matters (Women in Business Edition Volume 1)*, Torres features 18 top female professionals who share their lessons on business and leadership. In these pages, through inspiring stories, you'll discover:

- Why empathy and EQ is crucial in leadership
- How failure paves the way to success
- How to find your purpose
- How to turn your passion into your life's purpose
- What it means to turn challenges into gifts
- What value-based care means for cancer patients
- And much more!

Navigating the world of real estate can be stressful. Are you getting closer or further away from your goals? Adam Torres is here to help you move forward. In his latest edition of *Money Matters (Real Estate Edition Volume 3)*, Torres features 10 top professionals who share their lessons in real estate. In these pages, through inspiring stories, you'll discover:

- Different approaches to leadership and people management.
- Rules for success from a Green Beret.
- How to effectively manage a company full of millennial employees.
- How to transform your marketing mindset.
- Where customer success and employee success meet.
- What manifesting your success in business looks like.
- And much more.

....

Navigating the world of real estate can be stressful. Are you getting closer or further away from your goals? Adam Torres is here to help you move forward. In his latest edition of *Money Matters (Real Estate Edition Volume 2)*, Torres features 13 top professionals who share their lessons in real estate. In these pages, through inspiring stories, you'll discover:

- How to get more properties through syndication.
- How to implement servant leadership to have a more successful business.
- Why investing in real estate is not just for rich people.
- How important insurance is in real estate transactions and what to look for.
- Why using a private lender can help you in real estate transactions.
- What legal options you have to protect your assets.
- And much more!

Navigating the world of real estate can be stressful. Are you getting closer or further from your goals? Finance guru Adam Torres is here to help you move forward. His guide, Money Matters, features 15 top professionals who share lessons from their more than 250 years of combined experience.

Embracing diversity and inclusion in a rapidly changing business landscape can be challenging. Are you and your organization positioned properly for this new age of connectivity? Torres features 14 top Asian leaders who share their lessons on diversity, equality and inclusion.

In this clear, concise manual, financial expert Adam Torres goes over the basics of personal finance and investing and shows you how to grow your wealth. Torres makes sure you are prepared for whatever life throws your way. It's never too early to think about the future and his book will give you the right tools to tackle it.

This workbook has been designed specifically for individuals like you who are dedicated to improving the results in all areas of your life. By following the ideas and exercises presented to you in this transformational workbook, you can move yourself into the realm of top achievers worldwide.

Made in the USA
Coppell, TX
22 June 2023